EUROPEAN VISIONS FOR THE KNOWLEDGE AGE

A Quest for New Horizons in the Information Society

Paul T Kidd (Ed.)

Cheshire Henbury

Preface

Visions of the future are an important aid to the development of a world that people want, rather than one that is imposed on them by some external unseen hand of fate. Visions can also offer ideas and present alternatives that can stimulate creative thinking, trigger innovation, and provide some pointers to the types of issues that may need to be addressed in the future.

This book has been designed with these aspects of vision in mind. The aim is not to use visions to predict the future, but to explore different options and possibilities. The book is directed at stimulating a reflection on possible futures as society moves forward in the emerging *knowledge age*. Experts drawn from the fields of science, engineering, technology and humanities present their thoughts, ideas, and reflections on where society may be headed, covering a time scale up to 30 years ahead. The book offers a unique perspective of the intersections among knowledge, design, technology, communication, people, and society. Based on their own in-depth knowledge of current developments, the authors describe what they think *could* be, what they think *should* be, and sometimes warn about what they think *should not* be the future.

The strength of this book lies in its *independence*; it does not represent the official view of the authors' companies, or institutions, but rather the independent opinions of a range of thinkers and practitioners. Such an independent presentation of ideas can provide a valuable *mirror* for reflecting on current actions, or for laying the foundations of future ones.

In Europe there is a need to develop clearer visions of future society. The reflection and discussion about where to go needs to be extended far beyond acknowledged experts, to include a much broader spectrum of society. This book offers one starting point for such a broader discussion and reflection on society's future in the *knowledge age*.

The idea for this book originated with Jakub Wejchert who shaped the concept and recruited the contributors, tirelessly reviewed the contributions, and provided advice to the authors to enable each of them to arrive at quality contributions. Unfortunately changing work commitments and areas of responsibility meant that Jakub was no longer able to continue in the role of editor. When Jakub withdrew I was asked to step in and take over the role of editor to ensure that the valuable contributions contained within the book reached the intended readership. This I was happy to do, sure in the knowledge that the content represents a valuable resource for discussion about the future of society. Thus while I put the finishing touches to the book, preparing the introduction and arranging publication, the bulk of the credit for this book lies with Jakub. I would therefore like to express my thanks to Jakub for his commitment and efforts, and for giving me the opportunity to finish what he started. I hope that the finished product reflects well his original intentions.

Paul T Kidd
Macclesfield, United Kingdom
February 2007

Acknowledgements

The copyright of Figure 6.1 belongs to Laurent Beslay, and is reproduced with the copyright holder's permission. The copyright of Figure 11.1 belongs to José del R. Millán, and is reproduced with the copyright holder's permission. The copyright of Figure 13.1 belongs to Marc Luyckx and Verna Allee, and is reproduced with the copyright holders' permission. Thanks are due to Jakub Wejchert for undertaking the bulk of the work involved in creating this book, particularly finding the contributors and guiding each them towards the production of their final manuscripts.

Contents

Chapter 1

The Knowledge Age: Peering into the Future

Paul T Kidd

The Dawning of a New Era – The Knowledge Age

As society moves from the industrial era into the new *knowledge age*, old concerns, and some new ones, stand ready to challenge humanity as it strives to make sense of a rapidly changing and often confusing world. The *knowledge age* offers the prospect of creating wealth through brain power rather than muscle power. Using human intelligence, circumstances have been already been created where there is a stream of new ideas emerging from research laboratories, and as a result, technologies, products and services seem to be in a continual state of flux. There is always something new to buy, to use, to apply, and there is more to come. Novelty and innovation have become imperatives for business success and the drivers for economic growth and unprecedented widespread prosperity in the industrial world. People in the industrialised countries, have never had it so good, at least in material terms.

However there are dark clouds on the horizon: global warming, terrorism, environmental damage, cyber crime, schisms in society, and threats to privacy, are but a few. In material terms the citizens of the industrialised countries, and increasingly those in the developing nations, may be riding high, but is society heading in the right direction? What type of society will emerge as the knowledge age begins to mature, and will it be a society that people will really want to be part of?

These are broad questions, and there are several factors at play that will influence how the knowledge era develops and how it will impact upon society and peoples' lives. This book aims to address one of these factors, that of information and communication technologies, and then only modestly, for in itself, the subject is a vast one.

Information and communication technologies are one of the key enablers of the new *knowledge age*. But where are these technologies leading? What will be the result of their continuing development and even wider adoption in all aspects of life? Who will control these technologies, big business or citizens? What information and communication technologies will be shaping society further into the future? Will these technologies be threatening and alien to the human sprit or is it possible to produce a more human-centred technology? What new opportunities in work, leisure, healthcare, government, etc. will arise?

There are many questions, more than can be posed, and surely more than can be answered given the uncertainties that any effort to envision the future must involve. However, it is necessary at least to try to consider some of the questions and to find possible answers.

Why bother to think about the future? Surely there are enough existing problems in the world that need attention, without considering more, which may or may not, eventually materialise. No-one can predict the future, so surely in the end it must all just be speculation? To some extent this is of course true, but some people have insights and intuitions that provide a glimpse into the foggy and uncertain world that is the future. These insights and intuitions about the future are valuable.

Visions of the future are not crystal clear; they are inherently fuzzy notions that combine knowledge in a particular domain with a sense of what could develop, blended with a sense of what should be, or perhaps should not be. Visions encompass rational knowledge as well as intuitive elements, and their purpose is to light the paths to follow to the future. The process of vision building is clearly not the same as trying to predict the future analytically, or to analyse trends and statistics. These are all important tools for planning, but vision building is a complementary activity: visions for the future do not try to predict exactly what will happen, but rather offer options and explore ways that could be followed.

Thinking actively about the future can also help to provide a better understanding of the present, to envisage options that might otherwise not be considered, to reflect on these, and to map out and better set the compass for future steps forward. Humankind is gifted because it can use its intelligence to foresee difficulties that might perhaps be avoided. So without attempting to at least imagine some of the possible landscapes of the future, decisions may end up being made based on a limited and narrow view of the present, ultimately creating problems that future generations will have to deal with.

Visions also play a role in the innovation processes by fostering new ideas and concepts and stimulating new thinking. Visions of the future provide an opportunity for *out-of-the-box thinking*. Thus this book provides a fresh set of perspectives on the future, ones that can help you the reader, to think *outside the box* of the present. In this spirit, this book provides a diversity of views about technologies relating to human knowledge and communication and their role and influence in the world.

Exploring the Knowledge Age

The book presents a series of essays written by a set of leading researchers and thinkers, who in their articles, reflect on technologies, as well as consequences and implications, over a timescale upto 30 years ahead. These essays have a diversity of starting points some from technological perspectives, some from human or societal ones. Each one can be seen as a small *vision* of the future, written by a leading authority in their area.

Looking to the future can no longer be done from a prognosis of technology alone; a multi-faceted view is needed. It is also true that new breakthroughs often occur at the intersection of different disciplines. Therefore, an underlying aim of the book is to present a set of multidisciplinary and pluralistic perspectives, trying to avoid the trap of being either too socially-centred or too technology-centred. For these reasons the book has encouraged views that span across different disciplines and traditional viewpoints.

The presentation of this book is deliberately impressionistic. It presents a collection of independent views from a range of authors. It does not provide a consensus view, indeed within the collection of essays there are opposing views and arguments. An impressionistic glimpse of insights written by leading practitioners provides a special kind of awareness of future options, quite different to a strictly analytical approach. Some of the ideas may seem utopian, naïve, or even disturbing. If that is the case, then it is more likely that counter thoughts will be provoked, leading to a more stimulating book and avoiding the trap of a sterile academic work that serves no purpose other than to stimulate discussion among a select few. Indeed the contributions in this book have been written with a wider audience in mind, and care has been taken to make the essays accessible and free from technical jargon. Where technology is described it is done so in a way that will appeal to those without a detailed technical background, without alienating those that might have deeper understandings. Both the technically and the non-technically oriented will find elements in the essays that will challenge their world views and their

3

taken for granted assumptions, and inform them about many wide ranging issues.

Thus is the nature of the exploration of the knowledge age that the book presents. The collection of essays offers visions provided from different perspectives, including those of technologists, researchers, engineers, designers, scientists, and thinkers from the humanities. The perspectives are all European. Every contributor is either based in Europe or has strong links with Europe. The essays therefore provide an opportunity to discern the emergence of a uniquely European perspective on the future of the *knowledge age.*

Of course the contributions represent just a small sample of visions. Many topics are not covered since to do so would have resulted in a work of excessive length. However, the focus in each essay is on the essence of the subject matter addressed. Each chapter seeks to identify the fundamental issues. The details of specific visions may change with time as technologies develop and new ones emerge, but the deep underlying concerns and basic principles identified in the contributions will remain. It is in these more timeless areas that the lasting value of the book lies.

The contents are organised into five self-contained parts: *European Manufacturing 2035*; *Novel Perspectives for Networked Intelligence*; *The Future of Body and Mind*; *New Directions for Power and Participation*; and *The Distant Horizon*. Each section brings together a number of essays under a broad theme relevant to the future. Each section can be read independently.

The first part, *European Manufacturing 2035,* examines how in the future, information and knowledge is likely to become linked to the physical world in unexpected ways. It illustrates radically new systems of production, product-service systems, managed consumption, and manufacture based on micro particles and the atomic level. These could radically change patterns of consumption, and help move society towards a more sustainable future.

The first article by Paul Kidd, *The Future of European Manufacturing: Driven by Globalisation or Global Warming*, examines how global warming, fossil fuel depletion, and energy consumption need to become the primary drivers for the future of European manufacturing. Using data from respected agencies, the serious and growing nature of energy-related environmental problems is addressed, leading to the conclusion that nothing short of a radical transformation of manufacturing into a less energy consuming industry will be necessary to respond to these problems. A vision of new, non-fossil fuel based system of production, less transport intensive, and less energy consuming, is presented. This new system of production relies on virtual warehousing and distribution, on-the-spot manufacturing, product-service systems, and managed consumption. It may also offer an opportunity to revitalise European manufacturing industry.

Following on from this opening article, two closely linked contributions, *From Bits to Atoms*, by Roberto Saracco, and *Micro Fabrication* by Brahim Dahmani, describe some intriguing possibilities of how this new system of production might be realised. Both of these essays point to new forms of *local* manufacture, as well as the disassembly of physical goods that could reduce negative environmental impacts. By translating *bits into atoms*, everyday objects such as books, articles of clothing or even biological tissue could be *printed* on-demand, locally. With a simple scenario Brahim Dahmani illustrates how three-dimensional *printing* could transform the local production and re-cycling of clothes, and as the author suggests, these possibilities may not be as afar away in the future as they seem.

The second part, *Novel Perspectives for Networked Intelligence*, explores what the world will be like once computers have disappeared from view and information processing and exchange become part of an everyday networked life. What will be the features of such networked systems? Will such ambient systems be technology-centred, reducing human roles to insignificant acts, or will they be truly symbiotic, and enhance distinctive human abilities? How will people use these systems, and how will digital ownership be ensured? What are the implications and scenarios for future living? These are some the questions that this part of the book addresses.

The first contribution by Paul Kidd, *Human-Centred Ambient Intelligence: Human-computer Relationships for the Knowledge Era*, considers the relationship between people and computers. It addresses the values that designers bring to the development of such systems, and highlights the danger of designing systems for the *knowledge age* based on paradigms for human-computer relationships that emerged in the old industrial era. The article then proposes design concepts and principles for a human-centred relationship more appropriate to the *knowledge age*.

Some practical suggestions for being able to better manage ownership and privacy in a networked world, are taken up by Laurent Beslay and Hannu Hakala in *Digital Territory: Bubbles.* Socio-cultural norms, habits and legal rules provide guidelines for peoples' assessment of public or private spaces. Yet, networked technologies bring the private sphere into the public one and vice versa: work, home and school environments are no longer distinct environments. The article paints a vision of digital territories and the concepts necessary to manage emerging digital transactions and interactions.

In the following article, *Variations on Big Brother,* Walter Van de Velde takes up the issues of privacy and surveillance through two future scenarios. The author points out that many kinds of *Big Brother* scenarios are possible, some sinister and some with interesting twists. Two possible futures *Connectopolis and Egopoli* are presented and explored. Perhaps not all Big Brother visions are as expected?

To end the second part, Kazimierz Krzysztofek describes some of the social aspects of future networked worlds in his article, *The @lgorithmic Society: Digitarians of the World Unite*. He investigates the implications of algorithmic thinking on the social scale, and illustrates the ways in which the industrialised world is already moving towards a *post-information society*.

The third part, *The Future of Body and Mind*, considers the way that health and wellbeing determine the degree to which people can live fully in the world. Information and knowledge-based technologies are playing an increasing role in peoples' health, representing an increasing linkage between the body, mind and technology. Intelligent biomedical clothes, preventative medicine, body repair, intelligent drugs, may all lead to new heights of being *healthier than healthy*. At the same time, new possibilities of mind-computer interfaces could enable people to control machines through thought.

People are becoming more health conscious, taking care about what they eat, the exercise they do, and the medical care they follow. These concerns have all become parts of everyday life. In the article *myHealth*, André Dittmar outlines how a range of wearable health monitoring devices could help people with a number of acute or chronic conditions.

Enhancing the human capacities of hearing or sight have been established for a long time through such means as eyeglasses and hearing aids. Body repair is also evident in the many surgical techniques employed by modern medicine, such as transplant surgery, implants, and so forth. Yet the next generation of technologies will offer completely new forms of intelligent prosthesis and body components, as well as aesthetic enhancement. Using a descriptive scenario, Marc Bogdanowicz, paints a picture of body-friendly technologies in the article *Before the Cyborgs Come*. He also analyses some of differences between *repair* and *enhancement*, and discusses which seem socially acceptable.

The above two articles all deal with body, but what about the mind? Although, the human brain remains as one of the *last frontiers of medical science*, it is already possible to make connections between the mind and computers. Yet it is the human mind that remains an even more enigmatic entity. In the article *Tapping the Mind or Resonating Minds*? José del Millán describes some of the advances and potential implications of having human thoughts linked to machines. In doing so the author touches up on the classical dilemma of *objectivity* versus *subjectivity*; the material brain versus human consciousness that mysteriously resides within it.

In the fourth part of the book, *New Directions for Power and Participation*, important global issues such as the knowledge economy, globalisation, and democracy, are considered. The section explores some of the ways information and knowledge technologies may influence these global issues in the future. Democracy, the cornerstone of European society, is dependent on how peoples' participation in decision making is enabled. Intangible assets are changing the way trade is considered. Change and complexity are seen as inevitable. What are some of the prognoses for the future?

The first article, *Towards Democracy without Politics* by Ignace Snellen, portrays a contrasting perspective. Growing tensions between politics and democracy are described in terms of decision making, participation, and the roles that information and communication technologies are playing. What kinds of new relationships may exist between governments, citizens, and public administrations? What are the ways in which changes are likely to lead to increasing realisation of participatory democracy and the demise of representative democracy?

From a different perspective, Marc Luyckx outlines the ways in which the world is moving towards an *immaterial society*. His article *A Win-win Strategy for Europe in the Knowledge Society* considers how the role of intangible assets is changing the concepts of industrial trade. His vision suggests an emphasis on qualitative rather quantitative growth. Can information and communication technologies help realise this vision by contributing to more sustainable forms of development.

In the article, *Ecological Humanism and Technology as an Enabler for a Better World,* Alfonso Molina describes how society needs to move away from the mind-sets of power-maximisation, and tribal globalisation, towards visions which place *people and the planet* at the centre of reflection and action. The article interweaves several topics, such as the emerging trends in ecological thinking, the open-source software movement, global inclusion, and electronic governance, and envisages *intelligent interactivity* as one of driving forces for change.

The fifth and final part, *The Distant Horizon* looks further into the future. Thinking about where society is headed and why, is important, but not necessarily easy. Past choices and prevailing attitudes both determine the direction in which the future unfolds, for better or worse. The essays in the final section are perhaps the most speculative and questioning in this respect, but they also relate back to some of the topics taken up in contributions in preceding sections. Each author writes about a view of the possible futures, towards which society could, or should be moving, and what needs to be done to ensure that the distant horizon is potentially a happy and meaningful place.

In *Transport 2030: 20,000 Leagues Between Two Cities*, David Jeffery suggests two future scenarios. These both describe a journey between two cities, but in two very different futures. One is optimistic and the other much darker. The optimistic future describes a journey supported by automatically driven electric vehicles, leased to drivers on-demand, incorporating enhanced vehicle safety features, as well as satellite-based information and navigation systems. The second journey describes a frustrating world where chronic congestion is the norm, information systems are autonomous and uncoordinated, and environmental damage escalates.

In a different vein, Roman Galar's *Restarting the Evolutionary Drive* offers an original perspective on future social and economic developments, based on the perspective of complexity and evolutionary theory. He outlines how this perspective provides a vision of information and communication technologies that may in fact help move forward prevailing circumstances towards a *New Renaissance*.

In the third article, *The World as Computer*, Walter Van de Velde explores how to refocus thinking about algorithms, computing and the world in ways that redefine what computer science is all about.

To close part five, in the article *Creating Meaning: the Future of Human Happiness*, Liselotte Lyngsø and Anne Skare Nielsen paint a futurist's view of the future of happiness. The article examines the things in life that provide for happiness and what gives people value and meaning. The authors suggests that new thinking is needed in relation to how technologies of the future are conceived and designed.

~

Europe and the other industrialised societies have reached a significant point in their history. Major opportunities enabled by information and communication technologies lie ahead. But there are also significant challenges. How well society deals with these will determine how future generations will look back and judge the beginnings of the *knowledge age*. Will it be seen as a time of creativity, of throwing off constraints, of boldly building a better world for all? Or will it be assessed as an age of limited vision, of perpetuating the past, of missed opportunities? The answer is impossible to predict as it lies in the choices that will be made. If this book helps to illuminate these choices then it will have served its purpose well.

Part I: European Manufacturing 2035

The Future of European Manufacturing: Driven by Globalisation or Global Warming?

Paul T Kidd

Introduction

In the year 2035, European manufacturing industry will have declined to the point where it is no longer a significant contributor to the European economy! Why such a gloomy prediction? Is it because European manufacturing will be off-shored to China and other emerging economies in Asia? Or is it because no one will want to work in manufacturing, because of its (outdated) image as consisting largely of manual and dirty jobs? Or perhaps it is because European manufacturing industry does not have what it takes to compete in global markets? Certainly these are all issues which threaten to undermine and weaken European manufacturing capabilities. These however, are not the main explanations for predicting the demise of manufacturing in Europe by 2035. The reason is much subtler.

It is precisely because of the attention that is being paid to the above three matters that increases the risk of failure! Exploitation of global opportunities, transformation of the industry to knowledge intensive work, and achieving competitiveness in the face of global competition: these are all very important topics, but they are normally considered within the mindset of globalisation of the traditional industrial era system of production. This is what is wrong. Rather than globalisation being the driver and the logic for the future of manufacturing, based on a system of production as it is at the beginning of the 21st century, global warming is the main issue. This should be driving the development of a new system of production; one that is compatible with a low carbon economy, and one that is capable of revitalising the sector.

Global warming caused by an increase of greenhouse gases in the atmosphere, is however not the only potentially crippling issue impacting the future of manufacturing in Europe. Europe also has an addiction to non-renewable fossil fuels and an insatiable appetite for energy. Both of these issues have direct bearing on manufacturing futures. Thus, global warming, fossil fuel depletion, and increasing energy consumption; these are the main factors that will shape the future of manufacturing in Europe. Other matters seem to pail into insignificance when compared to these daunting problems. However, this not evident from the content of most manufacturing foresight, futures, roadmapping and visioning activities, even those published in a time when the destructive and serious nature of global warming have become much clearer.

That this is so however, is not very surprising, for most such studies only make passing reference to resource limitations, the need to improve environmental performance, and the conflict between growth and the environment [1]. Few studies analyse environmental problems in depth, or identify those features of the industrial era system of production that are an inherent source of environmental damage. Nor do such studies seek to identify priorities among the diffuse range of environmental challenges. This generally is the case both in Europe and in the United States.

Europe, and the rest of the industrialised world, as well as the industrialising nations, are fast approaching one of those decision points, a fork in the road so to speak, a moment in time, upon which the future of humanity will turn. Along one way the path is lined with the familiar. It is the path well trodden, of incremental changes that will not adequately address energy-related environmental concerns. This is the road that will ultimately lead to a crisis in manufacturing because it is founded on playing the global competitiveness game, on terms that are largely determined outside of Europe. This is the route to manufacturing decline and economic insignificance for the industry in Europe by the year 2035. The same old problems will persist, and faced with growing environmental regulation in Europe, the outcome is likely to be the demise of European manufacturing.

Along the other path however, the way in uncharted, unclear and the surrounding territory is alien. This road leads to a new system of production that is inherently low carbon emitting and low energy consuming. This is way froward and now is the time to begin to address this unfamiliar terrain, and to explore a new and different future for European manufacturing, one that might offer some hope that it will still be prosperous and economically significant in 2035.

So what could European manufacturing industry look like in 2035 if global warming and energy-related matters were positioned as the prime drivers for the sector's future? Before providing a glimpse of a possible answer to this question, an overview of the energy-related circumstances that prevail in 2006 is necessary to highlight the seriousness of the problems that will have to be addressed.

Global Energy Circumstances in 2006

It would be incorrect to state that nothing has been, or is being done, in Europe to deal with environmental problems created by manufacturing industry. Indeed, in a the comparative study on Environmentally Benign Manufacturing [2] undertaken in 2001 by the World Technology (WTEC) Division of the International Technology Research Institute in the United States, Europe emerged very well from a comparison with Japan and the United States.

European strengths in government-led activities were identified in areas such as product take-back legislation, development of lifecycle analysis tools and databases, co-operation with industry, landfill bans, recycling infrastructure, and economic incentives. In comparison, the main and only strength of the United States was in the area of financial and legal liability, and Japan, which although better than the United States in several area of activity, was still lagging behind Europe.

On the industrial side the picture that emerged was one of both European and Japanese manufacturing being more focussed on addressing environmental issues than US manufacturing industry, albeit there were differences in strengths between Japanese and European industries.

On the research side in Europe, even a cursory examination of the literature indicates that there is much going on in terms of research and pilot projects, at both national and European levels. This suggests a better future for manufacturing than the pessimistic opening statement to this chapter. Plastics from plant materials, energy efficiency projects, fuel cell technology, elimination of hazardous substances, and improvements to recycling technologies, etc. Theses are just a small sample of the environmentally advantageous developments taking place. On the energy supply side, new technologies are also emerging that promise zero carbon emissions from fossil fuels [3] using pre and post combustion carbon capture and storage. Renewable energy technologies that extract energy from the wind, waves and sunlight are also continually being improved, and there is also the nuclear option, as well as bio-fuels. Surely then, the future is bright? Is it not just a question of developing and applying such environmentally benign technologies, paving the way for manufacturing *business as normal*? This is not the case. What has, and is being done in Europe is of course very welcome, but the scale of the resources devoted to environmental issues fall far short of what is needed. The seriousness of the problems seems to be understated and underestimated. Digging deeper, beyond the technological research and pilot projects, into the data, statistics, and projections that are being produced by governments, agencies, and international organisations, quickly reveals that energy-related circumstances, both in Europe and globally, have already reached a serious state and are set to worsen, not to improve.

The challenges can be illustrated by considering the following:

An Insatiable Appetite for Energy

The International Energy Agency in its World Energy Outlook 2005 [4] predicted that if policies remain unchanged, world energy demand will increase by over 50% between 2005 and 2030. Whilst the International Energy Agency believes that world energy resources are adequate to meet this demand, such an increase in energy consumption will require a phenomenal investment of around 17 trillion United States dollars to bring these energy resources to consumers.

The European Environment Agency also reports [5] that energy consumption will continue to grow, making it more difficult to reduce energy-related environmental pressures. Energy consumption in the 25 Member States of the European Union increased by 11.6% between 1990 and 2003. Rising personal incomes and changes in lifestyle, with subsequent growing transport volumes, led to an increase in energy consumption of households, services, and transport, with transport becoming the largest consumer of energy. At the same time energy consumption in industry decreased, but electricity use however increased particularly rapidly in this period owing to its attractiveness and flexibility in end-use, and because of growth in the services sector and an increase in the ownership of electrical appliances. Growth in electricity consumption has in fact been twice as fast as the growth in energy use. All the signs are that these trends are set to continue unless additional energy saving measures are implemented.

A useful indicator for measuring progress in de-coupling economic growth from energy consumption is energy intensity, which is defined as the ratio of energy consumption to GDP. The energy intensity of the European Union's economy decreased by 15% between 1990 and 2003 owing to rising energy efficiency and structural changes taking place within the economy [5]. The efficiency of electricity production from fossil fuels also improved over the period, but since the share of electricity in energy consumption grew, this factor offset the reduced pressures on the environment derived from greater efficiency.

De-coupling of economic growth from rising energy consumption was most successful in the industry sector as a result of technical improvements and structural changes, while private households consumed more energy per capita owing to an increased number of (often larger) homes as well as more energy consuming appliances.

Improvements in the energy intensity of manufacturing industries over this period can be accounted for by several elements. Some improvements have clearly arisen from more energy efficient production processes and innovative technologies. However, economic factors have also played a role. In the new Member States the economic restructuring of the early 1990s led to a substantial initial decline in both energy consumption and the output of heavy industry. A decline in energy intensive industries within the European Union has also contributed to reduced energy intensity. However, much of this production has not ceased, just migrated to the emerging low-wage economies. This just creates additional needs for transportation, and combined with less stringent environmental regulation, the net result is invariably an increase in global energy intensity.

During the period considered, there has only been an insignificant de-coupling of transport energy consumption from economic growth in the European Union [5], with an average annual decrease in energy intensity of only 0.2%. This unwelcome fact is a result of rapid growth in road transport, which has led to rapid increases in energy consumption despite efforts to improve vehicle fuel efficiency. Transport growth has been influenced by various developments. In many regions growing urban sprawl has resulted in longer commuting distances. Infrastructure improvements have also made road transport more attractive, and rising disposable incomes have changed many lifestyles leading to more demand for travel and private cars. Furthermore, the development of the internal market in the European Union resulted in increased freight transport as companies sought to exploit the production cost advantages of different regions.

Fossil Fuel Addiction

In Europe, fossil fuels still continue to dominate energy production and consumption [5]. Combustion of fossil fuels accounts for almost 80% of total energy consumption and 55% of electricity production. Between 1990 and 2003 there was a shift from coal to cleaner natural gas in electricity production, although this fuel switch has slowed since 1999. Oil consumption grew as a result of increased transport volumes and oil continues to be the most important fuel in total energy consumption. The share of nuclear power remained almost constant. Shares of renewable energy in total energy and electricity consumption remain at low levels, despite large increases in the use of some types of renewable energy. The production of energy and electricity from renewable energy sources grew steadily between 1990 and 2003, with a particularly large increase in wind and solar electricity. However, the increase in the share of renewable energy in total energy and electricity consumption was limited by the fact that rising energy and electricity consumption offset to a large extent the increase in the use of renewable energy. In 2003, the share of renewable energy in total energy consumption and gross electricity consumption was 6% and 12.8%, respectively. The European Environment Agency therefore conclude that a significant further expansion will be needed to meet the European Union targets of a 12% share in total energy consumption and a 21% share in gross electricity consumption, by 2010.

With fossil fuels continuing to dominate energy production and transport, the issue of fossil fuel depletion must also be considered. Whilst the world seems to be well endowed with coal supplies, with the availability of resources extending hundreds of years into the future, the position with regard to oil supplies is not so reassuring.

For political and commercial reasons accurate public data on the world's oil reserves are hard to come by. There are various predictions about when oil supplies will cease to be commercially exploitable. In 2000, the United States Geographical Survey estimated, using geological data, that the world's remaining oil reserves amounted to 3,021 billion barrels [6]. To put this into perspective, about 918 billion barrels of oil were produced over the 40-year period between 1965 and 2005, according to oil industry statistics [7].

The United States Geographical Survey's figures for world oil resources comprise three categories of reserves. The first is remaining reserves, that is to say, oil that has been discovered but which has not yet been extracted. The second category is reserve growth, which is the expected increase in reserves resulting mainly from technological factors that enhance a field's recovery rate. The third category is undiscovered oil – the oil that remains to be found through exploration.

The reserve growth and undiscovered volumes are derived from United States Geographical Survey mean estimates, which are an average assessment over a wide range of uncertainty for reserve growth and undiscovered resources.

It is reported that the United States Government, based on the work of the United States Geographical Survey, believes that exhaustion of the remaining known oil reserves will occur sometime around 2055 [7].

However several oil depletion studies have been undertaken by numerous organisations, each producing widely differing conclusions [7]. One study, for example, predicts oil production peaking as early as 2010, remaining at a constant level for 10 years, and then falling to exhaustion level around 2075. Another study however, does not see peak production occurring until 2030, and then remaining at a constant level for 15 years, and eventually falling off to exhaustion levels sometime in the early part of the 22nd century.

In addition to the above mentioned lack of public data on world oil reserves, further uncertainties concerning the timing of peak production and exhaustion arise from several other factors. These include the possibility that significant new oil fields, not accounted for in the estimates, will be discovered thus moving the timing of peak production further forward into the future. However, increasing demand may do exactly the opposite. Other factors adding to the uncertainties are the long-term effects of oil price on the demand for oil, and the development and availability of competitive alternatives to fuels such petroleum.

Whilst there is no agreement about when oil will run out, there is however consensus that demand for oil is increasing. World demand for petroleum is set to increase 37% by 2030, according to the United States Energy Information Administration's 2006 International Annual Energy Outlook [8]. Demand is expected to hit 118 million barrels per day in 2030, up from 2003 levels of 80 million barrels, despite oil prices that are expected to be even higher than they were in 2005, and driven in large part by transport needs. Higher demand is also expected to come from Asia, especially India and China.

With regard to the long-term effects of oil price, though worldwide oil demand is forecast to increase, it is possible that higher prices might temper demand and boost the appeal of other sources of energy, such as coal, gas and renewable fuels. Oil represented nearly 38% of the world's total energy consumption in 2003, but is expected to fall to 33% by 2030.

Alternatives to crude oil, as the primary source of liquid fuels, are coal, shale oil, and oil sands. These three sources could potentially extend the use of petroleum type fuels for hundreds of years into the future. Some in the oil industry believe that the world has so far only tapped into 18% of the total global supply of crude oil.

These are all comforting thoughts for those who are worried about what will happen when crude oil supplies are exhausted, but not for those who are concerned about the damage that fossil fuel consumption is doing to the climate. This is to say nothing of the wisdom of relying on oil as a fuel and of leaving little of the substance for future generations, in the far distant future, to exploit.

17

Greenhouse Gas Emissions

The net result of this continued reliance on fossil fuels is that, according to International Energy Agency [4], energy-related carbon dioxide emissions, the most ubiquitous greenhouse gas, will also climb, and by 2030 emissions will be 52% higher than in 2005. These projected trends have important implications and lead to a future that is not sustainable from the perspectives of depletion, environmental damage, and energy-security. The International Energy Agency's conclusion: these outcomes must be changed by moving the planet onto a sustainable energy path.

The European Environment Agency reports that energy-related emissions of greenhouse gases in Europe are beginning to show upward trends after decreases in the 1990s, putting long-term reduction targets at risk [9]. Specifically, energy-related greenhouse gas emissions fell by 2.6% between 1990 and 2003, but have been rising slowly since 1999.

The United Kingdom Government's 2006 Energy Review Consultation Document [10] also notes that global emissions are continuing to increase. Between 1990 and 2003, emissions in the European Union and G7 countries, plus Australia, grew by 5.2%.

According to the European Environment Agency, a major contributing factor to these increases in Europe is a slow down in the switch to natural gas in electricity production, in favour of coal powered plants. In addition, there is a long-term trend of growing transport emissions owing to increased transport volumes. This has offset much of the improvements achieved in other sectors. Hence substantial decreases of energy-related greenhouse gas emissions are required to meet long-term emission reduction targets proposed by the European Union.

Total European Union greenhouse gas emissions rose slightly in 2004 by 0.3% compared to 2003 and were 5% below the 1990 level. With existing policies and measures, European Union greenhouse gas emissions are projected to be 2.1% below the 1990 level by 2010, falling short of the Kyoto targets.

Greenhouse gas emissions in the pre-2004 European Union Member States (the EU-15) in 2004 were 0.9% below the base-year level. This clearly shows that in 2004, the EU-15 was little more than one-tenth of the way towards achieving the 8% emissions reduction target required by 2008–2012 under the Kyoto Protocol. Latest projections for 2010 show that the combined effect of existing and additional domestic policies and measures, the Kyoto mechanisms, and carbon sinks (forests), would bring emissions down to 8.0% below the EU-15 base-year level. This corresponds exactly to the reduction required under the Kyoto Protocol. With existing domestic policies and measures, total EU-15 greenhouse gas emissions will only be 0.6% below base-year levels in 2010. Taking into account additional domestic policies and measures being planned by Member States, a total EU-15 emissions reduction of 4.6% is projected. This relies on the assumption that several Member States will cut emissions by more than is required to meet their national targets. The projected use of Kyoto mechanisms by ten Member States will reduce emissions by 2010 by a further 2.6%. Finally, the use of carbon sinks would contribute an additional 0.8% [9].

Two Member States are on track to achieve their burden-sharing targets by 2010, and project that existing domestic policies and measures alone will be sufficient to meet or even exceed their targets. Six more countries anticipate they will exceed or meet their commitment targets through the use of additional measures, or application of the Kyoto mechanisms, or use of carbon sinks, or a combination of these. The remaining seven Member States project that they will miss their targets despite the implementation of additional measures or the use of Kyoto mechanisms or carbon sinks.

From 1990 to 2004, the emission of greenhouse gases in the EU-15 decreased in most sectors, especially in waste management, industrial processes, and agriculture. Energy supply and use, excluding transport, saw lesser reductions taking place. EU-15 greenhouse gas emissions from energy supply and use, excluding transport, were 2.4% below 1990 levels in 2004 and are projected to stay at roughly the same level by 2010 if only existing policies and measures are used. However, greenhouse gas emissions in the EU-15 are projected to decline further in most sectors by 2010 compared to 2004 levels, if additional domestic policies and measures are used.

Between 1990 and 2004, carbon dioxide emissions from public electricity and heat production increased by 6% owing to an increase of 35% in electricity production in thermal power plants.

EU-15 greenhouse gas emissions from transport increased by 26% over the period 1990 and 2004, and are projected to increase further to 35% above 1990 levels by 2010 if only existing policies and measures are used. The average carbon dioxide emission of a new passenger car was reduced by about 12% from 1995 to 2004. However, 21% more cars were sold in the same period. As a result, this increase in the number of cars offset the emission reduction gains arising from technological improvements to vehicles.

One of the two European Member states that expect to exceed their greenhouse gas reduction targets by 2010, is the United Kingdom. At the beginning of 2006 the United Kingdom Government undertook an energy review consultation [10]. One of the short term goals of the United Kingdom is to contribute towards the European Union's obligations under the Kyoto Protocol, which requires the United Kingdom to reduce greenhouse gas emissions by 12.5% below base year levels by 2008-12. The consultation document reports that the United Kingdom is on track to deliver this. Estimates show that total United Kingdom greenhouse gas emissions in 2004 had fallen 14.6% below 1990 levels, and projections show that they should be about 20% below by 2010.

A second goal in the shorter term is to reduce carbon dioxide emissions by 20% on the 1990 level by 2010. However, the United Kingdom Government has noted that meeting this aim is proving to be challenging. Projections suggest that the United Kingdom will have only reduced carbon dioxide emissions to around 10% below 1990 levels by 2010. These projections are based on measures in place at the beginning of 2006, and do not take account of any new measures that might be introduced in the future.

The key message emerging from these figures, and one that is stressed in the consultation document, is that the projections highlight the size of the challenge in meeting longer-term carbon goals. By 2020, projected emissions lie in a range of 144 million tons to 148 million tons depending on assumptions made on fossil fuel prices. This is some 30 million tons above the level that has previously been set by the United Kingdom Government as representing real progress towards the 2050 goal of a 60% reduction in carbon dioxide emissions.

The size of the carbon challenge for 2050 is illustrated in the consultation document by using carbon intensity and energy intensity as measures, carbon intensity being the level of carbon emissions against GDP. The United Kingdom has improved considerably on both counts. Carbon intensity has improved by 55% since the early 1970s, a rate of almost 2% per annum. Energy intensity has improved by 40% in that period, largely as a result of energy efficiency improvements, the trend away from coal to gas plant for electricity generation, and the shift in the economy from heavy industry towards the commercial and services sectors.

Assuming that United Kingdom GDP grows on average by 2.5% per annum in the years to 2050, then carbon intensity in the United Kingdom would need to reduce to around 10% of 2006 levels if the target for 2050 is to be met. This is an extremely demanding goal. A striking fact presented in the consultation document is that, even if the United Kingdom had a completely carbon-free generation mix, but took no measures in other sectors, the United Kingdom would fall far short of its target for 2050. To make real progress towards the 2050 goal by 2020, not only will lower emissions from generation be required, but also continued and significant improvement in the efficiency with which energy is used in travel, homes and in business.

One of the conclusions of the energy review consultation is that, although present policies in the United Kingdom will result in the United Kingdom exceeding its target under the first commitment period of the Kyoto Protocol, strong economic performance has led to growing energy consumption. This growth, combined with higher levels of electricity generation from coal, will lead to higher carbon emissions in the United Kingdom [11].

Put another way, the growth in the economy and the resulting greenhouse gas emissions will far outstrip any gains made in reducing greenhouse gas emissions using the measures deployed so far. Something more radical is needed!

Some Implications for Manufacturing

The above is presented to paint a realistic picture of where Europe stands in terms of energy production and use with regard to three key issues: greenhouse gas emissions, addiction to non-renewable fossil fuels, and an insatiable appetite for energy. The challenges posed are daunting. Clearly is it not going to be sufficient to focus on supply-side issues such as switching over to low-carbon fuels and electricity generation; demand-side measures must also be taken.

The energy intensity of European manufacturing industries must be significantly reduced. Energy intensity is not however a measure of energy efficiency, since it is affected by a number of factors unrelated to measuring efficiency, such as the movement of large energy consuming industries outside of the European Union area. Improvements in energy efficiency indicate that less input energy is being used to provide a given output. Energy efficiency improvements alone however will not be enough to address the problems. The ultimate goal for European manufacturing should be, not only to improve energy efficiency and to reduce energy intensity, but also to achieve significant energy savings, thus reducing energy consumption in absolute terms.

Transport in particular is an obvious area where energy savings need to be sought.

Figures produced by Department for Transport at the end of 2005[12], show that goods vehicle transport has increased by 22% in the United Kingdom since 1993 and light van transport by 53% in the same period. This time scale covers the adoption by manufacturing industry of new logistics and supply chains methods and lean production techniques, the latter of which tend to emphasise smaller more frequent delivery of parts by suppliers.

Unfortunately data collected by governments does not indicate the extent to which modern manufacturing approaches in supply and distribution are further adding to greenhouse gas emissions. This highlights an omission in official statistics and a need to investigate the impacts that optimisation at the micro level (the individual enterprise) has upon performance at a macro level with respect to the energy and carbon intensity of manufacturing industry.

The link between economic growth in manufacturing and its demand for transport needs to be broken. In the context of manufacturing industry this will require the development of a system of production that is less reliant upon transportation and vehicle-kilometres driven. To encourage the development of a less transport intensive manufacturing industry, it would be beneficial to develop an internationally agreed transport-based emissions trading scheme for all manufactured goods. This would help to highlight the negative impacts of off-shoring European production to places such as China, and could help to drive developments towards more distributed smaller scale production facilities located closer to markets.

In addition it is clear that European manufacturing industries, as the producers of energy consuming devices and appliances used in homes and businesses, need to address energy intensity, energy efficiency, and energy reduction in the different sectors that they serve. This represents both a challenge and a market opportunity.

Manufacturing in a Low Carbon Economy

Demand-side improvements in response to energy-related concerns will require a paradigm shift in the way manufacturing is conducted, in terms of every aspect of manufacturing enterprise operations from customers and products, through actual manufacturing activities, to distribution, sales and after market support.

One possible solution lies in Product-Service Systems where pre-designed systems of products, services, and supporting infrastructures fulfil market needs in way that has a smaller environmental impact than separate products and services with the same function fulfilment. Another solution might lie in Eco-efficient Services. These are commercial market offerings aimed at fulfilling needs by selling the utilisation of a product or system instead of just providing the product. A further possibility is virtualisation of distribution and warehousing. Product data and designs would not be transformed into manufactured goods and then transported, but would be made available across information and communications technology networks. Physical items would only produced when needed and very close to the point of sale or use.

The following three cases indicate the possibilities:

The Future Generation Automobile Enterprise

During the 20th century car manufacturers in effect undertook the transformation of services into goods, by moving transportation expenditure from buses, trains and taxis to spending on car purchases. In so doing however they generated a growth in additional new services (finance, insurance, repairs, etc). Yet people who own and use cars still use buses, trains and taxis. In fact at different moments people have different needs which they satisfy with a changing mix of goods and services. These needs potentially shift from day to day, perhaps even from hour to hour, or minute to minute.

While some people buy automobiles because they like cars, many people purchase motor vehicles because they have transportation and communication needs. A car however is only one way of satisfying these needs.

Using a concept called *managed consumption* it might be possible to meet these changing needs with less energy use than is possible using the dominant business model based on outright purchase and ownership of a vehicle. Managed consumption is a systems approach applied to each individual customer's consumption of goods and services. It is a possible way of resolving the paradox of how to achieve economic growth without consuming large amounts of energy resources.

Managed consumption takes environmental responsiveness to a new level of sophistication by sharing resources between customers, only delivering a resource to a customer when they need it. It does not render recycling redundant. Materials will still need to be returned to their original forms or reused in manufacturing. Neither does managed consumption replace re-manufacturing. Cars will still be manufactured, and will need to be remanufactured to reduce waste.

Managed consumption is clearly not applicable to all manufactured goods, but is certainly relevant to automobiles. It is unlikely to entirely replace individual ownership of cars, but could provide a significant alternative. To be successful, managed consumption would need to be capable of delivering goods and services near instantaneously to meet quickly changing individual customer needs. It implies capabilities like: door step delivery of a vehicle, individually customised, when required and for as long as required; and capability to delivery multiple goods and services configured near instantaneously to meet rapidly changing individual customer needs.

On the Spot Manufacturing

There was a time when someone ordering a new pair of glasses had to wait several days for delivery, because production of the lenses and their assembly into frames was undertaken at a central facility. This is no longer the case. A new pair of glasses can be produced in less that an hour, because the work is now done at the optician's premises. Perhaps this is how much of manufacturing will be undertaken in the future?

Returning once again to the car, which in many ways is symbolic of the problems created by the mass ownership of energy consuming products. Back in the late 1980s, the notion of a car customised to individual requirements was raised in the scenario of the three-day car publicised by the Japanese.

The three-day car scenario arose from a study undertaken by some leading Japanese firms from numerous sectors. In 1987, ten representatives from different Japanese industries began meeting to discuss the future of Japanese manufacturing. Included in this group were some well-known names: Nissan Motors; Komatsu; NEC; and Toshiba. The main motivation behind the initiative was concern that the competitive advantages in leading Japanese manufacturers had reached maturity and that many of the techniques commonly associated with the Japanese approach were being copied by Western competitors.

Eventually the initiative acquired the name *Manufacturing 21*. As the work progressed, a clear objective emerged to develop a so-called post-just-in-time manufacturing paradigm that would be highly flexible to change and that would stimulate further changes. This was an early recognition is Japan of the notion that Japanese industry needed to undertake a paradigm shift.

One of the driving forces behind the three-day car was the expected transfer of automobile production from Japan to other parts of the globe. The expectation was that by 2001, annual car production in Japan would be as much as 20% lower than in 1986. A need was identified for the Japanese motor industry to learn how to make money on slightly higher value, special niche models selling fewer than 20,000 units over a lifetime – essentially a manufacturing strategy for low volume automobiles. In addition, the challenge would be to reduce delivery lead times for a new car from an average 21 days down to three days – this would apply to both standard vehicles and customised cars.

The notion of servicing a niche market of customers who wanted to be involved in the design of their own vehicles, so-called proactive consumers or *prosumers*, was emphasised in this scenario. Envisaged were vehicles that would accommodate: styling changes to body panels; modifications to instrument panel layouts; customer designed trim; car

24

lighting systems modified to particular tastes; tailor made seating; and sound and entertainment systems specified to exact individual requirements.

Also noted was the possibilities of customisation that would be enabled by the use of electronics, that is, on-board computerised systems. This opens up the possibility of adapting the performance of engines and suspension systems to individual requirements.

A central idea put forward by the groups working on the development of the three-day car scenario was that achieving this level of customisation would require changes to both product design and manufacturing facilities. Product designs would need to be modularised and new materials capable of being economically modified to the required style would be required. Extremely flexible manufacturing and logistics systems would also be needed, and manufacturing of the vehicle might need to be moved to the point of sale.

The concept of the three-day customised car was picked up in 1991 by a group working in the United States who developed the idea further and came up with the notion of the re-configurable automobile. This scenario foresaw vehicles being purchased for lifetime use and reconfigured as their owner's needs and lifestyles changed, and as new technologies became available.

Specifically the scenario suggested a modular product design providing: exchangeable body panels attached to a scalable body structure; attachable sub-assemblies such as fenders and hoods providing body styling choices; new options such as choice of dash panels and seating arrangements; easily replaceable engines, transmissions, suspensions, braking systems and interiors; exchange of engines as significant efficiency and emission improvements were introduced.

Such vehicles would not be manufactured in large mass-production facilities, but again as in the case of the Japanese scenario, in smaller distributed production facilities.

A similar proposal has been outlined for the production of spares for a variety of products and items as the following two scenarios illustrate [13]:

Scenario 1:
In this futuristic scenario set in the year 2035, Boston Trader is a large cargo ship, powered by hydrogen fuel cell technology, which regularly travels back and forward across the North Atlantic between Europe and North America. On a voyage to London it is forced to return to New York for emergency repairs to a water pump. Built in 2010, it is now 25 years old and many of the companies that manufactured components and systems for the vessel have long ceased to exist. However, thanks to the use of product data and lifecycle management systems during the design, construction, and operation of the ship, every item of product data that has

ever been created for the vessel – sketches, spreadsheets, drawings, bills of materials, manufacturing process routes, numerical control programmes, etc. – are still available and kept at the owner's computer resource centre in London. As the ship makes its way to New York, original product information for the pump has been sent electronically to a number of pre-qualified manufacturers in New York City, and an electronic bidding process has resulted in the selection of a contractor to manufacture and install the new pump. As soon as the ship arrives in port the new pump will be ready and waiting, will be quickly fitted and tested, and Boston Trader will depart within a few hours to continue its journey.

Scenario 2:
In this futuristic scenario, a car is in the garage for repairs. The engine needs a new piston, but the garage no longer holds stocks of engine components, nor does the vehicle manufacturer. Instead, the garage makes all the components they need in a matter of minutes, not using conventional subtractive technologies like a lathe or a milling machine, but using additive technologies, that were at one time called rapid prototyping and manufacturing processes. These construct components layer by layer. These machines are linked via the internet to the manufacturer's product data and lifecycle management systems, and produce the replacement component on the spot, as and when needed. Versions of these machines are also fitted into mobile repair vehicles, and using the internet and mobile communications technologies, roadside repair personnel are often able to produce some components that will do until a permanent repair can be made. Likewise, parts for domestic appliances are being manufactured in high street shops or outside homes in a service technician's vehicle, using similar techniques.

~

The additive manufacturing processes described in these scenarios, first appeared in the late 1980s, and over a period of 16 years they have moved towards a state when the manufacture of production grade metal components is becoming feasible. Often such processes use less energy and produce less scrap then the familiar subtractive processes.

Producer-Consumer Lifecycle Relationships

This scenario considers how the dominant business model of the late 20th century, based on purchase and ownership of products, may be superseded by a new business model, based on pay-per-use, offering significant energy saving benefits. The scenario considers the case of a washing machine, another example of mass ownership of energy consuming products.

Scenario 3:
A married couple's washing machine is broken. It is very old machine so the couple decide to buy a new one. Off they go to the local store, where on arrival they see lined up the usual array of products, but they immediately discover that none of them are for sale!

Surprisingly they discover that they can have any one of the products on show, or choose from several that are not in store, and have it delivered to, and installed in their home within four hours. And it will cost them nothing, well not immediately anyway. They will not pay anything until they start using it, and then they will only pay for the amount of use, with different rates applied depending on the time of day, thus encouraging them to economise by only using the machine when they have a full load and when electricity is avaiable at off-peak prices.

When they visit this futuristic store, they do not even need to speak to a sales person. They can use in-store computer screens to help them chose the washing machine that best suits their circumstances. They are asked about the number of people in their family, and how many times each week they use a washing machine. Based on the answers provided to such questions, they are offered a choice of products that best suits their requirements. On offer are the familiar brand names from the 20th century – Hoover, Hotpoint, Indesit, and several more – plus many brands that are relatively new market entrants from places such China, Malaysia and several other countries. However, unlike in the early part of the 21st century, all these companies now manufacture locally, close to markets, to avoid the significant greenhouse gas emissions associated with the transportation of goods over long distances.

In this interaction with the computer, what the couple do not see is any information on price, because the assumption is that they will not want to pay the high price tag that is attached to modern consumer products. The price is deliberately set high because it covers the cost of recycling the product once its useful life is over, as well as the true environmental cost of its production. The price is also high because it includes the cost of product upgrades that have to be provided, by law, over the period of use, to extend the useful life. Also factored into the high purchase price are the advanced technologies and electronics that will help to reduce energy usage, as well as the compulsory maintenance and repair costs that will keep the machine operating at optimum efficiency. Another significant factor in the high price is the legal requirement now in place that mandates a move away from economies of scale driven mass

27

production, that had previously locked manufacturing industry into environmentally damaging, priced-based, consumption oriented, business strategies.

With such a high purchase price, pay-per-use is extremely attractive to most consumers.

The next step in the selection process is provision of information about the couple's broadband internet connection, and if they have a wired or a wireless network in their home. The internet is a key component in the new way of using a washing machine. When it is installed, in addition to the usual power, water and drainage services, it will also be connected to the internet.

The operation of the machine will be continuously monitored using the internet so that any problems are quickly detected and a repair technician despatched before the user even experiences a breakdown. For those non-urgent washes, the internet will provide the means for the energy supply company to control the timing of the wash so that it makes use of electricity generated from renewable sources. This aspect is also part of a Europe-wide energy management scheme designed to ensure a more constant energy demand, which has resulted in a reduced need for natural gas and oil fired power stations devoted solely to handling demand peaks, thus reducing unwanted and harmful emissions of greenhouse gases.

The internet is also key to how the couple will pay for the service, for since they are not buying the washing machine, but paying on the basis of use, it is no longer considered a product, but a service.

On the in-store computer screen they are asked to identify their utility suppliers – gas, electric, water, telephone, and internet. Then they will see what the service will cost from each of their utility companies, for each of the products that have been identified as being suitable for their needs; the manufacturers of washing machines have teamed up with utility companies to deliver this service. Each utility will offer a deal based on specific circumstances, and payments will be collected through the monthly or quarterly bill from the utility company that is eventually selected.

Of course the couple did not need to visit an electrical appliance store to do all this; they could have done the same from home using internet shopping, or at their local supermarket, or any one of several outlets offering computerised shopping facilities.

The Role of Information and Communications Technologies

The enablers of manufacturing in a low carbon economy are numerous and varied. New business models will need to be developed. Consumer attitudes towards product ownership will need to be changed. Industry mindsets will also need to be addressed to overcome the inevitable scepticism resulting from over two hundred years of industrial development that has favoured energy consumption and high carbon emissions. New business strategies will need to be formulated by both equipment vendors who supply manufacturing industries, as well as manufacturers who use this equipment. High levels of responsiveness, a very strong focus on customer satisfaction, excellence service quality, and the ability to quickly satisfy individual customer demands, no matter how unusual, will be required.

Achieving a good understanding of the concept of a shift towards smaller scale production, on-the-spot manufacturing, etc. is also key. A simplistic interpretation is the industrial era factory system versus these new concepts. An *either or* circumstance. This is not the case. Between the two is a continuum, with positioning determined by technological feasibility, production economics, lifecycle carbon and energy analysis, safety issues, product characteristics, and so forth. The challenge will be to develop methods to determine where, along the continuum, manufacturing can take place.

There are many unknowns. How effective will the proposed approaches be in reducing energy use and carbon dioxide emissions? What sort of manufacturing best suits the approaches outlined above? What technological developments are needed to make the scenarios feasible? Can tax, legal, and carbon trading regimes be designed to foster the development of an alternative system of production? What steps need to be taken to ensure that developing economies such as China are not disadvantaged by the suggested developments?

In technological terms, research is required on several fronts. On-the-spot manufacturing requires further development of existing processes. New materials for these processes are also needed so that parts with the required properties, such as surface finish, strength, etc., can be manufactured. This inevitably will involve the use of nanotechnologies to create materials with the desired characteristics, as traditional materials are not adequate for the purpose. New, low energy joining and bonding methods, suitable for small-scale facilities, will also need to be developed. However, such technological developments will also raise a number of environmental issues in their own right. For example, will new materials based on nanotechnologies be more toxic than traditional materials? How will nano-based materials be recycled? Will joining and bonding technologies suitable for small-scale production be more difficult to undo, making separation of materials during recycling more difficult?

A key enabler of the alternative system of production envisaged will be information and communications technologies. In all of the scenarios described, these technologies play a central role.

Managed consumption for example, requires advanced information and communications technologies to support communications and the establishment and tracking of customer needs. All the scenarios will make use of broadband internet. Computerised systems that can analyse customers needs, provide product selection guidance, and offer design options, will all figure large in the range of tools that will be needed. This means that what can be described as, customer-facing systems, will take on a much more important role. Technologies to support simulation and visualisation of the use-experience will also probably be significant.

On the manufacturing side, many processes, unlike the familiar subtractive processes of the industrial era, such as lathes and milling machines, will be additive, where component parts are built up layer by layer. However there are already concerns about the suitability of modern computer-aided design and other software to support the existing generation of additive manufacturing processes, and these issues will need to be better defined and understood, leading to new software that is better suited to these processes.

Also mentioned in one of the scenarios is a Europe-wide energy management scheme. This concept is based on achieving a more constant energy demand. Information and communications technologies will provide the means to link energy consuming devices in the home, to remotely located control centres. These centres will initiate operation of the appliances to match the availability of spare renewable generating capacity during off-peak periods, thus avoiding fossil fuel consumption and the related carbon dioxide emissions.

Conclusions

Manufacturing developed in a world where energy intensity and carbon intensity were not of any concern. Many modern manufacturing practices, such as lean production and supply chain management, optimise performance at the level of the individual enterprise. Likewise, off-shoring of production offers opportunities for the individual enterprise to increase its profits, at least in the short term. The cost of all these practices in terms of energy and fossil fuel consumption, and the resulting contribution to climate change, is obvious, but hardly ever considered when the longer-term future of manufacturing is addressed.

There seems to be a tacit assumption that somehow, life in the world of manufacturing will go on much as normal in the future, and that whatever has to be done to respond to global warming, will not significantly affect the path that manufacturing will follow. This is nonsense.

The challenge of meeting longer-term greenhouse gas reduction targets requires a more fundamental approach as opposed to trying to improve the existing system of production. The future of manufacturing will be radically different to that which most people foresee. If it is not, it is likely to be because collectively the world was unable to solve the problem of global warming, and just continued along the present road, which seems to be heading towards a global catastrophe.

The effects of climate change will be significant and the scale of the problem is enormous. Within the problem however there is also an opportunity. There are concerns about European manufacturing; about the off-shoring of production, about attracting skilled people to work in the sector, and about competitiveness in world markets. There is a possibility however, that by focussing on these matters, Europe has lost sight of the real threats, which really lie in global warming, fossil fuel depletion, and increasing energy consumption. It is possible that by addressing these issues directly, through the development of a new system of production, that Europe might well find a way of dealing with the now familiar concerns that, during the opening years of the 21st century, have dominated discussions about the future of European manufacturing.

Ahead lies the opportunity to develop a low carbon, low energy intensity, non-fossil fuel based manufacturing sector. It is one of those grand challenges that do not come along very often. It is a challenge that each of the European Union Member States would have no chance of rising to on their own. Collectively, however, as the Europe Union, they can. Moreover, it is not as though the risk of investing in an alternative system of production is very high. For, through an intelligent focus of resources on technologies and developments that could have equal validity in other scenarios, the risks could easily be minimised.

Back in 1973, at the time of the first oil-shock, it was said by many that the industrialised world was too dependent upon oil, and this dependency should be broken. This has not happened. Exactly the opposite has occurred. Now the price of this folly is starting to become clear. There are those that do not accept that global warming is happening, and some that do, believe that it is not a result of human activity. There are also vested interests that do not want the industrialised world to switch away from fossil fuels such as oil. What will influence the future? Will it

31

be vested interests, or will it be the distinctive human attribute – intelligence – that allows humankind to foresee the consequences of its decisions and actions, and to shape the future to create more desirable outcomes for the plant and all its inhabitants?

References

[1] Sonntag, V. 2003, *Speed, Scale and Sustainability: An Inquiry into Technological Momentum and the Strategic Use of Advanced Manufacturing Technologies* (University of Maastrict, Maastrict)
[2] WTEC Panel Report, 2001, *Environmentally Benign Manufacturing* (World Technology Division of the International Technology Research Institute, Baltimore)
[3] Zero Emission Fossil Fuel Power Plants Technology Platform, 2006, *A Vision for Zero Emission Fossil Fuel Power Plants* (Office for Official Publications of the European Communities, Luxembourg)
[4] The International Energy Agency, 2005, *World Energy Outlook 2005*, (International Energy Agency, http://www.iea.org/Textbase/subjectqueries/index.asp)
[5] European Environment Agency, 2006, *Energy and Environment in the European Union: Tracking Progress towards Integration* (Office for Official Publications of the European Communities, Luxembourg)
[6] United States Geological Survey, 2000, *World Petroleum Assessment 2000: Description and Results*, (U.S. Geological Survey Digital Data Series - DDS-60, http://pubs.usgs.gov/dds/dds-060/)
[7] Wikipedia, 2006, *Oil Reserves* (http://en.wikipedia.org/wiki/Oil_reserves)
[8] Energy Information Administration, 2006, *Annual International Energy Outlook 2006* (Energy Information Administration, Washington DC, http://www.eia.doe.gov/oiaf/ieo/index.html)
[9] European Environment Agency, 2006, *Greenhouse Gas Emission Trends and Projections in Europe 2006* (Office for Official Publications of the European Communities, Luxembourg)
[10] United Kingdom Department of Trade and Industry, 2006, *Our Energy Challenge: Securing Clean, Affordable Energy for the Long-term* (Department of Trade and Industry, Energy Review Consultation Document, January 2006)
[11] United Kingdom Department of Trade and Industry, 2006, *The Energy Challenge: Energy Review Report 2006* (HMSO, London)
[12] Department of Transport, 2005, *Transport Statistics Bulletin, Traffic in Great Britain, Q4, 2005,* (http://www.dft.gov.uk/stellent/groups/dft_transstats/documents/page/dft_transsta ts_611128.hcsp)
[13] Kidd, P.T., 2001, *E-business Strategy: Case Studies, Benefits and Implementation* (Cheshire Henbury, Macclesfield)

Chapter 3

From Bits to Atoms

Roberto Saracco

Introduction

The human race has achieved spectacular progress through its capacity to conceptualise. Conceptualisation does not use atoms, but something intangible that goes on inside peoples' minds. Wording is an important part of this process; modelling is another. Understanding the boundaries of objects and capturing shapes are also part of conceptualisation.

Atoms are the starting point for many human activities, but adding a human touch moves beyond atoms. Take coding as an example. The activity of coding, be it in a written language, in a spoken one or in gestures, started at an early stage in human evolution. Over the past few hundred years, coding has become the object of scientific theories. Engineers and computer scientists have also made coding the foundation of their professions. They have exploited the tremendous power of conceptualisation and consequently created most of the objects that are associated with the modern world, from tiny electronic parts to huge skyscrapers. These have been conceived and designed, refined and finally planned with the help of computers.

Computers work by manipulating bits. Bits are digits, either one or zero. In computing, a bit is the smallest unit of information handled by a computer. These are represented physically by a very small pulse of electricity sent through a circuit, or a small point on a magnetic surface that can change state to represent either one or zero. Bits convey little information of use to humans, but they can be manipulated by computers to present information in a way that is useful to people.

The modern Boeing 777 aircraft was designed from the very start using computers, that is to say, by manipulating bits, rather than using physical mock-ups. Bits have also helped achieve spectacular progress in medicine because scientists have been able to capture and model the inner working of the body and to gain understanding through conceptualisation. The decoding of the human genome, the complete collection of human genetic material, was achieved through the use of computers, and the result is but a first step in a healthcare revolution that will have a significant impact in the future.

Because of the value of bits, the past 40 years have been focused mostly on the way to represent anything in bits and in creating the means, often in the form of machines, to transform atoms into bits. Sound, pictures, temperature and many other measurements, are all examples of things that have been converted from the physical into bits stored in computers.

There are however, many areas where significant work is still needed to create bit representations. One example is the representation of emotions. There will be continuing progress towards representation in bits; researchers are working to capture single atoms and to code them. At the same time they are learning how to manipulate single atoms.

In the future it is possible that two big research areas connected to bits may come to fruition. Both are likely to change the world in very significant ways: the understanding of bits and their transformation into atoms.

The abundance of bits will stimulate research into these two topics. The first area of research will help make sense out of the deluge of information. Understanding what is in an image and how the various elements relate to other information will greatly increase the use that can be made of bits. The second area, the one addressed in this chapter, recognises that atoms satisfy many human needs: bits belong to the perception of reality, and atoms are the reality.

People and Atoms

People are made of atoms, live in a world of atoms and interact through atoms. Progress has made an impact on people because there have been ways of translating bits into atoms. The digitised voice is returned into coherent vibrations of atoms that can be heard; billions of printed pages capture digital information making it visible and useful; pills are swallowed, not the concepts on which the medication is based, and so on.

There is nothing new in translating bits into atoms, just as there was nothing new in Johann Gutenberg's printing press based on moveable type. But that press changed the world by making it easy and cost effective to produce printed material.

A similar revolution is in the making. New machines are likely to become available in the future to bring a new level of effectiveness to the translation of bits into atoms.

Imaging this scenario. What if consumers, after seeing chinaware on the internet, can have them made in their living rooms? What if doctors can capture the essence of their patient and their ailments, and create the right medicine for each one? What if ladies, fancying new dresses in the morning, can get them made in their bedrooms, ready to be donned?

People relate to their environment through atoms. It is essential to convert bits into something that can be perceived such as light, sound, forces, and so forth. Picking up a computer storage disk does not tell anything about the information it contains. For this, sophisticated devices (the disk reading heads in the computer) are needed to capture the information and send it to a device that can translate it into perceivable and understandable information.

There are two main approaches to bridge the gap between the bits and reality. One is to convert bits into atoms (the focus of this chapter); the other is the conversion of bits into signals that can be conveyed to human brains. In the first case the reliance will be on peoples' senses (hearing, sight, taste, touch, smell) to understand the bits. In the second case human senses are disposed of in favour of a direct connection to the brain.

Although enhancing human senses is an interesting area, in normal life, improving the conversion of bits into atoms and then using human senses is the way forward. Thus, from here forth the chapter will focus on this latter area.

Converting Bits into Atoms

Representation in bits, of objects, can be reproduced on computer screens. These views let the viewer examine the third dimension by rotating the image and special gloves may provide both the sensation of touching the object on the screen and the feeling of turning the object around in space. Computer generated pictures may also be used to look inside an object by making its outside layer transparent or semi-transparent. Such views deliver more information than can be provided by holding the actual object.

Nevertheless, no matter how precise and life-like the computer representation and the interaction with the object are, the object remains in the realm of bits. If people want to eat from a magnificent bowl that they have seen on the computer screen, then it needs to be converted from bits into atoms.

This is already possible, and being done, in most manufacturing processes. The objects are manufactured from information about the product stored in a computer, and then produced using computer-controlled machinery. The product is designed, simulated and often shown to prospective clients using a computer. Once everything is ready, the bits that represent the product are transformed into atoms by, often sophisticated and expensive, production processes.

The phrase is *sophisticated and expensive production processes.* In the future there will be a radical increase in the sophistication of production processes and at the same time there will be a dramatic reduction in both the cost of this production machinery and the manufactured product. These two advances will make it possible to have the production process in peoples' homes, and to eliminate many factories and the associated complex distribution chains. This is going to be a major revolution, similar in the scale of its effects to those brought by the first industrial revolution in the 18th century.

Is this going to happen? The emergence of the factory system was one of the significant features of the first industrial revolution. Will the next industrial revolution be based on the demise of factories? How likely is this? The answer is that this is a very feasible scenario, and this can be seen from developments that are taking place in a field that is called three-dimensional printing.

Before explaining what three-dimensional printing means, it is worthwhile examining developments that have occurred in the area of conventional printing.

Printing was once a very costly process. Only 50 years ago, the number of publications at the news-stand could be counted on the fingers of two hands, but the number of publications is now counted in the hundreds. And this represents just a small quantity of the amount of material being printed.

Computers and low-cost ink-jet printers have made it possible to produce printed material everywhere. The paper industry has consistently seen its market increase, even more than the computer industry.

Colour printing used to be the realm of specialised and expensive machines. A colour printer has however, become the *de facto* standard for any computer and the printer may cost as little as €20. The main revenue flow for the printer manufacturer no longer lies in the sale of the printer, but rather in selling paper and ink. Complex printers have given way to ink cartridges (for ink-jet printers) that have embedded in them all the printing complexity, leaving to the printer the job of positioning the printing head.

The task of sending extremely small drops of the right colour ink, to the required spot on the paper is completely managed by the ink

36

cartridge. How is it then, that by moving complexity from the printer to the cartridge, there has been such dramatic decrease in cost? The answer lies in volume.

Previously the market was for printers, and it is only possible to sell a certain number before market saturation occurs. There was however a change to a market for cartridges, and colour ink-jet printers require two (one for black and one for coloured inks), and often more. Multiply two cartridges by the number of times the cartridges are changed over the life time of a printer, and the result is at least an order of magnitude increase in the market. And when markets change by this amount, the rules of the game become different.

The production of ever increasing amounts of printed material says a lot about the longing that people have for atoms. Much of the paper used for printing could potentially have been saved if there was acceptance of reading the information on a computer screen. For a number of reasons many people like to have sheets in their hand to read from.

Three-dimensional printing, or the printing of objects, is quite a different business. First a few words about the meaning of this term. Three-dimensional printers are not science fiction. They exist and are used in manufacturing industry and elsewhere. They belong to a class of processes called layer or additive manufacturing. When these machines first appeared in the late 1980s they were called rapid prototyping technologies, a term which reflected their primary use at that time. The technologies however quickly advanced to the point where they could be used in the manufacture of products, and this is an area where developments continue to be made.

The machines work by building up a product layer-by-layer, with one thin layer of material bonded to the previous thin layer. There are many different technologies in use, but usually they work by creating a layer, one small piece at a time, and often involve adding material drop by drop. This is why the term three-dimensional printing is used as they clearly work in a way that is similar to ink-jet printing.

Three-dimensional printers are expensive, costing €100,000 and more. This is a similar price that a colour printer would have cost in late 1970s, but by 2020 it is reasonable to expect that three-dimensional printers, able to print a vast array of objects, will be at the €500 (possibly even lower) price level. This will enable them to become a widespread commodity item.

The main issue is whether there can be such a low price. In this case, a shift from the printer to the material cartridge cannot to be taken for granted. The difficulties introduced by a third dimension will always mean that a certain level of complexity will have to reside in the printer itself. However, given the time span, it is safe to assume that one way or another there will be some breakthrough resulting in the slashing of costs.

Clearly, the possibility of printing a glass in a living room is going to reduce markedly the need for supply chains, for transport, and for retailers. And the need for the producer will also be reduced: manufacturing will have become a process that consumers control themselves.

Where is the value and who gets paid for the glass that can be materialised out of bits? The answer is that the value will remain in the conceptual object, the thing represented in bits, for example, a fashion dress, and possibly in the *ink*, that is to say, the plastics, ceramics, metals, micro beads, etc. that will used by three-dimensional printers. These *inks* will be priced to subsidise the printer cost, as it is for two-dimensional ink-jet printers.

It can be expected that the object itself will be downloaded from a designer's web site, for a payment, and then manufactured (printed) in the home. Thus new pieces of chinaware will be printed on-demand, just in time for a special occasion.

Depending on the quality desired different kinds of ink might be used and paid for. With an ink-jet printer the quality of a printed image is dependent mostly on the paper used, but in object printing the ink will make all the difference. Cheap ink may be used (for example, plastic material) for chinaware that will be used once and then thrown away. Alternatively, special ink that can be reused may be preferred. Once the customer has finished with an object, it will be placed into a machine that will decompose it into the original materials, with those materials that cannot be recycled being disposed of. The number of disposable objects may then increase at the same pace as the adoption of recycling machines. There will be no need to use a dishwasher with this latter scenario. Dishes will be printed, and after being used, they will be thrown into a recycling machine that will refill the printer's cartridges.

Amazing progress may derive from a completely new approach to the creation of objects. Parallel to the evolution of three-dimensional printers there may be an evolution to self-assembling production technologies. Nanotechnology is particularly interesting in this respect. The field of nanotechnology is concerned with working at extremely small scales, of the order of one thousand millionth of a metre. It involves manipulating individual atoms and molecules to create, for example, new electronic devices, or extremely small machines, or materials with novel properties. The technology has the potential for wide application.

In the area of drug design and production, nano-techniques are being used. In the production of some electronic parts, self-assembling techniques developed by scientists will soon be adopted. Significant progress will be made in this field in the future, thus enabling many new products, techniques and applications.

Smart materials will become increasingly common and some of this smart material will be created in the initial phase through three-dimensional printing, with self-assembly being used to complete the production process. Elemental materials will self assemble into more complex structures, which will be further processed through three-dimensional printing, into more complex objects.

An example where both processes occur is in the construction of human tissue. Construction of human tissue or organs, is a topic of research. First a cell solution is grown. The cells may be taken from the patient and possibly manipulated to correct genetic problems, to obtain the required *ink*. A three-dimensional printer then creates the scaffolding for the tissue and injects the required cells and nutrients. A self-assembly process then takes place to create the tissue.

The demarcation line between a self-assembly process and the creation of interacting objects that form a self-standing community is extremely thin. Research in the area of smart dust is an example of this possible evolution. Here a microscopic grain of material containing computer processing, storage and communications parts, and others to provide power, movement, sensing, can be printed and then they can be let loose to self assemble into a community of interacting entities. Thousands of these particles can cover wide areas, sensing the environment and providing information. They become almost a living being, interacting with the environment and changing its response accordingly.

Some Possible Directions to Consider – Present and Future

Clearly the availability of three-dimensional printers may disrupt the supply chain by enabling the local production of many goods. The first signs can be seen in the book business. A number of bookstores are starting to offer printing on-demand thus multiplying the number of books offered to customers, while cutting stocks and also reducing the number of books sold off cheaply because they have not sold very well. In India, specially equipped vans tour the country providing print on-demand of books that are stored in bit form onboard the van, or which are downloaded via a satellite link.

Value will reside increasingly in intellectual property (the design of the object and its usability) and less in the physical object itself. Clearly there are unexplored issues related to the accountability for the objects. If a product does not work, then who will take responsibility? Will this be the printer manufacturer, or will responsibility rest with those who created and provided the object specification? Probably the latter will need to take responsibility and to provide support to solve problems, since the relationship is going to be a direct one between the object provider and the customer, with the printers fading into the background.

Printed objects will need to be more sophisticated compared with the products people are familiar with, which can be bough from a retailer. Printed objects will need to be able to communicate with the provider, for example, to enable customer support, aftercare and so on. The value of most objects will lie in the intellectual property and in the attached services, rather than in the material object itself. This will be a further revolution.

Drivers

Three-dimensional printing technologies are evolving under the pressure of cheaper manufacturing processes. In addition there are areas, like nanotechnology and biosciences, where three-dimensional printing and self-assembly are the right approaches. In this progress there will be an increase in the capability to produce a variety of goods, and a decrease in cost. Economies of scale will drive the offer to a wider market and will contribute to the success in the mass market.

The availability of local three-dimensional printing will start to make a dent into the distribution chain. First it can be expected that three-dimensional printing of objects will take place, not at the consumers' premises, but at some retail outlet. In-store production already takes place, such as customised paints and printing on T-shirts. Three-dimensional printing will considerably extend this type of activity. For example, production of clothing on-demand may become an interesting area that may be pioneered by large fashion brands such as Levis, Benetton, Diesel, and others.

The interesting aspect of printing on-demand is that the consumer, or the retailer, can add to the specification to obtain a customised product. This will be a value-added service opening up interesting markets. Printing on-demand will shortening the life of products and will also likely increase product turnover, particularly if workable and effective recycling were part of the business proposition.

This increased turnover will place even more value on intellectual property and stimulate innovations, since bigger markets will be created.

Obstacles

The availability of the technology is obviously the first obstacle. However, the technology will come and the evolution will be towards making it cheap, although this will take time. The price will also have to drop radically, but again over a period of ten years this will happen to the point where three-dimensional printing will be within reach of the mass market.

New products are needed to supply the variety of *inks* that will be used in three-dimensional printing. This is a brand new sector, and one that is far more complex than that of ink-jet cartridges. Business plans need to be devised to make a full set of components affordable. In ink-jet printing, the ink subsidises the printer, but not the content being printed. For three-dimensional printing, some of the ink may be very cheap compared with the product being printed, but in some case it may be too expensive to make it practical. Think of printing a disposable dish of plastic. An equivalent plastic dish may cost less than one cent, but the ink for printing it may be much more expensive. On the other hand, a ceramic dish may cost over €10, but the ink that will be used to print it may be significantly cheaper than this. Therefore, business models that take into account what is to be printed are probably necessary to make this type of business successful.

Impact

There are many possible impacts on conventional business practices. The dividing line between products and services will become blurred. New value chains will appear and old ones may suffer as a result. More value will be placed on the intellectual property, while manufacturing will tend to become a commodity, and distribution, as it is known, will be largely unnecessary.

As the value of the intellectual property increases the issue of defending that property will become crucial. What will be the difference between printing one or ten plates? Will people pay based on the number of plates produced, or just for the specification for the plate? What if consumers add their own designs to the plate specification, and therefore include their own value? Will this additional value be transferred to another person, or piggy backed on to the value of the original specification? There are a host of new issues to be addressed, beyond the obvious one of protecting the original intellectual property.

An Example Future Scenario

Having discussed the technology and its drivers and implications, it is appropriate to close this chapter by looking at a possible future scenario, where three-dimensional printing of bits into atoms opens new possibilities. The example is chinaware, but other products will also be produced in a similar way.

Chinaware in the wallet

The sight of some marvellous chinaware in a china shop in Delft in the Netherlands results in the purchase of a card containing a specification of the chinaware. Back at home, the card is plugged into a three-dimensional printer, enabling the production of chinaware, in the quantities allowed by the card.

Window-shopping led to a dream of owing delightful chinaware. After examining the china in the shop, including handling the products, the customer connects to the home to retrieve information and images of furniture and home decorations to confirm visually how well the chinaware will match with the décor. After confirming that appropriateness of the china, a purchase is made. But there is no need to carry the china home. The customer leaves the shop with a card containing the specification for printing the items at home.

The shop provides the customer with the address of a company that can provide the raw materials needed to get exactly the same china as seen in the shop. The more material that is purchased, the more china that can be made, up to the limit agreed with the shop. The size of the plates is left to the customer to decide.

The customer will keep the card for future use. When a piece of china is damaged or broken a new piece will be created. If more material is needed then the supplier will deliver more for a fee. The card will also be useful when selecting a new set of table cutlery, to help ensure a match between the designs of the two products. The card will also be useful if at anytime the customer wants to engage in any customisation of the design.

One day the customer receives a greeting card from the far away shop in Delft, pointing out a new collection of chinaware which can be viewed on the company's web site. The customer is invited to make a purchase. Possibly there may be a deal to recycle the old chinaware. This is possible because the new materials will contain a solvent that can be used to recycle the old items and partially reuse them to create the new set.

Conclusions

Printing of chinaware, or other products such as clothes, is not something that will happen for many years. For some products, this approach may have little appeal. However, progress in the area of production of goods is clearly moving towards increased flexibility. Some of this will undoubtedly result in greater customisation capability. This may lead spontaneously to having products manufactured based on a very precise specification at a given moment in time.

Cost will be one of the main hurdles to overcome: mass production is much easier to optimise and therefore results in lower cost. It is cheaper to have pictures from a digital camera printed at a shop, than to do it at home. But the latter, for many, is more convenient. The same will happen for other kinds of object printing.

Research in the area of three-dimensional printing is addressing better manufacturing tools and new software, for example, software for copying and manipulating images of objects. In the long run the cost element will become less significant. However, other issues, like the complexity in manoeuvring the machine, will remain. These are possibly the greatest challenges. It is much simpler to look at objects in a shop and decide upon something that is wanted and liked, than to create an object in the mind and then to explain it to a machine. Because of this, the designer's role and creativity is unlikely to be at risk. Therefore, there is likely to be a flourishing business of providing catalogues of *ideas* and *parts* that can be easily translated into machine commands to make predefined objects.

Information and communication technologies will play a significant role in the vision described. Clearly, printers as such are part of information and communication technologies. More important however, is the set of technologies related to software. It is the availability of easy to use modelling techniques for three-dimensional representation, and the resulting virtual look and feel, which will make it possible for users to decide what they want to print. This is important since object printing is obviously going to be more costly than printing paper and people will want to be sure that they want to print an object and not to waste money on printing items that are unsuitable or not wanted. Software will also be needed to provide the digital watermarking necessary to identify the ownership of designs.

Applications of GRID computing, that is to say, the linking together of numerous computers around the globe to provide increased computing capabilities and resources, is also going to play an important role. This is a crucial area, comparable in effect to the invention of the World Wide Web, and the standardised means of creating web pages and the web browser to read these pages. The invention of ways to easily combine existing applications into one that yields the desired functionality will increase productivity, cut cost through reuse, and create incentives for the sharing of applications by rewarding the owners through a completely new marketplace (similar in scope to the one created by eBay). The word invention is used here on purpose. There is as yet no clear idea how to achieve this. Possibly, information and communication technology research in several software fields will stimulate ideas on this.

The printing of an object in a personalised environment makes much more sense if such an object is unique (and thus does not leverage on large scale cost savings) and to be unique it must be a personalised version derived from one or several blueprints. This is where GRID computing becomes useful, by providing a way to mix different components into a single object.

Chapter 4

Micro Fabrication

Brahim Dahmani

Introduction

Many things have been converted into a digital stream of data, and more will follow. Bits are everywhere! A bit (either a one or a zero) is the smallest unit of information handled by a computer. These are represented physically by a very small pulse of electricity sent through a circuit, or a small point on a magnetic surface that can change state to represent either one or zero. Bits convey little information of use to humans, but they can be manipulated by computers to present information in a way that is useful to people.

In the future, individuals will have at home, as attachments to internet broadband connections, not only entertaining audio-video equipment, but also micro fabrication systems. These will be able to generate three-dimensional objects as good as the ones bought in shops or delivered by express couriers such as DHL, UPS or Fedex.

This latter aspect is much less well documented, since there is still a trend to value much more the digital content and the intellectual part, than the objects and the hardware. These are considered as a degraded state, cumbersome, expensive to duplicate and heavy to transport. All the value is thought to be in the immaterial: in the bits. Atoms are seen to be remnants from the past: something to be eliminated if possible. This thinking has been very much developed and exemplified in Nicholas Negroponte's famous book entitled *Being Digital* [1]. Nevertheless people are not always listening to music, or watching movies coming from remote and often unknown locations. People still drive cars, wear clothes and eat food.

The conceptualisation of an object in the mind precedes its actual construction. This scheme will still be true in the information society. Smart objects will include not only intelligence in their embodiment, but also during conception, production and recycling.

Sustainable Clothing in a New High Technology Environment

A Scenario

The smell of fresh coffee and the sound of soft music gently stimulate John's senses. Slowly he begins to wake. The artificial sky projected on to the ceiling above his bed displays the subtle colours of sunrise.

John rises from his bed, pours a coffee and savours the rich aroma. He takes a sip, then another. It will take a few minutes before the caffeine starts acting, stimulating his brain, and driving away the sleepiness that still dulls his thoughts.

Intelligent software, instructed to respond to John's presence near to the coffee machine, begins to comment on the agenda for the day. The first item is physical exercise, before a day of working from home. In the evening John will relax with some friends at a restaurant in the town centre.

For the physical exercise John will require a jogging suit, then later, after a shower, he will need some comfortable casual clothes. For the evening a trendy suit is required.

The caffeine has now done its job, and John is fully alert and asks the software to propose some designs for the suit. John's local data storage has sufficient designs for the first two items. The designs for the suits held in local storage are two-months old, and out of fashion. The system alerts John to this. John smiles to himself. In the last decades fashion has accelerated at such pace that styles one-year old look like they belong in a museum.

John speaks to the software instructing it to contact an on-line tailor that already has, on record, John's personal data: size, measurements, colour taste, usual mood, and so on. The online tailor automatically suggests a customised suit for the occasion, taking into account the people John will meet and the weather. John eventually chooses something simple and elegant, and leaves some of the details to be selected randomly, just to be sure of the uniqueness of the result.

During the time John has been drinking his coffee and having a suit design created, a clothing robot has manufactured a jogging suit

46

perfectly fitting John's body measurements. The material is a non-woven anti bacterial and thermo-regulating one. While John is out jogging the robot will continue to work, producing the casual clothes that have been specified.

On returning from jogging, John throws the exercise suit in the recycling drawer of the clothing robot, and for a few brief moments watches the still warm material vanishing under the glowing light. The novelty of this has still not worn off, and John still finds the whole process fascinating. The basic molecules of the fibres will be sorted and reused at some point in the future.

John takes a shower. When finished, a hot air blower does the job that once towels were used for. John thinks back to the old times when people had to have cumbersome equipment to keep clothes clean and fresh. Past generations spent countless hours washing, drying, ironing and folding clothes: in John's opinion this was time wasted! He is not alone in thinking this. And all that wasted space used for storage!

A green light is blinking on the ready drawer of the clothing robot. John's casual clothes are ready. The material has special characteristics providing anti stress properties. These have been designed into the fabric using nanotechnology, which involves manipulating individual atoms to create the desired effect.

At the end of the day John is tired. His work has included a few teleconference calls to colleagues, and now John is looking forward to the dinner. The wall in his home office comes to life with a message. It is time to get ready. There is just enough time to change into his new suit, which is ready in the clothing robot.

Just at the right time, a rented car with fully automated driving capability pulls up outside John's home. A time slot has been reserved for the journey along the highway into town. Within a few minutes John is on his way, dressed in the suit that was designed and made for him that very day, secure in the knowledge that the car will take him safely and on-time to the restaurant where his friends will be waiting for him.

Some Comments on the Scenario

The production of a customised suit described in the scenario can be broken down into five steps: online choice of a design; customisation of the design; micro fabrication; recycling; and, more of the same.

Step one, online choice of a design, is the simplest part of the process. Early versions of this step came into use at the beginning of the 21st century. Choice of a style via an online catalogue can of course be generalised to other products and will likely have an impact on many aspects of human behaviour. Selection can be done by style, with a lot of software help to advise on suitability for each individual.

At the end of this first step, instructions will be sent to the computer in the home, describing how to make the suit from some basic materials. The design can be used once and then deleted from the system, or kept for future use.

For step two, customisation of the design, intelligent software will add to the manufacturing instructions, information about personal details (measurements, colour preferences, etc). The system *knows* about the people in the home and what other clothes (shirt, tie, etc.) are to be worn with the suit, and will ensure that the colours match. The software will certainly also include more advanced information like favourite after-shave, preferred feel of the fabric, and so on. The software will communicate with several other advanced functions to establish the weather, the place to be visited and the activities to be undertaken.

Step three is micro fabrication. A machine, using the instructions, will form the desired piece of clothing, using appropriate materials held in a storage area. The machine will have to be small, inexpensive and able to fulfil the needs of a family.

At step four, clothes produced in step three will be recycled. After being worn, perhaps only once, the clothes will be returned back to the original materials that were used to create them. There will be no more washing, drying, ironing, or any need for the equipment associated with these activities. Very little clothes storage space will be required.

The recycling will involve purification to remove any unwanted materials such as dirt. This cleaning will be done at the level of molecules and atoms, and will be much more efficient than any other type of cleaning.

Step five is simply more of the same. The clothing machine will form new items as and when needed for the whole family.

The drivers – what will make it happen?

Some people began buying clothes online in the late 1990s, the main advantage for the online buyers being to avoid busy shops. However, except for choice and payment, the rest of the buying process was very traditional. The items purchased existed in a warehouse somewhere and were delivered by postal services. An argument against this online shopping model is that the pleasure of going out shopping is lost, but similar remarks were made about television shows. It was claimed that they would never be popular because people enjoyed going to the theatre.

Clothes bought in a shop are usually based on designs and fashions created several months earlier. The ideas that designers are inventing at any moment in time will not appear in the shops for several months, or at best, several weeks. There will therefore be room for enterprises that will short cut the usual distribution chains and create value by providing online customers with the clothes based on up-to-date designs. Perhaps in the early stages this will be directed at people willing to pay a high premium, but later on this may be made available to a wider market at lower prices.

The value chain in the clothing and textile industry has been split between the conceptual part, which is undertaken in high income countries, and the manufacturing part that is done in low income countries. The pressure on the manufacturing cost is so high that production has to be undertaken in countries far removed from the main markets. This is a continuing process, with companies looking for even lower-cost places to locate manufacturing.

Moreover, with the shift of production to remote regions, transport cost has become a more important part of the total cost. And it is likely at some point that global environmental regulations will oblige the taxation of transport to pay for the environmental consequences and to discourage the movement of goods over long distances. When this occurs, the price of clothes will start to increase. And at this point there will be an incentive to invest in a different mode of production.

Manufacturing may then have to shift to fully automated robotic mass-customised production facilities, located closer to the main markets. This will involve achieving, in someway, the production of individual items, customised to size and taste, using industrial scale standardised mass production technology. Alternatively, personal micro fabrication machines, based in homes, or in local shops, may appear. These will provide individual choice and customisation, but at the costs associated with industrial mass production of clothes.

The consequences – what it will change?

The business model of the whole textile industry will change significantly. The value will no more be in the items, but in their design. This has been partly true for sometime, but will be even more so with the scenario described.

Of course, some designs of simple clothes will be quickly turned into commodity items and will be widely replicated, probably being available for free or for the payment of some small fee. The music recording industry experienced a similar phenomenon in the late 1990s and the early part of the 21st century.

What will protect the industry much more than a strict copyright enforcement, will be the constant need for new creative designs. A fashion

49

creator will have many more ways to achieve fame than in the past. It will be easier to provide online services to multiple customers, than to have contact with them individually in a shop. And people will be as eager as ever to find a personal style that will differentiate them from other people. Fashion will still be a rapidly changing marketplace, but its pace will no longer depend on cumbersome production methods.

The raw materials will no longer be produced and delivered to factories. Basic chemicals will be in cartridges. These will be the raw materials used by the home clothing production machines. A whole new industry selling and maintaining micro fabrication clothing machines will appear. This will not happen in a short period of time. More likely there will be several phases of development. The first generation of machines will be too expensive for the average home, and will thus be based in local fashion shops, and be used for a fee. However, to gain the ultimate advantages of the approach, low-cost home equipment will need to emerge.

Advantages

Recycling will be included in the technology and not be an added part to be dealt with later.

The cloth will be disassembled and purified and then re-used to make new clothes. The recycling of the fibres will be a first step, before something more ultimate like disassembling down to the basic molecules and atoms.

There will be no more housekeeping tasks like washing, drying, and ironing. The machines required for these tasks will no longer be required. Cleaning will be done at molecular and atomic levels as part of the recycling process. Clothing storage facilities will be minimal.

The desire for labour saving appliances in the home, to eliminate or reduce the amount of housekeeping tasks, has been a very powerful driver in the introduction of home technologies and devices. Micro fabrication will satisfy this desire even further, and as a result will easily gain wide acceptance.

Conclusions

Surprisingly much of the technology needed to make the proposed scenario is close to becoming a reality. Some of it has already been developed. Online shopping for customised clothes has been achieved. Software to advise on the suitability of items is feasible and similar software has been used in hairdressers and also in opticians to help select glasses. Instructions, in the form of programs describing how to make a piece of clothing, are very similar to those used for automatic knitting machines. Such programs are shared and distributed over the internet. Of course, these have to become transparent for the user, so that they do not need to be a tailor. Moreover, high quality fibres with special properties, for example on the thermo-regulating fibres, are available. Fabric with anti stress features to release stress from the body is also available.

The spinning wheel can be seen as an ancestor of the modern knitting machine. Many hundreds of years and an enormous amount of technological development separate the two. The modern knitting machine will become an ancestor of personal clothing equipment, but the distance in time between the two will not be too great. Technology for forming fibres from chemicals, is already a reality in industrial manufacturing of stockings. On the other hand, the disassembly process will probably need much attention. It is not very well documented, but in 2004, about 24% of used fabrics were recycled to fibres. What is needed therefore is research effort focused on developing fully recyclable products. For chemical companies, such materials are likely to provide new opportunities to sell products into new markets.

References

[1] Nicholas Negroponte, 1995, *Being Digital*, (Knopf, New York)

Part II: Novel Perspectives for Networked Intelligence

Human-centred Ambient Intelligence: Human-computer Relationships for the Knowledge Era

Paul T Kidd

Introduction

This chapter deals with the topic of a different type of compute-based technology, different that is, to the one that people have become familiar with. The envisioned computer-based technology can be described as human-centred, that is to say, as opposed to the technology-centred technology that has become so ubiquitous in the early part of the 21st century.

The road to achieving such a human-centred technology is lined with many obstacles. But first, what is the starting point? Where does the journey begin?

Information and communication technologies are in the process of becoming a taken-for-granted part of everyday life. Steadily, digital technologies are being incorporated into the fabric of society: medical services, banking, retailing, manufacturing, transport, entertainment, education, and many other activities, have all become highly dependent on information and communication technologies. Without digital technologies, society would be unable to function in the way that people have become use to. The technologies have provided the means by which people have been able to increase their participation in many social activities. Moreover, businesses operate in ways that are only made possible through the use of information and communication technologies. In addition, professionals in all disciplines use computers as an integral part of their everyday activities. And most importantly, innovation in this field, and continued take-up of new technology, is a driver for economic growth and improvements in productivity: failure to ensure that this innovation and technology take-up is sustained will be very damaging for the economies of both the industrialised and the developing nations.

This diffusion of information and communication technologies into everyday objects is sometimes referred to as pervasive computing. The view of the computer as *boxes on desks or in computer rooms* is now very much outdated and misleading. Computers can be found just about everywhere, but their presence is not noticed, because the technologies are often embedded within items. And the information and communication technology content of many products, for example, cars, is continuing to increase. Thus, information and communication technologies have already started to move out from boxes, and are becoming an aspect of the built environment: they are part of products, services, and artefacts, and are adding intelligence to the surroundings, thus leading to the beginnings of so-called ambient intelligence.

Ambient intelligence is a European vision that places human beings at the centre of future development of the knowledge-based society and information and communication technologies. Computing devices will be embedded in many everyday objects, many of which will be networked together, and these technologies will be almost invisible to those who use them, and interfaces will be easy and natural to use. Ambient intelligence also demands contextual understanding on the part of computers, as they must in some way understand the user and the circumstances that apply at a particular point of interaction.

Ambient intelligence is a European perspective on how the trend towards pervasive computing can be shaped to Europe's advantage, and to the benefit of its businesses and citizens. It is a vision of what lies beyond the computer as *boxes on desks or in computer rooms.*

However the vision of ambient intelligence poses a number of concerns. Some are obvious and have already become important worries with the advent of the internet age: protection of privacy, creating trust, ensuring security, preventing the hijacking of the technologies for criminal purposes. Yet there is one matter that is perhaps less obvious, but which may prove to be a major roadblock.

A belief has been expressed [1] that ambient intelligence will not be widely accepted and used, unless users are deeply involved in the shaping of these technologies. Developers, it is proposed, need to do more than just bring new technologies to users to ask them what they think. A novel two-way relationship needs to be established between those that develop new technologies and those that use them. Users should be integrated into the processes of research and development, and new product creation and introduction. Users should be part of the innovation process, a source of ideas, and not just a resource to evaluate ideas generated by professionals. In effect what is being proposed is the development of a new approach to research and technology development, and the later activity of developing and introducing new commercial ambient intelligence products and services.

This new way of undertaking these activities can be summarised as design, by, with and for users. But is this enough to ensure acceptance? Possibly not! For no matter how much users are involved, a key issue is that, technologists bring to their work a set of values, and those values tend to devalue human roles and contributions, and emphasise the importance of technology as being in someway superior to humans. Put succinctly, computers are better than people are, and if people are involved in someway, then they represent a weakness in the design.

The above, of course, is an age old issue, but it is not one that has gone away. Over the years it has surfaced from time to time, and then slipped from view. But it is nevertheless still very important, and not a matter that has ever been satisfactorily resolved. The topic has been formalised with the Human Factors community under the name of allocation of functions (between man and machine). But this approach has been subject to significant criticism. The critique can be summarised by stating that allocation of functions does not correspond with much of the reality of technology systems design, and most importantly, ignores the central role of values in design. And it is in values, in the relationship between computers and people, where the solutions to the problems lie.

The knowledge era is heralded as a new age for humankind, implying some sort of transition from the past, to a new and different future, one based on the value of information and knowledge. The age that is being left behind, the industrial era, was, to a large extent, based on subjugation of human skills, knowledge, expertise, and purpose to the demands of a resource-intensive system of mass production. This led to a relationship between people and machines, where the needs of machines were predominant, and technology was designed, as far as possible, to eliminate the need for human intelligence, or to move this need to a select group of people within organisations, such as engineers and managers.

To move forward into the knowledge era, involves leaving behind the baggage of the industrial age. But how can this be done? What concepts are important and what fundamental principles apply?

Contextual understanding on the part of computers is probably the key to the creation of an ambient intelligence that serves people, rather than one that places people in a position of subservience to machines. But to achieve contextual understanding in a broad sense, allowing room for specific human characteristics such as a desire to play or to experiment, requires a new vision of the relationships between people and computers, one that could be termed an intelligent human-computer relationship, leading to a human-centred ambient intelligence. And the remainder of the chapter charts the way forward, starting with the topic called allocation of functions.

The Relevance of Allocation of Functions to the Design of Ambient Intelligence

Given the vision of ambient intelligence described in previous section, and the key importance that values play in the design of technology, it can be questioned if allocation of functions is a useful concept that has any relevance at all to the design of ambient intelligence.

This question needs to be considered as a case can be made that in many circumstances, except safety or mission critical applications (for example, air traffic control), that the concept has little relevance.

Much has been written about allocation of functions and several methods have been proposed. Normally the approach adopted is based on making comparisons between people and computers, for example, computers are better at undertaking rapid calculations, people are better at exercising judgement, and so on. What has to be addressed is whether these methods are useful and relevant.

Chapanis [2] has pointed to a number of issues that are often ignored in the allocation of functions. Some of these now seem very relevant given the needs to address ambient intelligence. Chapanis originally addressed his remarks to the issue of humans and machines, but machines now equate to computers or computer-based systems, and his three main points are as follows:

First, to make general human-computer comparisons is frequently the wrong thing to do, for example, although computers may be good at undertaking calculations, this is not a good reason for always using a computer to do calculations. Second, deciding whether a person or a computer can do a particular task better is not always important as all that may be necessary is to use that component which is adequate. Third, when general comparisons between people and computers are made, no consideration is given to trade-offs.

Chapanis also mentions a number of other concerns. First, allocation of functions in human-computer systems is determined in part by social, economic and political values that may vary from country to country. Thus, a design that works in one country may not work in another. This is an important issue given the trend towards globalisation of markets and technologies. Second, assignment of functions must be continually re-evaluated, because technology is forever changing and what is not possible now, may well be in the near future. Third, many of the difficulties experienced in making allocation decisions arise from engineering uncertainties. Designers tend to make changes throughout the design, and sometimes work on the basis of trial and error, thus creating uncertainties about the final design and its implementation in hardware and software.

Chapanis' recommendation is that allocation of functions be approached by first preparing a complete and detailed specification. This step should be followed with an analysis of all system functions. Some tentative assignments can then be made. This should then be followed by an evaluation of the total functions allocated to people to make sure that there is neither over- nor under-loading of people.

What is wrong with this recommendation? It seems that there are a number of points that make the concept of formal allocation of function procedures unrealistic, both from the perspective of practical design circumstances and the needs imposed by ambient intelligence.

First, design experience suggests that it is almost impossible to write a complete and detailed specification. Some constraints and goals are difficult to formulate and often cannot be clearly expressed until a model or a mock-up or a prototype system has been built. If a specification is written and presented to a client, it is likely that it will be accepted. When the system is built it is likely that the client will say that it is not exactly what is wanted or expected. The reason for this is that some goals and constraints remain tacit and only become explicit when the goals have not been met or the constraints have been violated.

Second, design is not an orderly process proceeding from specification to implementation. It is highly iterative and much more complex than is often portrayed by simple linear or even iterative models. Specifications are also often changed as the design proceeds, as it becomes apparent that some things may not be feasible or because someone comes up with a better idea. These changes are of course subject to formal controls, but a design specification is rarely static.

Third, many aspects of design are of course subconscious processes involving creative activity. People may suddenly come up with new ideas. These are explored and discussed. Some experimentation is undertaken. The ideas get modified, and so on. As this creative process takes place, allocation of function decisions are being taken, not explicitly, but in a more implicit way.

Fourth, technological innovations often start in a research laboratory. This process might involve elements of curiosity driven research, for example, to investigate what can be done with a particular technology. Some research ideas may then find their way into products, which are then bought by customers who add them to their existing systems. Thus, even when starting from a greenfield position, much software and hardware is bought in off-the-shelf, and is not customised. Control over allocation of functions is therefore restricted because detailed design is in effect undertaken by several third parties, who may have been more concerned with achieving technological innovation, than with addressing issues of human-computer interaction.

Fifth, allocation of functions only determines what people and the computers will do. It says nothing about how the computers operate. This means that allocation of functions has little influence on computer architectures and the detailed operation of software, that is to say, what the algorithms do and how this functionality is achieved via procedures and different programming paradigms.

Sixth, allocation of functions says nothing about the goals of the system, which are often a dominant factor in determining what people are expected to do. For example, knowledge-based systems can be used to attempt to achieve automated activities, possibly in real time. Alternatively, knowledge-based systems can be used in a more passive way to act as a system to expand users' understanding of the characteristics of a problem. When the goal of using knowledge-based systems to achieve automated activities is pursued, constraints are imposed on what people are expected to do. Allocation of function methods make no cognisance of this fact and could be said to be concerned with the secondary more detailed allocation decisions that stem from the major design decisions which have already been taken in the form of objectives, long before allocation of functions becomes a design issue.

Finally, design is a mixture of art and science, rather than being just pure science [3]. It involves a mixture of formal and informal methods, analysis, mathematics, and elements of judgement and experience. Designers often know from experience what has to be done to achieve a given result. With experience it should not be necessary to undertake detailed analysis of tasks to create satisfactory circumstances for people.

From this picture it can be seen that design is not a straightforward process. Simple models that depict a process of clearly defined stages, starting with the development of a requirement specification and ending with the testing of the built system, do not represent the full complexity of design.

Design is also a dynamic and evolutionary process. It involves a lot of creative thought, which is followed by a process of elimination and the build up of the design detail. All the time, prototyping, simulation and experimentation may be going on. As the process of building up the detail continues, there are bursts of more creative activity as unexpected problems arise which need to be resolved.

System designs, therefore, take shape over a long period. In this complex process there is no point where someone sits down and says people will do this and computers this. It just does not happen like that and cannot happen like this way because there is no point in the design process where it can happen, unless the design process is made very formal and over restrictive. One day the design is finished. Somewhere along the road the process of allocation of functions happened. Nobody can pin point the moment, because it did not exist. It happened on a continuing basis and it involved trade-offs between various aspects of the design.

However, it was Jordan [4], clearly believing that allocation of functions is not very relevant, who raised some of the most important issues concerning the relevance of allocation of functions. In his paper he points out that the term allocation of tasks to people and computers is meaningless because this assumes that people and computers are comparable. Jordan argues that they are not comparable, but rather that they are complementary. The problem is not therefore one of deciding what each should do, but of designing a system so that activities are done by people and computers.

According to Jordan this requires new formats for systems analysis and design. Jordan suggests that designing from a tool perspective will be part of this new approach, an approach that has been turned into practice, within a research setting (for example see [5]), but which has yet to make the transition into everyday design practices.

Jordan also indirectly mentions in his work that interdisciplinary design will form part of this new approach, by suggesting that computer-based systems should be designed to take account of peoples' need for motivation, learning, enjoyment, etc., that is to say, insights from psychology should be used in the design of computer-based systems.

It is these above two points that are the most interesting. Instead of allocating functions between people and computer-based systems, designers should be considering ways in which computers (and systems) can be designed as tools according to psychological and organisational criteria. This does not involve explicit allocation of functions. Rather it involves designing technology in a way that achieves certain desirable psychological and organisational results, as well as the more normal technical and economic benefits.

This approach also addresses some of the points raised by Chapanis. It avoids asking which is better at doing a particular task. It does not assume that design decisions are independent of the culture of the society in which the technology is to be used. And, it involves trade-offs between technical, economic, organisational, and psychological considerations.

Technologies for Ambient Intelligence

The scenario for the future considered in this chapter, so-called ambient intelligence, involves computers embedded into everyday objects, responding to actions and wishes of people in the environment, and understanding the context for particular circumstances of use. This implies a lot of change, uncertainty and unpredictability, for it is very hard to foretell what people may want to do. This suggests a different form of technology to that which people are used to; a technology that is specifically designed not only to be easy to use, but one that also acknowledges that future uses cannot be predefined in great detail. Technologies will, therefore, have to be designed to be open. Thus, rather than focusing on allocation of functions, as happened in the industrial era, the knowledge-age needs to address the design of systems as tools that can adapt to users and their particular circumstances, and to be open to different uses, styles, wants, and needs.

To achieve this goal four things are important: the open systems concept; open systems applied to human-computer interaction; user defined human-computer relationships; and evaluative and generative systems.

The Open Systems Concept

The concept of an open system comes from general systems theory and describes a system that receives inputs from and sends outputs to the systems environment. The concept of an open system is, however, also used in management science to describe organisational structures that take into account and respond to the environment. The idea can, however, have a much broader application. It can be applied not only to system architectures and organisational structures, but also to work practices, technologies, human-computer interfaces and the relationship between people and technologies such as control systems, decision support systems, etc.

Technologies, as with organisational structures, can be designed to be open systems. In this context, open systems technology is defined as one that allows people a very large degree of freedom to define the mode of operation of the system and the nature and form of the interaction

62

between the subsystems and between the system and its environment. The term basically implies a system that is extremely adaptive.

Open Systems Applied to Human-computer Interaction

The aim then, when designing ambient intelligent technologies will not be to use computers to substitute for, or to eliminate the skills and knowledge of people, but rather to enhance their skills and knowledge and to make these more productive and effective. In other words, the technology will be used to lever the skills and knowledge of people in whatever circumstances they find themselves. Thus the goal will be to combine the power, speed and accuracy of computers with the skills, knowledge, judgement, and creativity of people [6].

This will require that the designers of technologies stop trying to create systems that reduce peoples' scope to exercise their skills, knowledge and judgement. Traditional technology design practices require designers to specify, usually in detail and often in mathematical form, the system constraints and the required functionality. This will no longer be appropriate.

It will no longer be sufficient, when designing technologies, to consider the way in which the burden of the work will be shared between people and the computer. The aim will not be for designers themselves to predefine a technology that results in circumstances such that the user and the computer each makes an appropriate contribution to activities or the solution of problems. The aim will be to define a technology that allows users to determine for themselves a fruitful and effective symbiotic relationship with the computer. Users will do this in relation to the requirements in force at a particular moment in time.

This means that designers need to move beyond simplistic notions that the power, speed and accuracy of computers be used to support people. This is likely only to lead to circumstances where the computer does most of an activity based on an assumption that the designers will know in advance what activities will be undertaken.

This sort of thinking is based solely on the notion of doing something as fast as possible. Humans tend to be slow, and since computers are better at examining a large number of options and can do so very quickly, designers tend to conclude that computers and not people should do activities like these. This is an example of what Jordan has referred to as *man-machine comparability*. This comparability perspective ignores the needs of the people who will use the computer. In particular, these needs relate to the ability to respond to such things as change, uncertainty and unpredictability, as well as learning, enjoyment, and the opportunity to exercise and to lever skills, knowledge and judgement.

Thus, it is not enough just to be sympathetic to the idea that people, as computer users, should be in control of activities. Designers need, of course, to believe that computers should support human activities, rather than just being used to automate these activities. The *informating* power of computer technology [7] needs to be utilised, that is to say, bringing information forward to enable human actions and decisions. However, this is still not enough. Designers also need to break away from their conventional approach of designing computer-based systems on the basis that either the computer does something or people do it.

What is needed is a more relevant vision of the human-computer relationship. In ambient intelligence it is necessary to move beyond the principle of human-computer comparability and start thinking about complementarity. The way to do this is not to design the technology as in the past, so that the human-computer relationship is predefined. Rather, users should be left to determine their own relationship with the computer, so that they can work in a way that is appropriate to a given set of circumstances.

User Defined Human-computer Relationships

Many computer-based systems have been designed as closed system. A closed system is one where designers have determined, through the system design, the allowed actions. This is done to a degree that is more than is required, say, by hardware, or software or performance constraints. In other words, a closed system is one in which the user-computer relationship is *over-determined*.

A closed system typically restricts peoples' freedom of action, or forces them to use the computer-based system in a particular way that is of the designer's choosing and not necessarily of the user's choosing.

An open system approach can lead to a different type of system, one that is more suited to an environment characterised by change, uncertainty and unpredictability, or where people want to act in a way that is unique to themselves. With an open system people are not unnecessarily restricted in what they can do. For example, if people want to violate some constraint, then with a closed system this would not be allowed, while with an open system it would. Of course appropriate warnings would need to be given, and a design decision whether to allow this would be subject to considerations such as safety and the consequences of potential system failure. In some circumstances, this unrestricted approach could not be allowed, but there are likely to be many circumstances where this is entirely feasible.

More fundamentally, however, an open system in not characterised by circumstances where an activity is either done by the computer acting alone, or by the user largely acting alone. Between these two extremes there are an infinite number of possibilities. An open system would allow people to make use of any of these possibilities.

In essence therefore, an open system is one where the relationship between people and computers is determined by each individual user and not by the designers of the technology. The role of the designers of technical systems is to create a technology that will satisfy peoples' personal preferences and allow them to work in ways that they find most appropriate given the wide range of circumstances that they might have to deal with.

In ambient intelligence, computer-based systems should not be designed as closed systems, but as open systems. This means avoiding restrictions, using decision support systems in a way that is highly interactive and which allows sharing of the decision making process in a way that is unique to each person and to each circumstance. This is a real paradigm shift, but it is also very challenging as it will require an ability to develop complex, efficient and error free software, but this aspect is another story and not one that can be explored further in this chapter.

Evaluative and Generative Systems

To more fully understand how an open systems approach can be used to design a human-computer relationship, it is helpful to introduce the concepts of evaluative and generative decision support systems. An evaluative decision support system is one that takes a set of proposed decisions and evaluates and predicts the results of these decisions. A generative decision support system is one that takes a set of criteria and constraints and generates a set of decisions.

The problem that has to be faced is to break out of the evaluative versus generative dichotomy. There is no logical reason for this problem; it is just a mater of tradition. There is no reason why a system cannot be designed to be both evaluative and generative. Between these two opposite modes of operation there is a continuum of operating possibilities. The only problem is that systems are not designed to operate within this continuum, because designers are used to defining the mode of operation of the system in great detail. They are not accustomed to thinking about the possibility of letting people determine their own operating modes.

There is in fact, an important principle here and it is the principle of combining opposites. This involves moving beyond either/or constructs and considering oxymorons, that is to say, seemingly contradictory notions achieved simultaneously [8]. Combination of opposites is, for example, what *mass customisation* (cost efficient manufacturing of individually customised products) is about [9].

Conclusions

Ambient intelligence as a subject is still at an early stage of development. The topic takes technologists into a domain where fundamental and taken for granted assumptions are challenged. Ambient intelligence is a paradigm shift and before moving forwards it is necessary to understand the existing paradigm and to face up to the often painful task of accepting that established practices and beliefs are no longer appropriate or relevant. This in itself, is a major change exercise, but one that is vital to the successful development of ambient intelligence.

A new and different sort of technology is needed for ambient intelligence, but such a technology will not begin to emerge until people really understand that it is possible to design a different type of technology, one that is open to different uses in different circumstances.

Industrial society is founded on specialisation, division of labour, and what are often opposing roles. There are many of these roles: managers and workers, business executives and technical experts, strategist and implementers, technologists and social scientists, technology designers and technology users, and so on. Separation of designer and user, is a key issue, but it is something that is deep rooted. It is possible therefore that until the integration of users and designers is achieved, the type of technology envisioned in this chapter will not come about. But it also seems that achieving this type of technology will require that the ideas be institutionalised into the education system and the values of society. In the end it comes down to culture, norms and values. These are all challenging matters, and bringing about a change in these will be no easy matter. Nevertheless, they are key to achieving the vision of ambient intelligence.

In 20 years time people will look back and see all this as obvious and will be puzzled why so many people in the early part of the 21st century could not see the obvious. Ambient intelligence is a paradigm shift that implies that old ideas need to be re-evaluated, modified and in some cases abandoned. Allocation of functions seems to be one such concept that requires radical reformulation. It needs replacing with a set of design principles: among them the principle of combining opposites, open systems design, user-defined human-computer relationships, and a new way of integrating users into research and design. Based on these principles it should be possible to design and implement truly human-centred ambient intelligence.

References

[1] ISTAG, 2004, *Experience and Application Research: Involving Users in the Development of Ambient Intelligence*, http://www.cordis.lu/ist/istag-reports.htm

[2] Chapanis A. 1965, On the allocation of functions between men and machines, *Occupational Psychology*, 39(1), pp. 1-11

[3] Jones, J.C., 1981, *Design Methods: Seeds of Human Futures* (John Wiley, Chichester)

[4] Jordan, N., 1963, Allocation of functions between man and machine in automated systems, *Journal of Applied Psychology*, 47(3), pp. 161-165

[5] Kidd, P.T., 1988, The social shaping of technology: The case of a CNC lathe, *Behaviour and Information Technology*, 7(2), pp. 193-204

[6] Kidd, P.T., 1992, Interdisciplinary design of skill based computer aided technologies: interfacing in depth, *International Journal of Human Factors in Manufacturing*, 2(3), pp. 209-228

[7] Zuboff, S., 1988, *In the Age of the Smart Machine: The Future of Work and Power* (Basic Books, New York)

[8] Davis, S., 1987, *Future Perfect* (Addison-Wesley, Reading, MA)

[9] Pine, B.J., 1993, *Mass Customization: The New Frontier in Business Competition* (Harvard Business School Press, Boston)

Chapter 6

Digital Territory: Bubbles

Laurent Beslay and Hannu Hakala

Introduction

Digital territory is a vision. It introduces the notions of *space* and *borders* and other concepts to better understand and manage future, everyday digital environments. Digitisation is growing and becoming increasingly ubiquitous; in addition, the younger generations are more familiar with the digital world than previous ones.

Almost all personal data are now networked and thus available at distant locations. Simultaneously, the boundaries between traditionally distinct environments, for example, work, home, and school, are also disappearing as private activities are brought into the public arena and vice versa. Although the distinction between private and public areas is not always clear-cut, people are aware of the boundaries between them, and of the grey zones, and take informed or intuitive decisions on how to act accordingly.

The vision promoting the implementation of a *digital territory* aims for a better clarification of all kinds of interactions in the future information society. Without digital boundaries, the fundamental notion of privacy or the feeling of *being at home* will not take place. Supported by technologies, the demarcation in digital territory among personal, private and public spaces will be decisive for its acceptance and sustained usage. Without digital boundaries, the information society will remain a parallel world, *the cyberspace* that was described by William Gibson [1], rather than becoming fully integrated with everyday life.

To illustrate the vision of digital territory, the following sections describe *layers* of everyday activities, and where it is possible place digital boundaries. These range from the most intimate and private *territories*, such as near the skin, through to family spaces, and through to interaction between public and private space. The following examples are intended to illustrate the digitisation of the various physical territories. The primary concept is that of a *bubble*.

The Notion of Territory and its Digitisation

Personal space (an area of privacy) is usually translated into *physical distance* from others. Depending on the context, someone may, for example, try to reduce the distance to a goddess of beauty in a bar, to its minimum socially accepted (and even less) level, to *get* more information and eventually to start a conversation to charm the goddess of beauty. But even when much closer, a success considering the challenge, there is much valuable, and maybe forbidden data that is not available, except in a digitised environment.

By claiming territoriality on a specific space, people tend to stabilise and to regulate the social systems, which surround them. Depending on the distances and the nature of these territorial changes, their owners have decreasing control. Altman defined three main categories of territory that will be useful to illustrate later the different digital territories [2].

Closest to the person is the *primary territory* in which the individual has complete control; the management of the individual's body and its relative nakedness illustrates this. In the *secondary territory* the individual or a group has some control, ownership and regulatory power, but as a result of negotiations and transactions. Peoples' homes are clear examples of this secondary territory. This space has either been bought or rented, which gives the resident specific and personal rights in it, but it is still included in and regulated by a commonly established social, legal and even cultural framework. Finally, *public* territory is characterised by a temporary quality and free access. Obviously, a public bathroom is a place that can be used freely, for a limited time, during which this space is completely private. These places are regulated by public *social contracts* of use.

By digitising the personal domain, but also its boundaries, the vision of digital territory offers the opportunity to introduce the notion of territory, property and space in a digital environment. The objective is to provide a tool that enables users to manage proximity and distance with others in this future ambient intelligence space, both in a legal and a social sense, as in the physical world.

Ambient intelligence is a vision that places human beings at the centre of future development of the knowledge-based society and information and communication technologies. These technologies will be embedded in everyday objects, and be almost invisible to those who use them, and the interfaces will be easy and natural to use.

Ambient intelligence spaces will be a collection of technologies, infrastructures, applications and services across different ambient intelligence systems; car, home, the neighbourhood, the city, etc. This computing environment aims to facilitate and enhance peoples' everyday life by collecting a tremendous amount of data, analysing it, and providing an exclusive personalised environment better suited to the occupants. For example, a coffee cup may adopt specific colours depending on the temperature of the beverage, or the level of sugar according to diet guidelines. The information and data needed for social or business transaction will follow people and be accessible everywhere.

In the coming knowledge age, the crucial issue will be to design this digital territory such that user-control over the distance with others will be preserved, otherwise the exercise of charm described above, will become a nightmare. Indeed, partly illustrated in the famous movie Gattaca, a beauty target can almost be scanned by the admirer's desires. Helped by enhanced sensors with real-time analysis capability, the DNA (deoxyribonucleic acid) compatibility of this goddess can be discovered. Using profiles stored in various databases, to which the admirer has access, it may be possible to determine, before a single word is exchanged, if the goddess of beauty is socially free, or not.

Bubbles

A bubble is a temporary, but well-defined, space that can be used to limit the information coming into and leaving the bubble in the digital domain. It can be also understood as a digitisation of personal space, as described by the psychologist Robert Sommer [3] who used the analogy of a *soap bubble*. The idea of the bubble is defined to gather together all the interfaces, formats and agreements needed for the management of personal, group and public data and informational interactions.

The functionality of a bubble can be understood through two examples. The first example is mobile telephones and the second is access rights to a computer in a network.

Mobile telephones include a selection mechanism for personal profiles. These are used to control the ringing tones of the telephone, thus decreasing or increasing the possibility to reach the user. In this case the bubble corresponds to the personal profile settings which control both incoming and outgoing data flows; in this case, telephone calls which can be silenced or amplified.

71

The access rights to a computer in a network can have different levels. These will be different for an administrator, a normal user, or a visitor, and each will have different functions and properties – in effect there is a different *bubble* for each type of user of the computer network.

The bubble can be used to make filtering and selection of data. This contextual activity can be based on privacy, personalisation, priority, location, membership, ambience, circumstances, and time. The bubble may be described as a semi-transparent membrane that can be tuned to function differently depending on the direction of the movement of data. Filtering outwards is based on what people want to tell to external parties about information being stored inside the bubble, or about themselves. Information flow into the bubble is tuned based on information needs and requests.

A bubble can be created whenever it necessary for personal, community or global use. The bubbles can be shared between individuals or groups, for example, common bubbles for people having similar hobbies or bubbles for working teams. Bubbles can be seen both as a way to share views and experiences, but also as a means to limit the access rights of everybody in a proper way. Sharing of views can be widened not only to expressions of the present time, but also to the past. It can be seen as sharing personal images with others; images can be watched as moments in time, recording important milestones, or images can be used as a means of personal expression.

The number of existing bubbles is not restricted, but will probably be naturally limited. This can be compared to the number of email folders, which depends very much of the ways of using them. The bubbles can be used as a manageable concept for various interfacing occasions; surfaces of the bubbles can be interpreted as a means of communication for all inputs and outputs. This emotional content has both spatial and temporal aspects.

In the future, wireless tags (extremely tiny devices that can store information about the item to which they are attached, and which can communicate with the outside world) are likely to be embedded in a multitude of items of everyday life. Such tags represent a great source of knowledge for the user to be better informed about their nearby environment, but they may also, if precautions are not taken, communicate a lot of sensitive information about a person. The implementation of future *bubbles* may help to better control the data delivered by the tags to avoid invasion of privacy. For example, if tags are not allowed to communicate their information outside the bubble, under specific conditions defined by the user, this will take care of the issue of access rights to the tag's information. Security threats may then be avoided: a mobile tag reader cannot inform thieves of the potential value of goods and money

(European Central Bank has planned to embed wireless tags in euro bank notes) carried by their target, because of the opacity of the bubble for this specific data. In the future, users could better create and manage their own digital boundaries – through the appropriate design of *personal bubbles*.

Virtual Residence

The concept of a *virtual residence* is basically a representation of a home. It may be used as a mental map to manage security and privacy, both remotely and from within the home. A physical residence constitutes a legal sanctuary, and protects the citizen, at least in democratic countries, from outside interference or invasive measures. In some countries, citizens are even allowed to shoot someone who places a foot inside the boundaries of the home.

With the advent of the information society and its digitisation effects, values protected by the inviolability of the domicile will also need protection outside the physical limitation of the house. This requires the implementation of a virtual residence with digital boundaries as an extension of the legal sanctuary constituted by the home. Indeed, the digitisation of the everyday life environment tends to blur the borders defining the home (grass, fences etc.). When the home network is connected to the internet, the domain under consideration is no longer the home.

The problem is that in the digital world, there are very few social and legal indicators of what constitutes a private space. There are no clear labels to help internet users estimate where private digital territories start or end. Nor are there many social norms, such as the *netiquette*, to discourage people from entering private online spaces without authorisation. This lack of indicators not only implies technological challenges, but also underlines the need for a clarification of the social and legal framework of future ambient intelligence systems.

The concept of a virtual residence is therefore proposed as a means of tackling new concerns about identity, privacy and security within an ambient intelligence space that encompasses physical, online and virtual lives, and the embedding of computing in everyday objects. It consists therefore, of the following three elements: the future ambient intelligent and connected home considered as the main platform of the virtual residence vision; the online lives of people, families, households and their virtual representation and mobility; and interoperability between different ambient intelligence systems or ambient intelligence spaces.

The future intelligent home will contain many smart devices able to sense activity and to communicate this information to other appliances, people and networks, both within the home and outside the home. Within the home, domestic infrastructures can be regarded as the backbone of all these connections. It consists of wired, wireless and mobile technologies, among others.

This smart home will have complex and intertwined networks to increase the connectivity, the interaction, and the *intelligence* of home devices and services. Security issues will be at the heart of this development. In most cases, the inhabitants of the smart home will not be able to effectively administrate these networks and their potential failures because of their complexity. External service providers will probably do residential network administration, and as a result, domestic networks will be extended beyond the physical boundaries of the residence.

The above highlights the need to define a new digital territory, that is to say, a virtual residence that will encompass external network administration, be it automated or human driven. Because of the amount of interconnectivity of home networks and devices, disruptions will affect the whole network and will therefore, become *critical*. The criticality of the residence is of course also the result of the growing dependency of the smart home's inhabitants on networked home facilities and applications.

A monitoring system will be needed to conduct remote diagnostics. Future intrusion detection systems will be based both on network and physical sensors. Alarm functions will be a key element of the domestic critical infrastructure management. This latest example illustrates also the future bridge between the physical and the digital and their growing interdependency.

Virtual residence will also be used to represent the online private space of people, families or households in the information society and may enable the creation of new ways of living in cyberspace. Legal frameworks on music (Compact Disk) or movies (Digital Versatile Disk (DVD)) for instance, expect that these are used only for private listening and viewing, that is to say, only inside the family circle. A person can watch a purchased DVD wherever they like, at home, in the car, at work, in a hotel, as long as the person carries the disk with them.

In the future, it is expected that digital storage of entertainment and large bandwidth will increase and that viewing or listening will therefore not be restricted to use of the actual disk. It is easy to imagine the digital storage of family entertainment on a family computer, which is accessible not only in the home, but also outside from any location. Virtual residence will be the virtual space repository where all the family's private and commercial entertainment is stored. This will grant legal and social access to its use by the members of the family, who may be at different locations, for example, at university, or in a hotel room, eating in a restaurant, etc.

Finally, the notion of physical *residence* has evolved, in some countries to encompass other mobile spaces such as the car. Thus, virtual residences and associated software that may be located in various places in cyberspace also need to be seen as a mobile and dynamic concept travelling through different ambient intelligence systems.

Privacy, Security and Identity

When the French philosopher Jean-Paul Sartre declared "l'enfer c'est les autres!" (meaning "hell is the others!"), he did not suspect that his claim would be so consolidated and potentially implemented by the advent of the information society where everyone tends to become naked, not only physically (through powerful and tiny sensors), but digitally as well, when all personal data are under the permanent and pervasive scrutiny of others.

The construction of this vision is motivated by important issues like privacy, security and identity, which may be raised from the digitisation of everyday life. The building process of this digital world may indeed generate mainly two kinds of threats for the respect of privacy, identity, and security of the users.

The first is a lack of digital territoriality and therefore no protective boundaries. Four borders can be identified [4], and the crossing of one or more of these borders usually implies that people feel that their privacy is invaded. These borders are *natural borders; social borders; spatial or temporal borders or both; and ephemeral or transitory borders.* If these borders are quite well defined in the physical world, the digital environment is still characterised by the absence of these borders, which means that any abuse or violation of these borders cannot even be noticed.

The second threat is a multiplication of invisible and uncontrolled bridges between the real and the digital environments. A growing number of emerging technologies, such as location-based services, fourth generation mobile telephones, closed-circuit television, biometrics, etc., tend to establish links and bridges between a specific physical location and digitised knowledge and information. If the added value for the user is obvious, the potential new threats are not always highlighted. The following example describes a *positive* application of these bridges.

People are continuously creating their own views of the surroundings, but they are not able to share these views with others. When the ability to reference the real world with the digital space, tools and methods will be available that can be used for sharing these views with others. One idea to illustrate this is the concept of virtual notes; in the future people will be able to leave virtual yellow *Post-It stickers* where they want to. The only difference is in the visibility; they may be *seen* by everybody, or only those who are allowed, or only those who are able to see them.

Public Spaces and Private Spaces

The digitisation process of the information society also concerns public spaces. Public territory is seen as a free access space with a temporary quality. It offers the user a limited jurisdiction in terms of time and space. When a telephone call is made from a public telephone box, the users obtain jurisdiction of this territory for the time of the call. They control the access rights in this public place for a brief period of time and for a particular purpose.

The marking of private space is used to express that individuals have the right to do with that particular space what they want. Core parts of this private space are kept either inside the second skin (wearable computing device), or at the most they are shared among the family, that is to say, they constitute the inside information of the family bubble (residence). Some parts of this private space may be published temporarily to all the residents of a community, that is to say, made public, which is similar to, for example, arranging an open meeting at home for everybody in a neighbourhood.

The difference between private and public space is defined clearly on some occasions, like concerts or theatrical performances. The audience has the right to share the experience, that is to say, be there and enjoy, but cannot make recording or take pictures. There are other cases where the borderline is not this clear. The concert may not be arranged commercially, but still there is no right for those attending to make a recording of the performance and to sell it without permission. Many of the issues near the borderline between private and public spaces are such that their uses require some negotiation or agreement between the users of the spaces and the owners of the rights of the spaces. The grey zone is then defined as specific territory where a negotiation or transaction is required to obtain the jurisdiction of the targeted space.

Real world locations can be used to access both private and public virtual spaces. Some people may *see* information that is accessible to everybody, but at the same time some of them may have their own private information delivered through the same channel, and that information is only *visible* to them.

The interactions between public and private spaces in the future digital world and the significant role of digital territory can be also illustrated with the controversial example of a street crime.

Imaging that a murder has been committed in the street in front of a house. Alerted by the emergency call service, the police arrive at the crime scene a few minutes after the tragic event and undertake the investigation by collecting evidence and testimonies. Up to this point, the description of this scene is traditional.

Now, consider what happens within the vision of a digital territory. To obtain maximum information, the police not only define the physical boundaries of the crime scene with the well-known plastic tape, but also the digital boundaries surrounding the crime. They create a bubble (see Figure 6.1) around the victim, an information sphere or *infosphere*.

Figure 6.1: Bubble used at a crime scene. *Source*: Laurent Beslay, Copyright 2003. Reproduced with permission.

This digital crime space encompasses other peoples' digital territories, such as the personal bubble of the citizens who were in the street. This defines information from devices such as mobile telephones with *always on* cameras, wearable computers with detection facilities and proximity communication systems, etc. It also encompasses the houses in the street near the crime scene, and therefore the virtual residences near to where the crime took place. These include residential gateway systems, intrusion detection agents, etc. Finally, the *infosphere* also encompasses the digital part of the public space constituted by the street, including thermal sensors, closed-circuit televisions, global positioning systems of public transport, etc.

All these territories have collected and stored, with their sensors, a huge amount of data, which may be useful for the detection of the offender. The clear drawing of several and specific digital boundaries and territories, and of course, the democratic nature of the country where the crime took place, will permit the preservation and respect of the fundamental rights of the owners of these territories. At the same time, the police will have access to the data only under specific conditions and perhaps with a particular process, for example, to protect the identity of the witnesses or the legal sanctuary nature of the virtual residence as part of the residence.

Conclusions

In the case of the internet, it is already becoming clear that people contrast what is *online* to what is *offline* to a much lesser extent than perhaps initially expected. However, in the future, information and knowledge will become increasingly *embedded* in everyday things and everyday life. The individual, the nearby environment, physical residence, bubbles, and virtual residence, may become intertwined, paradoxically perhaps, by establishing clear indicators and boundaries for the digital territory.

By defining these kinds of boundaries, safe territory can begin to be created, spanning across the physical world and digitised counterparts. In the future, there will be an increasing amount of bridges between the physical and the digital. Through the construction of well-designed digital boundaries, emerging location-based services, wireless tags, body implants, ambient sensors, will form environments that are both trustworthy and that can become *domesticated*.

There is already the beginning of a blurring between traditional society that coexists with a digital counterpart removed from it, and a single society where people have accepted and adopted the fusion of physical and digital realities. In such a future society, people will still be able to control and manage distance and privacy from others, with new tools provided by intelligent technologies.

References

[1] William Gibson, 1984, *Neuromancer*, Ace edition, July
[2] Altman, I., 1975, *The Environment and Social Behaviour*, Brooks/Cole Monterrey
[3] Sommer, R., 1969, *Personal Space: The Behavioral Basis of Design*, Prentice Hall Trade
[4] Marx, G.T., 2001, Murky conceptual waters: the Public and the Private, *Ethics and Information Technology*, Vol. 3, No. 3, pp. 157-169

Chapter 7

Variations on Big Brother

Walter Van de Velde

Introduction – Big Brother Visions

Big Brother visions have well-known roots in literature, with Orwell (*1984*), Kafka (*Das Schloss*) and Kubrick's HAL (*2001 A Space Odyssey*) as primary pointers. The idea is also present in religion. Many will remember the Christian icon of an eye, with the inscription "God sees everything". The post-modern God of television has adapted the idea of Big Brother with similarly strong impact.

This small sample shows that no two Big Brothers are the same. The Big Brother in *Das Schloss* is an invisible bureaucracy that derives its power from its absurdity. Orwell's is an omnipresent observer that perpetuates an established order. Kubrick's Big Brother is willing to destroy the order to preserve itself. All inspire awe, and stimulate obeisance and subordination. In the Big Brother television series, on the other hand, the *eye* becomes public. It stimulates spectacle and trespassing of social norms, not obeisance.

Big Brother visions are usually distopian. They restrict privacy and freedom to the presumed benefit of some higher good, explicit or not. Their strength is in the subtle psychological nature of that restriction. They constrain without use of physical force, that is to say, by bending the mind rather than the body through reason or other means. This is well illustrated in Foucault's analysis of the Panopticon prison, an architectural realisation of an omnipotent observer that cannot be seen.

Big Brothers are not just fiction. The internet, for one, has been analysed as a digital panopticon. Digital transactions, from looking at web pages to buying online, leave their traces. It is technically possible to understand the digital trace of someone's life by piecing together information that is dispersed in various databases, routers and servers. Businesses and governments alike are tempted by the wealth of information that this can provide.

Technology has always been a driver for this type of surveillance. Closed-circuit television-camera security-systems, web cams, geographic positioning systems, image analysis, and environmental monitoring are all potential Big Brother technologies. One example of the power brought about by these technologies is the plan for the London Underground system to have 9000 cameras by 2005, with specialised image analysis software to detect suspicious behaviours. Ambient intelligence systems can also be seen in the same light, with computing devices embedded in everyday objects, responding in an unseen way to the presence of people to anticipate their needs. This blurs the boundary of the locus of initiative and thus easily drifts from service to soft coercion.

Surveillance systems are usually set up for specific occasions, but then have a tendency to stay. An increasing demand for more security from citizens is interpreted often as a demand for more control and surveillance. To allow authorities to track down the suspicious few, entire populations are sacrificing privacy and freedom to make sure that they fit safely within the norms.

Do Big Brothers necessarily restrict privacy and freedom? Or can something else be done with them, now or in the future? To answer these questions two scenarios, set in the distant future, are considered: Connectopolis and Egopoli. Connectopolis describes the experiences and impressions of a visitor from Egopoli, and Egopoli the experiences and impressions of a visitor from Connectopolis.

Connectopolis

When I decided to visit Connectopolis, my official reasons were of a professional nature. But my true motivation was curiosity. My great-grand parents had lived there before they moved south. I had learned of this region through friends and relatives that had passed through it. Thanks to the continental network of high-speed on-demand flains (*flowing trains*), it is easy to get to. So that is what I did.

A stay in Connectopolis has its discomforts for a citizen of Egopoli, such as myself. Of course there is the climate, with its infinite shades of grey, its gusty winds and the, occasionally spectacular, play of rainbows and rain curtains. For an Egopolian who is used to Mediterranean weather this is a change. But I sense a more subtle feeling of not being at home; the causes of which are initially difficult to pin down. It has something to do with the contradiction of an enormous capacity to absorb from other cultures on the one hand, and on the other, a closure upon itself. It sometimes feels as if a magical hand is staging before my eyes a surrealistic theatre play of randomly selected everyday scripts, the players not always understanding why themselves. After a couple of days it dawns on me that this is indeed the way of life in Connectopolis.

The district of Connectopolis, some call it a reserve, is not very big. It spans over 12,000 square kilometres and has around 7.5 million residents. It is mostly flat, surrounded by sea to the west and hills to the east. Little remains of its natural condition, though this is not apparent at first sight. I find the environment rather pleasing, with its mixture of small and large towns, a variety of rivers, woods and agricultural areas. The general impression is that it is fragmented, since a dense network of highways, byways and other lines of transport traverse the territory of Connectopolis. The uninformed visitor often sees this as the explanation for its name: every place seems to be directly connected to every other. But the nature of connectivity in Connectopolis reaches much deeper into the heart of this singular society.

Folders that promote the district to tourists and investors invariably highlight it as being *connected*. It is, but not in the *digital* sense in which this was meant in the internet age, as some call it in hyped techno-geological jargon. It is true that the district of Connectopolis, even before it was called this, had a strong tradition of digital connectivity. At the end of the 20th century it was one of the first places to be *wired* with optical fibre and coaxial cabling. It realised its ambition to connect every home. It was also successful in developing the suite of electronic services based on the internet and the World Wide Web: electronic commerce, electronic government, electronic learning, etc. including their mobile and ubiquitous variants. But these *e*-services, as they were called at that time, failed to create new synergistic effects in society. They remained virtual surrogates for existing and age-old social practices, at best leading to efficiency gains. In retrospect this *e*-wave of electronic services, roughly between 1995 and 2015, was a red herring, a false lead that was mainly invented to boost technology vendors' sales and those of their allies, but which misdirected expectations for its users. It led mostly to social isolation and disruption rather than to happiness or wealth, except for a few.

The first thing that surprised me about Connectopolis is that, like Egopoli, it is full of sensors. All kinds of observing devices can be seen in streets, in buildings, in shops, in public spaces and in many of the homes. Twice a year, in spring and in autumn, a mix of biodegradable smart dust, tiny electronic devices based on nanotechnologies and biotechnologies, are spread from the air to cover Connectopolis with an *ad hoc* network of

81

snuffers for soil condition, air and light quality, temperature, micro-biological characteristics, and so on. Sensors and electronic markers in livestock, food supplies, packaging, distribution systems and shops track food chains. Interaction among people is traced, thanks to electronic identity cards and the invisible propagation of data through overlapping personal area networks. Cameras are relatively absent and clearly marked, image-based information being used only for strict surveillance and recognition, mostly of *aliens*, like me, or in case of accidents and disaster.

I find the citizens of Connectopolis rather undisturbed by this constant observation. The Government managed to convince them that data would be stored only for as long as necessary and that it would only be used for the benefit of the individual and society. Legislation was enacted, giving citizens the right to access their data and to know who uses it and for what reason. The positive effects this helped to create quickly outbalanced initial worries about this *digital mirroring*. In spite of its relatively dense population, traffic in Connectopolis is smooth, and one always finds a parking spot. Flexible resource management is commonplace: there never seems to be too much or too little of anything (food supplies, theatre places, train seats). Epidemics are easily traced and halted. Ecosystems maintain their delicate balance in spite of human omnipresence.

All this is the result of the *fluidity-wave*, or *f-wave*, which occurred roughly between 2010 and 2025, and had a much greater impact on quality of life in Connectopolis than the *e*-wave. After decades of blind techno-delirium, information networks were finally understood for what they really are; meaningful *augmentations* of social, ecological, economic, sanitary, energy or transport networks. The resulting techno-social hybrids would *grow* on to real-life activity, gradually transforming it, but without disruption.

This image of a self-regulating territory may sound like the ultimate technocrat's dream, but my story is just halfway. The real power of the techno-social hybrid became clear when citizens obtained access to the data. This started from a group of *hackers* that managed to tap into the data and made it widely available. This initially subversive act launched a paradigm shift: *the digital mirror of Connectopolis had become visible to all.* The Government had tried to stop this, but was punished in the elections for doing so: the times when citizens could be treated as being too dumb to deal with the complexity of reality were definitively over.

Today it is difficult to ignore the status of Connectopolis: it can be seen everywhere. I am used to weather information back in Egopoli. In Connectopolis it is not just the weather, but the entire state of territory and society that is charted, analysed, annotated, animated and commented upon. Specialised media companies add value to the never ending data-streams that capture life in Connectopolis. Dynamically changing billboards provide, apart from publicity, overviews or more detailed information, and reveal trends and patterns in society. It takes a while to get used to, but once you grasp the colours and symbols, and learn to manage your attention through the multi-layered holographic displays, the effect is quite impressive. One gets a view of Connectopolis in all its multiple facets in the blink of an eye.

The right and obligation to know the state of Connectopolis is the cornerstone of its citizenship. In an important covered *plaza* that I visited this is most dramatically illustrated. The space is rectangular and, as the robotic guide kindly explained, measures 40.93 metres long by 13.41 metres wide, a clear reference to the Sistine Chapel in the Vatican and the Temple of Solomon described in the Old Testament. Its ceiling consists of a honeycomb structure with 42 high-resolution screens, each with a surface of several square metres. It reminds me of some old Palazzi back in Egopoli where the painted ceilings depict some ideal for the enlightened Renaissance man: the synthesis of nature (what is), geometry (how it is seen), science (how it is understood) and art (how it is re-created toward an essential ideal). Everyday-life goes on down on the ground, but looking up, one sees *the big picture* and feels part of it, inspired to contribute to its continuing construction.

As if the result of a second Renaissance, five centuries after the first, this ceiling in a Connectopolis town hall shows, presumably in real-time, a multi-faceted synthesis of the state of life and everything else in Connectopolis. This includes its economy, ecology, traffic, but also the health of its citizens, their activities, social exchanges, aspirations, joy, play, tensions, creativity, and so on. These different *facets* are democratically negotiated to reflect the shifting concerns and society values of the citizens of Connectopolis. Each facet of the ceiling highlights, by the symbolism I mentioned before, the tensions and frictions that any such aspect is subjected to. It is, just like those Palazzi ceilings, a permanent invitation to the citizen to reflect upon, and to take concrete action in society. And they do.

The media in Connectopolis have a significant role. What used to be radio and television for my great-grand parents, have become personalised news and advice channels. The public displays aim to bias attention in one way or another, but it is basically up to individuals to decide for themselves which aspects of Connectopolis to attend to at any given time. Individual *value channels* promote ideas of things to do, be it established patterns or professions, or new ones. Data mining techniques find regularities that can be enforced or counteracted, by providing to citizens, small scripts or role models.

Being original is one way to attract the sufficient critical mass to have an impact on the state of Connectopolis. This explains an emphasis on creativity and the seemingly enormous absorption capacity of foreign influences. Connectopolians are keen to try new things, and preferably do so in tribes. The result is a Boy Scout's interpretation of a rave-party: occasionally one can see people flocking to places where their *patterns*, professional or other, can be usefully employed to re-enforce weaker ones or to counter others. Social Mobilisation Systems (SMS), one of several peer-to-peer community information and communication systems, help ensure maximum reactivity and satisfaction. This phenomenon, essential to the Connectopolis way of life, is possible thanks to the fact that residents of Connectopolis are very mobile and easily commute over the moderate distances that are afforded by fluid transport and the small size of the territory.

This is the paradox of Connectopolis: it is a permanent experiment in living together, but at the same time it is blind to the meanings of its many imported and self-imposed rituals. Connectopolis has realised the panoptic utopia as a way to converge toward what is best for society. It is a constant invention of itself, the ultimate creative district. But being a world under permanent construction, it also risks the permanent self-destruction of its citizens' identity.

4 April 2043

Egopoli

I am a tourist in Egopoli, having a short break to enjoy spring in the south, while the weather is cold and wet in Connectopolis. The days are beautiful, the city magnificent, and I promised my boyfriend to send lots of pictures.

I know my camera has a *piggyback* feature, but I have never been in a place where it can be used. Here, in Egopoli, standing on a beautiful long-stretched triangular piazza, I switch on my camera. The digital screen instantly shows a mosaic of tiny images: they are all of myself, standing in the piazza, seen from different perspectives! I switch to *scan perspectives*, and the display cycles through the different shots, allowing me to choose the best one. I select the image that frames myself nicely in front of the church's roman façade, and zoom in a bit more. I have taken control of a whole network of cameras, all ready to take *my* picture. I am *piggybacking* on the other cameras as if they were mine.

In the first decade of the 21st century Egopoli, like most important cities in Europe, had been equipped with a dense public surveillance infrastructure. Digital cameras were installed all over town and sophisticated software was used to recognise suspicious events. Egopolians, known for their strong identity and political independence, saw this more as an act of aggression from the Central Government, but in the prevailing *esprit-du-temps* there was little that could be done against that. When international peace returned, the Mayor of Egopoli had had the idea of recycling the digital surveillance technology for more useful purposes. His idea was: "If some form of surveillance seems to be necessary for security, the resistance against surveillance is based on a fear of losing privacy. What a third party is observing leaves the private sphere. What would happen if the third party were in the private sphere itself?"

This is the experiment of Egopoli. It became a landmark that launched a whole new service industry.

So, I take the picture. It is sent to my camera and, from the several options provided I chose just to send it on to my boyfriend, with sound and ambient parameters (temperature, light, smell) included so he will be able to immerse himself in the same experience as me, almost.

The thing that surprises me about Egopoli is that there is no permanent observation. Instead, people are responsible for their own surveillance. Everywhere in the city it is possible to check what modes of self-observation are available: camera or others. One, several, or none of them can be used, as each citizen wishes, and they can choose what to do with the self-observation data. This is what I did with my camera. Egopolians typically use moving images instead of stills, and they apply a much wider range of methods.

The basic service, known as Guardian Angel, is available free, to anyone. There is a follow-me option by which they can automatically switch from camera to camera when moving through town. There is the multi-view option, which aims to collect data from multiple perspectives at the same time and, with the virtual-view option, can reconstruct an image from an arbitrary perspective. Citizens can define zones of the town where they want to be observed, or others where they do not want or need to be observed. Similarly, time-slots can be defined in which observation is wanted. The flashback option allows triggers to be defined that request observation to role back for a maximum of two minutes when triggered. All data is kept on servers for mass storage. I do not know where, and it does not matter to me. All that matters is that only I can access it. There are various ways to inspect and structure it, but no way to erase it. Indexing can be done manually or can be based on higher level information derived from time stamps, place stamps, contextual analysis, or other forms of more sophisticated content extraction.

To use the Guardian Angel I picked up an interactive smart card from the tourist office. It contains a limited range of sensors, especially for orientation, positioning and physical movement. It also allows recognition by the Guardian Angel infrastructure and communications with it. It comes with a set of five tags to keep track of personal belongings. This feature was the first to be made available, and after three decades Egopolians still invent new uses for it. It automatically triggers multi-view flashback observation when one of the tags is removed to more than arms length distance from the card. If somebody were to steal my handbag, I would have a trace of what happened, and the smart card would sound a beep tone to warn me. It was triggered just once during my stay when I forgot my coat in a bar: useless anyway.

At all times individuals are responsible and in control of their own data collection. The *owner* of the collected data is the one on whose life the data is collected: me. No link with the collecting *device* or its owner remains in the log. All of this data is continuously collected and stored. The resulting *life stream* is a hyper-perspective, a mosaic movie of oneself and surroundings, and one's own state and activity. I browsed my life stream a couple of times, and used some material to send to my boyfriend, but he agrees that it is not interesting as a documentary exercise. It does however show a glimpse of how the technology works. For example, some individuals are invisible on the images because they activated the ghost option, a digital trick on the images that can only be reversed under certain conditions and following strict privacy procedures.

But surveillance, personal security, or tourist photography are no longer the primary uses of the Egopoli system. Healthcare and independent living now represent a large share of uses. But sports, entertainment and lifestyle management has taken over as killer-applications; not the least because there is big money to be made from these.

Having data about ones' life is one thing, knowing what to do with it is another. The interactive smart card lets one buy time on a whole range of services. By linking my life-streams to one of those services, I delegate the right to analyse and add value to it, but not ownership of the original data or any of the results. At the end of each day I can access a web site that combines not only a trace of my day, but also a history of activities, annotated with recommendations for my wellbeing, as well as for the wellbeing of shops, restaurants and bars in Egopoli. This is delightful because it builds up in a very consistent way throughout my stay, and it is as if I could Google my short stay in Egopoli.

Simpler? Yes there is something very simple. I tried on the newest collection of the local designers in what is probably Egopolis' most hype fashion store. I tried on combinations, looked at them in an electronic mirror with two seconds delay, very convenient, and got real-time advice and hints on combinations. I could only afford a piece or two, but the shopping experience was cool.

Too egocentric? With one of the newest services, groups of people can agree access to one another's data. Teenagers regularly do, and so do families, mostly those with children. I have seen groups of people playing around to produce their own Big Brother holographic reality show for a closed group.

A competing service provider came up with a variation that is based on linking different people's lives. You buy time in the life of a fictitious personage that you can contribute to by picking up her life strand from another *player*. By close proximity of the smart card the life strand hops over from one player to another one.

Numerous lifestyle services are available as well. They link up a user with a person that has direct access to the streams that are being collected and provides all kind of advice based on this. The advice is delivered on handheld mobile devices or wearable audio-devices, called parrots.

Others have learned to use life stream services for marketing purposes. Research into consumer behaviour is largely achieved by plugging into, and paying for, data streams from consumers. Specialised consulting houses provide analyses of data that is captured, including that from sensors and products or service delivery points with the aim of understanding preference, ergonomic considerations, and new and unexpected uses. Half a century ago such uses would have caused an outcry from consumer protection organisations. We have come a long way indeed.

26 August 2046

Conclusions – Big Brother Variations

The scenarios of Connectopolis and Egopoli illustrate two Big Brother visions without the obvious distopian character of the classical versions. The Egopoli scenario is a radical alternative to a centralised Big Brother. There is an infrastructure that allows observation, but the person who is observed owns the information generated. It is also individuals who decide when and how to be observed. On top of this simple scheme, a range of services can be imagined that citizens can access or subscribe to, outsourcing the analysis and interpretation of data to trusted third parties. Egopoli has an egocentric flavour. Although certain services imply groups, there is not a community effect: it is each one on its own. The nodes in this network society remain individuals, at best as members of groups, but never of real communities.

In Connectopolis community plays a much stronger role. It is a vision in which the Big Brother folds back into the society that is being observed, and relies on its collective creativity to shape it. This is interesting in a post-modern perspective where universal codes and meta-narratives are broken down in favour of a technological and utilitarian rational.

Both scenarios make assumptions about people's attitudes and aspirations. Connectopolis supposes an active citizenship in which everybody is trying to shape society by inventing, importing and enacting social games. It has a multi-faceted mirror for the society. In Egopoli the mirror is scattered into a million pieces, one for each individual. What remains of social life is an almost perverse desire of watching and of being watched, at the limit, only by oneself. It is not obvious that this is what people want.

There will be, in any scenario, secondary effects that may be so strong as to invalidate the entire exercise. For example, in Connectopolis different balances in values may lead to territorial effects as dramatic as cultural borders and ghetto formation. Moreover, every Big Brother system will induce some kind of *Big Brother effect*: those that are being observed will change their behaviour to circumvent or disrupt the system. There is plenty of room for this in both scenarios. A Connectopolian may try to stay out of the observation ranges of cameras and sensors, or may offer a service to make people *invisible* to the observation system. Groups of Egopolians may stage a large-scale use of a service that will force it to shutdown. The absurdity of the system may also be demonstrated by using it against itself, for instance, by offering services that clean the images of any trace of people, or replaces them with cartoons or unrelated images.

Connectopolis and Egopoli both make sense technically, especially within a generous time horizon of 40 years. They are unlikely to find fertile ground in modern social and political contexts. Connectopolis is probably too idealistic and, with techno-optimism and political indifference, risks being reduced to a purely technocratic tool. Egopoli may be more in line with liberal trends and some of its services would make sense in the modern world. Its large-scale realisation would conflict with privacy concerns, as well as with the *Swiss pocket-knife* trend in personal, mobile information and communication products and services.

In the foreseeable future Big Brother type infrastructures and applications will continue to come forward, both for the technological drive behind them and for the prevailing geopolitical and social circumstances that motivate them. But a sustainable society cannot be built on fear. Modern Big Brothers may seem an inevitable consequence of technological possibility and the socio-economic need for safety. In the long run they will not survive if they do not contribute to individual or social fulfilment for everyone.

Chapter 8

The @lgorithmic Society: Digitarians of the World Unite

Kazimierz Krzysztofek

Introduction

The information society, the knowledge society, the post-capitalist society, the post-mass production society, ... The list of terms describing future society seems endless; and grows longer. People using these labels normally single out and expose one or more features of such a society. No-one has been able to encompass society as a whole, even though many have tried.

The feature of future society that is essential can be expressed by the name, the algorithmic society: algorithmic beyond real needs. The tendencies leading to this stage seem quite clear. This announces some benefits for the future, but also many complications.

"In the beginning there was Algorithm." So announced the well-known mathematician Steven Wolfram. Those who are not convinced by such biblical paraphrases can find something similar in leftist *holy texts*: the spectrum of algorithm is spinning around the world.

Algorithms are real. They are defined procedures. They usually refer to computer programs, but they also explain the behaviour of living organisms. In these cases they are genetic or hormonal algorithms. The term is rarely used for people even though humans are also equipped with genetic and hormonal programs. But people are also products of cultures, which gives them both desirable and undesirable features.

The notion of algorithm may be fruitful in explaining some cultural phenomena. Throughout history, people have been programmed via community cultures, cultures of fate, which did not leave much room for individual decisions, private consciousness, morality and identity. The history of European cultures can be interpreted as a long-lasting process of freeing human beings from these cultural algorithms. The most outstanding achievements date back to the age of the Enlightenment, when millions of educated people started to guide themselves by their own mind and free will. Yet, there were constant attempts to assimilate the chaos brought about by freedom of thinking and acting through certain endeavours meant to re-impose algorithms on people. In the industrial society it was the mass, redundant culture. In the 20th century, Nazi and Communist totalitarianism were particular cases of this; these imposed strict procedures of thinking and acting. This imposition of algorithmic thinking did not fully succeed, yet it was detrimental to both society and individuals: the victims of these systems.

The algorithm, seen as learned behaviour, is necessary for the functioning of humans. Without it people would waste their intellectual energy analysing all their actions, even those that are minor and insignificant. Without such algorithms humans would have never left the pre-human stage of their development, before the emergence of homo sapiens.

However, algorithms are perplexing. On the one hand the increasing use of algorithms will ease life, yet on the other there are doubts, considering the scale that will be achieved in the future, if they will be beneficial to humankind in the longer term.

Behavioural automatism protects people against unnecessary intellectual processing and, owing to this, it gives people a chance to use their minds for creativity, innovation and invention. Yet, there is a concern that a decreasing number of people will be able to be creative. A striking contradiction of 20th century civilisation was that on one side there was an imperative to *be creative and innovative*, but on the other there was rising pressure for predictable human behaviour, since unpredictability gives birth to chaos which is difficult to manage.

The problem of algorithms was relatively less important when technologies of the mechanical age imposed procedures on muscles and senses. Information and communication technologies however replace some functions of brain, for instance memory, calculation, processing, etc., which makes the problem much more complex and provokes anxieties.

It is possible that the near future will see a move to information algorithmic-behaviour of people. Those who succeed in freeing themselves from it will produce algorithms to program people – the algorithmic masses. This will not occur because of some *Matrix*, as in the film of that name, will but because of the very nature and logic of the bio-techno sphere. Its impetus makes futile any attempt to stop this machine.

Are Humans Unreliable?

In the next generation humans will have to deal with information of a different nature, separated from the real world and context. The analogue person derived information from nature, from data registered by the senses and intellectually processed. Moving in the physical, analogue world, people absorbed information from the environment, from street signs, maps, directions from other people, etc. In the future people will absorb data from anonymous databases, remotely located, and managed by unknown people. Data will be provided by omnipresent satellite-based geographic positioning systems, information embedded in everyday objects, wearable computers, implanted electronic circuits, mobile telephones, etc. This will be a *plug-into-the-world* environment, or using another metaphor, an *electronic universal Swiss pocket-knife*.

There are grounds to believe that third generation mobile telephones will be the first devices to resolve the problem of the *last mile connection*. These will have capabilities that will enable a whole range of new services that are not possible with the second-generation mobile telephones in use at the beginning of the 21st century. These third generation mobile telephones will be an *omni-medium,* integrating dozens of functions performed by several tools such as digital cameras, electronic money, etc. These databases will offer behaviour algorithms: "nearby there is a Chinese restaurant, and the opposite side there is a computer games arcade". In the places where people are travelling, railway or bus stations, airports and other familiar or unfamiliar places, the algorithms will be delivered in the same way. People will not be looking for analogue sources of information, for example, from fellow travellers. The traditional opinion leaders and information broadcasters, along with narrowcasters where people can select the information they want to receive, will lose their meaning since the source will be beyond theme. People will become more *single*. The rapid growth of information and communication technologies clearly leads in this direction. When a human being has an awareness of meagre power and control over the environment, then that person instinctively seeks a supporting community. When people feel more empowered and have a sense of control over the environment, then fellow creatures seem less necessary.

Information served in this way is undergoing alienation and automation. This process will be the more rapid as bioelectronic hybridisation of humans transforms them into symbiotic creatures that are quite comfortable and happy with anthropo-technologies, knowing that they will provide more empowerment.

Humans will not need external control, as they will be provided with their own algorithms. They will not be any more a reliable source of information for the systems collecting data on them, to make them even more algorithmic, as the information and communication technology itself is seen more reliable and creditworthy. This lack of confidence in humans accounts for the practice of engaging computers to obtain trustworthy data, or when to control and measure the productivity, integrity and probity, and commitment of an employed person. It is becoming more profitable to derive information from objective systems independent from individuals. There are however some people who hold strong convictions that this will deepen the erosion of trust among people, thus weakening social capital. The more algorithms are used to guide people, the more productive they will become, therefore the better human capital.

This leads to a discomforting and discouraging conclusion, that increasingly intelligent tools will require increasingly less human intelligence on the mass scale. This is far from concluding that people will become barcode-steered bioelectronic hybrids. This would be the full triumph of algorithm. Yet, it is beyond question that the scientific approach to survival is an imperative for civilisation: science along with digitisation. The latter is visible: it is hard to imagine a modern people without their personal identification number (PIN) code. PINs are algorithms in a pure shape. The *locus of control* will shift outside to impersonal centres of control. Artificial computer-based intelligence will facilitate everyday life, but this will be a further production of the algorithm. The more intelligent the house becomes, the less intelligent will be the dwellers.

The techno-pessimists claim that expansion of the computer civilisation is a race between the software manufacturers, who produce friendly programs for stupid consumers who are often referred to as end-users, and the world which produces the improved species of stupid people. It is possible to say therefore, that the information age differs from the Palaeolithic era only in that the then humanoids did not use intelligent tools: that is why to survive the humanoid creatures of that time must have been intelligent.

There is a tendency to assess barbarians as pre-reflexive creatures forgetting that *digitarians* who fill the computer memories with vast quantities of data everyday will be, in the not too distant future, post-reflexive people. Humankind achieved the peak of reflexive knowledge in the age of the Renaissance and the Enlightenment. Barbarians and savages formed, in a way, a society of knowledge; to survive they must have absorbed the whole output of their cultures. Is it possible to claim a right to call the future society that of knowledge, in the age of *on-off-push button user-friendly technologies?* Thus the knowledge society can be seen in a historical context: decreasing amounts of knowledge mastered by an individual in relation to the total volume of knowledge. The knowledge acquired by members of modern and post-modern societies is that which is materialised in the knowledge created by other people: in books, intelligent tools, software, networks, that is to say, accumulated algorithms.

An important question arises. How long will these algorithms accelerate incessantly? Moore's Law predicts that computing power doubles every 18 months. Human intellectual power of course develops much more slowly. The point is that there will be a *digital divide* in the coming years. An ever-decreasing number of people will program the ever increasing number of people, providing them with algorithms. Starting from the simple calculators back in the 1970s, every new generation of information and communication technology pushes more people out, eventually reaching beyond higher and higher intellectual frontiers. What will be left will be a decreasing minority: the majority will be less intelligent than computers.

Millions of *end-users* will decreasingly process information consciously and the human brain will take on the functions of algorithms at the expense of consciousness. Data and information will be shifted from the zone of awareness of processing and *value-added* creativity, towards the zone of algorithmic behaviour. In the age of mechanics the machine replaced man wherever human labour became algorithmic and routine. Washing machines replaced manual washing, sowing machines replaced the hand sowing of crops, weaving machines replaced weavers, digging machines replaced manual digging, etc. In future generations a similar thing will happen in the sphere of routine intellectual work that is subject to application of algorithms. This announces a revolution in offices. Human intelligence will be needed to teach or program computers that in turn will teach and program humans.

This will bring about a further elimination of hierarchical layers and intermediaries in society. In the previous types of society, political parties, journalists, scientists, clergymen, teachers, shopkeepers, and others, helped people: citizens, consumers, the faithful, etc., to make choices and decisions. These institutions played the role of information filters and exercised control through censorship, consulting, editing, selection, etc. of the flows of material and symbolic goods from producers to receivers. Among them there were trusted authorities.

With every new supermarket, fast food establishment etc., the number of intermediaries diminished. This also refers to the early stage of the information society, which reduced the number of intermediaries. The information consumer with access to the internet in the home, communicates directly with the source. People buy, learn and vote at home. They take control of the act of communication, have video on-demand, create their own theme channels, operate their remote control devices, become *turn-the-channel* people, and senders and receivers.

Large-scale vertical hierarchical links are giving way to large-scale horizontal, decentralised, network contacts. Owing to de-monopolisation of information centres, the information itself is ceasing to be a scarcity. From the era of scarcity, a new age of information overabundance and redundancy has begun.

Paradoxically this redundancy of information brings about similar effects as its scarcity. This produces a society where unsolicited communications, referred to as *spam* in the internet world, predominate. Navigation through the information mass then demands better *spam elimination*. There seems to be a constant race between improving the filtering programs that remove *spam*, and the *spam generators* whose programs retrieve and use email addresses from databases. This is like an impersonal information war. *Spam*, it seems, is becoming a danger to culture, knowledge and communication in the network society.

In the age of mass media and mass society, people are bombarded by flows of information. Interactive media allow people to choose information, on-demand. It is possible in the near future that people will *demand no information*. The very notion of the *right to information* will lose its sense. Is the future a post-information society?

Many people feel helpless in the face of information overload. Many are not able to control it, in particular the less educated and skilled. Paradoxically, once again, there emerges a need for new intermediaries. But these are intermediaries of a different kind than those mentioned previously. The new generation of go-betweens will not just filter the information stream, but will also place it into context, and analyse, authenticate and integrate it with users' knowledge. They are necessary to deal with the excess of information.

These new intermediaries are still sought after, but there are signs indicating that by 2015 they will be replaced by digital intermediaries; software that will serve people, learn about them and know increasingly more about their *masters*. They will be perfectly aware of peoples' needs, and their intellectual and emotional profiles. And the software will provide people with algorithms.

Creators of this software will be the elite of future society. The algorithms produced by them will be very valuable intellectual property. The owners of such a huge business based on this software will have concentrated in their hands a large amount of symbolic power. Such a concentration of representational power means that groups of ordinary people will be on their way to losing their self-representation through culture, and be doomed to be portrayed by other narratives in which they do not find their own problems and dilemmas. This self-portraying is

94

difficult since the marketplace becomes a universal locus of legitimacy. It takes over the power of communicating and gives meanings.

The effects of algorithms on culture will emerge as they did when previous inventions were introduced. Diffusion of print brought about change in language algorithms; systems of education adopted the pattern of discourse from books; change in syntax forced people to speak according to the written language rules. The latter became more standardised as unification of national languages came to effect, at the expense of regional dialects, tongues of small ethnic or sub-ethnic groups. Mass media accelerated this process of nation-state building. The linear nature of reading with its transport of thought, line-by-line, paragraph after paragraph, imposed linear thinking and acting on people.

In the digital age there will be enormous simplification of the communication code, that is to say, its further submission to algorithms. Linguists notice decreasing use of subordinate clauses in writing and speaking. Media imitate this simplified code in their vital interest, to be understood by their audiences. Subject matter is being dispersed into the computerised world of the internet, into what is called cyberspace. Being online affects what people do when they return to the off-line world.

As the *pre-computer generation* begins to slowly disappear, and the digital one grows, there will be a decreasing number people who are resistant to algorithms. This will be a practical knowledge society, full of information jams, chaos and narrow meaning, but not one of wise knowledge.

A Black Scenario?

Is the above a black scenario? This is not necessarily the case. The intention is not to predict an apocalypse. However, the bright future dreamt of by those who believe in a vision of a creative Europe, cannot be taken for granted.

The use of algorithms is simply a necessity. It grows out of the need for predictability and escape from chaos. Without algorithms societies may not manage to master the synergetic effect of individual freedom and powerful tools offered by information and communication technologies. It is not the *Matrix* that subjugates people with algorithms. *The Matrix* is people. At stake is soft governance, without hard totalitarianism, the lessons of which everyone is familiar with.

The use of algorithms is inescapable since the absorption of the bio-socio sphere by the bio-techno sphere is an evolution with its logic. This evolution is not moral or leading aims, since no evolution is ever so. What is at stake is technical civilisation protecting itself against *integral collapse*. It is an attempt to create order, and protection against chaos. The coming age will not be that of simple structures with built-in algorithms, but an age of complex systems. For these systems, what will count most is not so much the structure itself, but: chaotic flows, turbulence, instability, disorder, erosion, tensions, globalisation, fragmentation, decomposition, networks, bifurcation, attractors, discontinuities, fractals, streams, conflicts, dependencies, etc.

This is the splitting of a polycentric structure. Processes generated by the system of states, overlap with processes running counter to them and, furthermore, both undergo institutionalisation. Thus there is a host of forces at work, many of them with conflicting, mutually neutralising vectors, which makes it difficult to arrive at a clear-cut resultant direction. They give rise to tensions and conflicts. They overturn established norms, and complicate or even completely thwart global governance. This greatly intensifies the risk, uncertainty, unpredictability and non-transparency of processes with a global compass. It also gives rise to huge heuristic problems and positively provokes the question of just how to investigate these processes.

The whole existing edifice of knowledge has been built on implicit belief in the linear type of analysis. But when a variable can be transformed overnight from dependent to independent, or when the status of the world at a particular point in time has changed by the time an analysis is published, then it is no longer possible to rely on standard research tools. Some grounds for optimism can be seen in the advances in chaos theory without which any prognostication, starting with weather forecasts, seems to be impossible. If this theory is to be further developed, then the engagement of a whole task force of information scientists aided by powerful computers will be indispensable. The problem is that the scholars who study global processes are not the most noted information and communication technology specialists.

In trying to measure up to the challenges of inquiry, a number of other problems are encountered. One of the most troublesome is the inadequacy of the language of analysis. The need to label certain forces with conflicting, but constantly interacting vectors, leads to the coining of internally contradictory blended words, such as *glocalisation* (combining the opposites of global and local), or the more recently minted *fragtegration* (simultaneous integration and disintegration in the world) and *chaorder* (chaos and order combined). There are many others: *coopetition* (co-operation and competition,) *mass customisation* (customised products at mass production costs), *refolution* (reform and revolution), and prosumption (production and consumption). And there are terms such as timeless time and spaceless space, space of flows, polilog, telepresence, mass non-corformism, etc., whatever they may mean. These and similar terms are unacceptable to analysts engaged in a nostalgic quest for a positivistic clarity. People can hardly manage to diagnose the *magnetic storm* that society is experiencing.

These chaotic and complex systems must be provided with algorithms to protect them against the catastrophe caused by the proverbial *butterfly wings*; a butterfly flaps its wings in Beijing and sometime later it rains in New York. Such is the nature of a chaotic world.

Such an event occurred in September 2001. When comparing the energy and power of the United States with that of the terrorist network, it is easy to call this *the butterfly effect*. And yet, the latter succeeded in freeing an enormous energy of the group-network process. The attack on World Trade Centre changed the world. One of its direct consequences is the restriction of freedom in the name of the war against terror. This means imposing new algorithms on American and global society to make it more controllable and predictable, for example the Global Awareness System. People on the whole will accept this, as they prefer the security given by algorithms rather than freedom. No-one however can guarantee security in return for loss of freedom. Both may be lost.

The measurement of complexity demands an enormous processing power. At the busiest airports there are over 100,000 takeoffs and landings yearly, which demands computing power to manage these. Therefore there arises a necessity for increasing computer power, that is to say, to improve artificial computer-based intelligence, much of which may be embedded into everyday objects. Is this not a classical example of a positive feedback? The more the system is complex, the more computers are needed. But the more computers are used, the more complex a given system becomes. When algorithms are used in social processes, what is at stake is not so much feedback as feed-forward, that is to say, intelligent systems that are able to manage the chaos via self-replication of algorithms.

Hence society will not be more intelligent, but more intelligently managed by algorithms. Millions of dollars were invested in creating the supercomputer *Deep Blue*. This was not for the purpose of showing its superiority over the world chess champion, but to test it and benefit from the test, to build even more powerful computers equipped with better, more infallible algorithms managing people as the part of bio-techno system.

There is an attempt to make societies a complex self-regulating system as perfect as the human brain. The flaw in old social systems is that they appear to be insufficiently intelligent and reflexive. Wolf Singer, a philosopher and logician, and a member of the Pontifical Academy of Sciences, claimed that old social systems lacked meta-intelligence and thus underwent decomposition. The old algorithms did not resist stormy changes. The hierarchical system must collapse sooner or later when achieving a certain degree of complexity, and everyone does. Institutions of such a system do not learn because the most important actors and players of the system do not worry about the system's survival.

Intellectuals efforts will be directed at examining what system is optimum, and what proportions of hierarchy and networking are the most functional. The quest is to find principles for organising and stabilising the system, that is to say, the most intelligent algorithm that can be imagined, which is the human brain. It is possible to imagine an analogy between the structure of society and that of the brain. A lot can be learnt in terms of modelling the social structure on the brain's structure and its functioning: interactivity, self-optimisation of neural network links, de-fragmentation and the like.

Costs

Interestingly enough the idea of collective or connected intelligence on networks attracts more attention than the question of non-algorithmic freedom. Is the said collective intelligence a matter of freedom, or the common algorithm of humankind? Arun Netravali, of Bell Laboratories, claimed that the new generation of people would live their adult lives in a world where everything is connected by intelligent networks. Omnipresent sensors will transmit data directly to the networks like nerves transmitting information to the brain. The earth will then be a different planet, algorithmic, and society will be intelligent owing to the collective intelligence. Individual ants or bees are not intelligent, but societies of ants or bees demonstrate genetically programmed social intelligence. The mass society of the industrial age was not a smart mob, but information and communication technology makes its smarter.

Will the information society be smarter than the industrial society? The conventional wisdom about the information society is that it will enhance freedom and individualism. The reality seems different; the information society will establish its own electronic pecking order. It will be heading for a superstructure over the electronic assembly line and control over intellectual work. People will have to work according to an algorithm. If anyone has a whim to do something else, the system will detect it immediately. Computers demand algorithmic discipline in teamwork to manage and control *workflows*. If anyone does not understand this logic they behave like a deserter abandoning the assembly line. The difference between the assembly line of the industrial era and that of the information age is not qualitative. The former was based on workers using mechanical tools, and at the latter will be based on symbolic tools that demand more complex activities. In both cases the tools are at hand, in the first case hand tools in pockets, in the second, on a hard disk or on the internet. Is this *déjà vu*?

The algorithm is then, the way to control chaos, but the price is high: the margin of conscious decision-making and human responsibility is ever decreasing. Humans become post-decisive and post- reflexive. Objectively, what is taking place is subjugation of the intellect to the algorithm, however people may think of it as intellectualisation of the algorithm.

Try to do something in an office where the computers are out-of-order. In such circumstances attempts to do anything will fail: nothing can be done, as the computers (often called servers) will have stopped serving. Simply speaking, computer algorithms do not operate and people are not able to use their own *human* algorithm.

The future will complicate circumstances even more. Information and communication technologies will not be solely a tool; they will become a part of the techno-human system that operates only as a whole, and each sub-system separately will be useless. It will be groundless to say that a digital appliance is only a tool. A person becomes tool of the tool. Next will be the dethroning of humanity.

This will bring about serious consequences. Dreams of the self-sustainable development must be abandoned. The notion of *self-sustainability* will lose its meaning. Nothing will be self-renewable; everything must be renewable artificially since the environment of life will be increasingly artificial. In generations to come, people will have to adapt more to the artificial environment than to the natural one. This adaptation will need increasingly technological extensions built into humans, while what is intellectual in human beings will be transferred to the global network. This complex system will be doomed to constant transformation; without it the system will not survive. The implementation of sustainable development will require the *standstill of algorithms*, but there is no energy to do it.

Once again history will close the cycle. The dualism of technology-culture versus arts will recede into the past and there will be a return to *technic*, meaning technique (from the Greek *tekhnikos*), which for the ancient Greeks meant many things: crafts, skills, arts, technique. They did know the word *arts*; *art* is derived from a Latin word. In the digital age artists can be software producers and vice versa. *Art for art's sake* will be replaced by *technology for technology's sake.*

Hopes – How to Tread Different Paths

The imposition of algorithms for the sake of more effective governance and self-governance will not be free of conflicts and tensions. The future will be a constant struggle against the omnipotent algorithms; people will be defending themselves against them and will make their cultures to produce antibodies. Very helpful will be natural *software*: languages. These have evolved throughout human history. The bigger the variety and diversity of languages, then the better the chance people will have of self-defence. Unfortunately this diversity is ever diminishing despite efforts to preserve it. The domination of the English language, increasingly becoming algorithmic to meet the needs of computing, markedly weakens the chance of self-defence.

It may sound heretical, but hackers may have an important role to play in self-defence. Hackers are animated by an ideological mission, *gift giving*; to give the *netizens* (citizens of the internet) as many tools of self-protection and control over business and electronic governments, as these have to control *netizens*. Hackers and the *copy left* movement engaged in breaking software codes, protect culture and knowledge from being frozen in their existing shape. If, as humankind, people are who they are, it is mainly because cultural codes have never been frozen. An important role will be played by *open-source software*, which provides *freedom* to change and improve the computer code behind the computer applications that people use, for example, word processing tools. Owing to this, people of the digital age will know the art of computer programming. Without it, individual expression will be hard to achieve. Circumstances in the early part of the 21st century are reminiscent of the past when people, lacking literacy, were deprived the opportunity of written expression.

Much will depend on what culture the new generations will need. The future will depend on how many people there are like Linus Thordvalds, one of the founders of the open-source software movement, who can challenge the software establishment: the *gatekeepers* of the old way of producing software. There is a need for people who can produce algorithms for all to counterbalance the empires of companies such as Microsoft and the tycoons of the information business. Much will depend upon the extent that this counterbalancing can be achieved.

Attempts at socialising intellectual property can be expected. History will then be repeating itself. An increasing number of young people will believe that socialism on the internet is feasible. It did not succeed when applied in the real world and led to many tears, but they will think that it is worth trying it again, this time as a new version: dotcom(munism) with Leninux (Linux) software as the collective algorithm.

There is one problem with the hacking: it tries to create chaos in the system, seeing it as chance for more freedom. This, however, complicates life in the digital age and turns millions of net-users against hackers. They are doomed to operate within the system; both sides need each other.

Towards the Post-information Society

To conclude it is worth asking a slightly provocative question. Are developments heading towards the post-information society? The question may sound nonsensical as all human societies at the every stage of their evolution collected and processed information to create knowledge indispensable for survival. These societies are, not infrequently, called pre-information ones to contrast them with the late modern information societies for which information is the main resource, and technologies to process this, the most important tool. Logic requires that the question be asked, of why evolution may end at the information stage. Using the three-stage development model, from pre-modern through modern to post-modern, demands consequences.

The post-information age means a counteraction to digitisation. In the industrial society people started to regard handcraft very highly, because they were bored with assembly line produced goods. Something similar will happen in the information age: the analogue job will be held in high esteem. Possession of analogue goods will increase social status. Analogue will no longer be a synonym for social exclusion. History once again will close a cycle.

Conclusions – A Plea for Brighter Europe: A Non-algorithm Manifesto

A truth is that younger Europeans and new European immigrant generations will create the future of European cultures. In past decades and centuries the *corpus culturae* was formed by values, ideas, patterns, norms and imagery transmitted from generation to generation. New generations did not substantially change the inherited culture. A question arises whether this will be the case for the generation of younger Europeans. European cultures over the last couple of decades were shaped predominantly by institutions and the market, the two main regimes of social regulation. Societies, including young people, were provided with a cultural offer created by the professional producers and distributors, moguls and tycoons of the culture industries. Several phenomena indicate that this will change markedly.

For centuries people themselves created their own cultures, which grew out of individual and group experience, strife, belief, etc. In the industrial age there emerged an elite of professional culture producers and distributors who started to provide masses of people with entertainment and popular culture. In the digital age, once again, millions of people, notably the young, all over the world, are producing cultures by themselves and for themselves. A cycle has been closed. It remains to be seen what this new culture will be like. To know this, a deeper insight into this process is needed.

The culture of young Europeans is increasingly created in social networks and spread out within these. These networks are reinforced by information and communication technologies; this is the text message generation. Cultural activities of young Europeans flow out of institutions into networks in which the social and cultural capital of Europe is vented; networks of self-organising and self-regulating people, creating cultures.

These cultures show strong individuality and specific communication codes, which make enormously for cultural variety. Citizenship is defined increasingly by cultural features, affiliation to *choice groups* rather than to nation-states. New tribes, to use a term coined by Michel Maffesoli, are *producers* of new cultures.

Information and communication technologies allow people to return to spontaneous communication. Billions of text messages, and the more recent multimedia equivalents, emails, chats and blogs (online diaries) and many of thousands of discussion groups on the internet, lead to the belief that in the age of individualism, a certain form of *collective intelligence and culture* is emerging. New cultures are being created which demand a new anthropology to study them. The new culture is that of chat, dispersed over the networks, non-hierarchical, canon-free, overcoming time and distance; the culture of social action rather than that of institution.

Will this culture change Europe? There are of course worries such as *fortress Europe* or *Europe as a globalised colony.* A question worth answering is whether the new cultures promise *a network Europe.* This may be a Europe that offers much more for coming generations than was offered to past generations. And it may provide a chance that Europe will not be built only on hierarchies, institutions and markets, as was previously the case.

What culture is emerging in youth networks? What are the cultural activities of young people and what future for Europe will they create? How will young people feature in European integration, thus influencing future trends of cultural development? In what degree will there be continuity with the past, and in what measure will new cultures change Europe? There are no answers as yet.

Part III: The Future of Body and Mind

Chapter 9

myHealth

André Dittmar

Introduction

People are concerned about their health, and this concern is growing every year. Furthermore, society, health policy and patients' requirements are changing. The basic needs of human beings are intrinsically *negative*: that is to say, people have sought to avoid cold, heat, hunger, and thirst. Improvements in the standard of living have changed these needs, which are becoming increasingly *positive*: citizens' needs are now about comfort, pleasure, health and quality of life. In western society in particular, there is a fundamental shift taking place from a concentration on basic human needs, to a more positive involvement of citizens in their own quality of life and health.

Scientific progress in chemistry, physics, and genetics enables the development of these positive needs. Wearable health devices are becoming more sophisticated, and the care they provide is increasingly individualised. But do the risks counterbalance the benefits? Is developing a healthy lifestyle just a personal option, or can it also become a social obligation? Are biomedical sensors for citizens' health, such as an analyser to help control diet and food intake, friends or spies?

It may be difficult to answer all these questions; however, in the future, healthcare monitoring is likely to move towards the use of sophisticated wearable devices, that are appropriately designed, simple and easy to use – but which also minimise risks. A range of possible future developments is described in this chapter.

Overview of Sciences and Technologies that may Affect Future Health Delivery

There has been immense progress in the scientific and technological developments that support modern health provision and care, particularly in genetics, chemistry, physics, and information and telecommunications. The majority of therapeutic medicines still use chemistry and physics, but new knowledge and particularity genetics are changing this landscape.

Chemistry has brought the largest number of solutions: human beings have used plants and animals molecules for thousands of years for medicine, but modern medicine is based on the creation of artificial molecules. Physics brought the possibility of optics, mechanics, electronics and recently the access to small size, thanks to micro and nanotechnologies, the latter being the manipulation of individual atoms and molecules.

Genetics is potentially a form of *magic* that has numerous and theoretically unlimited possibilities; for example, repairing, optimising, and increasing natural defences using genetically engineered vaccines. The relative importance in biomedical engineering of genetics will increase progressively and will replace many chemical or physical investigation methods and devices.

In the growing domain of *wearable health devices*, more individualised, specialised forms of healthcare are coming to the fore. The influence of a bio-inspired approach to biomedical engineering is paramount to this development. However, a paradox arises from the sophistication of the devices that can be developed: the greater the needs for security, the more precautions are required.

Innovation in biomedical engineering is a *game* played by two groups: on the one hand there are *inventors and researchers* and on the other hand *users*. The directly concerned users are patients and physicians. Everybody agrees with the main rule; innovation and new devices must not lead to risk for patients. Therefore, innovation has to be tested and validated. Testing molecules is an old problem that is solved by lengthy procedures and a large army of protocols, good practices and ethical rules. Many thousands and thousands of molecules are tested every year, but they have many common points. This is a biochemical dialogue between living tissues and the molecules.

For biomedical devices the problem is different: the large variety of fundamental principles and theories, for example, optics, mechanics, thermodynamics and electricity induce long and difficult tests. Long development time is also inherent to the difficult communication between the engineer and the physician. Doctors typically have biochemical knowledge that supports exchanges with pharmaceutical laboratories, whereas multidisciplinary knowledge is essential to understanding biomedical device operation.

A device must not be used on human beings if it has not been tested in real conditions. Mathematical models, physical models, experimentation on animals are only a part of the response to this difficulty. The higher the need of security of the patient, the more precaution and prevention are reinforced.

The choice of methodology and technology is crucial for a biomedical project and particularly when the duration of the project is longer than the technological evolution. The main question is what is the time between the expression of the need, to the availability of the corresponding product on the market. For example, the first insulin pump (without sensor) that could be implanted in the body appeared during the 1980s for the treatment of diabetes. At that time several scientists and futurologists said that it was too late for insulin pumps: the progress of genetics would lead to artificial pancreas in a few years. After 20 years there was still no automatic micro insulin pump with sensors able to effectively measure the rate of glucose over several days, and also, no genetic pancreas available! The lesson to be learnt from this example is that the speed of progress of biomedical technologies is not constant and is difficult to foretell.

Advances in physics will lead to new components and particularly to micro technologies for designing and making smart miniaturised pumps, actuators, stimulators, multi-sensors, and high-power autonomy wearable devices and those that can be implanted. Under certain conditions it is possible to stimulate the secretion of local specific organs or tissues, for example, those of the nervous system. These devices can operate automatically in association with sensors, under the remote control of the patient or the physician. They may be particularly useful for chronic diseases, persons with disabilities and elderly people. The spectrum of application is very wide, for example, therapy, vigilance, sleep status, behaviour monitoring, and early diagnosis.

The rapidly growing bio-inspired approach consists of studying the concepts, mechanisms, materials, information and signal processing of living beings. The aim is to develop a more creative and imaginative design for biomedical engineering.

This new approach is not about copying nature, but takes advantage of the more recent progress in materials, signal processing and the potential offered by micro and nanotechnologies to build devices on the same scale as nature. This gives access to the possibilities and concepts attached to small size phenomena.

Biological sensors are available in very large quantity; they are self-repairable, self-adaptive, intelligent and multipurpose structures, have energy economy, small volume energy storage, and are recyclable, and so on. All these concepts and devices are working and have been tested for million of years. Bio-inspired designing is particularly convenient for biomedical engineering using a natural and biocompatible approach. It is not a religion, but a new way of thinking out of the overly classical *old highways of thinking*.

The bio-inspired approach is a second-degree methodology giving added value to the existing methodology. Usable in almost all the spectrum of knowledge, and particularly with micro and nanotechnologies, the bio-inspired approach is compatible with chemistry, genetics, and micro and nanotechnologies.

Wearable Devices, Smart Clothes, Home Care – The Benefits of Technological Progress

With the growth of wearable devices, for example, wrist and web-enabled mobile telephones, people may start finding simple and practical solutions to their healthcare needs. Wireless wearable devices and the internet are affecting a large spectrum of patient issues from managing chronic conditions to caring for loved ones and achieving health and wellbeing goals.

For example, a 63-year-old man takes several medications a day to control his heart condition. But he is often so absorbed in his work, that he forgets to take his pills or does not take them at the scheduled time, jeopardising his health. With his mobile telephone and his wearable dispenser he can receive reminders and appropriate medication doses through the day.

Another example is a 40-year-old woman who was diagnosed as having diabetes and has to measure blood sugar level and communicate it to the physician. Thanks to wearable technology and biomedical sensors, glucose levels can be measured continuously and reliably. Automatic solutions for personalised glucose monitoring and insulin infusion with adjustment of insulin dosage are not far from reality.

In the future, the people are likely to benefit, on the spot, from a whole range of health related information, for example, genetic, clinical, early warnings and prognosis, but also decision support, with or without involvement of the physician. A whole range of health related computer resources, such as databases, special computer programs, health records, medical devices, will be networked together to provide healthcare services.

By the year 2020, patients and citizens are likely to experience a completely different healthcare and wellbeing environment; starting from the organisation of health and healthcare services, through regulation and electronic facilities, to culture and security. New structures, operating separately from the classical hospital-based care will grow, allowing electronic health services, delivered over the internet, at home and anywhere as well as *doctor on-demand* services and access to personal health records. Chronically ill patients will be their own health providers (self-care) with the support of family and friends.

Citizens will be more *health educated* and *health active* and will build a partnership with doctors with respect to decisions. Total quality control will be applied to health providers, and patients will allocate marks to their general practitioner and healthcare institutions. Finally, electronic health expenses will be sufficiently covered through individualised insurance programmes and services including prevention and monitoring.

New possibilities for home care and ambulatory monitoring will be provided trough smart clothes. Modern telemonitoring devices are not available on the market. Smart clothes that provide a complete solution of telemonitoring do not exist.

Smart clothes are wearable devices, with a special interest. Clothes are in contact with about $1.5m^2$ of skin. So they are particularly appropriate for the fixing of sensors, micro-devices, wires, electrodes, etc. Smart clothes are particularly user friendly and adapted for a daily use by the patient.

Mainly, there are two kinds of smart clothes. First there are smart clothes with sensors close to the skin, which are used for biomedical purpose. The sensors are enclosed in the layers of fabric, or at the surface, or in the fabric itself, which is used as a sensor. Piezo-resistive yarns, optic fibres, coloured multi-layers (textiles with multiple layers that change their colour according to the applied mechanical stress), etc. can be used as sensors. These biomedical smart clothes have several advantages. They avoid the necessity of the nurse or doctor attaching the sensors, and the sensors are located at the right place. Furthermore, the sensors are protected, they are not visible, and they are user-friendly and particularly adapted for monitoring in case of chronic diseases and monitoring of disabled and elderly people. Biomedical clothes are also suitable for use during professional, sport and military activities.

Second there are smart clothes with sensor devices in pockets, and on the outer surface of the fabric. A lot of new functions can be added to clothes using to micro-technologies, micro-radios, microcomputers, flexible television screens, micro-cellular telephones, but also solar cells, energy recovery systems (in shoes generally), and flexible keyboards. These devices are used mainly for communication, displaying colours, pictures, indications of mood, messages, etc. But some devices or sensors used for monitoring can be placed in the clothes in special pockets (satellite-based location devices, fall detectors, data loggers, accelerometer, activity detectors, etc.)

Both ways of using smart clothes are compatible and complementary. However, are intelligent biomedical clothes the enabling human interface?

Heart diseases remain the main cause of death and are expected to maintain the same rates in the future. A sustainable solution to fight systematically the origin of this disease is to empower citizens in a lifelong process to limit their individual risk profile, to enable early detection of complications, and to prevent acute events that can cause serious heart damage.

The starting point of the scenario is to gain knowledge of a citizen's health status. This can be done through continuous monitoring of vital signs. The approach of wearing intelligent clothes is therefore to integrate system solutions into functional clothes with integrated textile sensors.

Intelligent biomedical clothes will act preliminarily as a source of patients' data on their behavioural profile as it affects the heart disease risk profile like activity, stress, sleep and nutrition. Intelligent context-aware personalised algorithms will not only determine the circumstances, but also provide adequate feedback for the users on how to change their behaviour across all possible disease states. Intelligent biomedical clothes act as a human interface for the ever-increasing knowledge about health, and translate this knowledge into personalised feedback for the user in any circumstances, and with any disease status.

For healthy subjects, interactive gaming and other self-motivated programs will help the user to enjoy a healthier lifestyle. The system will not only help the user to adapt to a healthier, lifestyle, but will also effectively improve personal performance owing to better fitness and more effective ways of coping with stress.

For citizens at risk the system will provide adequate information on how to deal with individual risk factors. It will give advice on ways to reduce risks like hypertension, overweight, diabetes, physical inactivity and stress, through personalised training plans and motivation to change behaviour. Early detection through long-term trend analysis will drastically reduce the damage from severe events. For example, it will reduce the time to respond to myocardial infraction (destruction of a portion of heart tissue owing to interruption of its blood-supply) or a stroke.

For post event patients these kinds of system can significantly improve the rehabilitation processes and detect any complications at an early state. Daily monitoring will enable new forms of personalised drug treatment and the self-administration of medication according to the specific behaviour and circumstances of each individual.

For chronically ill patients, intelligent biomedical clothes empower the user to better understand and self-manage the disease state. Early detection will limit acute events and complications that may lead to hospitalisation and extended hospital treatment. The rehabilitation process will become a lifelong process in which patients and families are also actively involved.

The use of intelligent biomedical clothes will not only improve circumstances for the user, but will also enable medical professionals to react in a timely and appropriate way to the patient's illnesses, by significantly improved timely diagnosis and new ways of therapy and personalised treatment. It will help to improve the effectiveness of the healthcare system by cost-efficient access to the best care and it will empower each individual to have a longer and healthier life, with increased personal performance. Intelligent biomedical clothes can act as a key enabler for a lifelong continuous health improvement process for all individuals.

A Healthy Lifestyle – A Personal Option or a Social Obligation

Every day, experimental measurements and the statistics show that new arguments confirm the influence of food and of lifestyle on human health. The risk factors for cancer or heart diseases, but also for mental disturbances, are related to these parameters. For a long time, lifestyle was part of private life and considered a personal option. The origins of diseases were unknown and no efficient treatment existed.

The therapeutic and surgical treatments of significant diseases are increasingly efficient, but also more expensive. Disease prevention through healthy lifestyle and compliance with risk management rules will be placed under the responsibility of each individual. The impact of such practices will have a great societal and economic impact. Healthy lifestyle will in the future be a social obligation. A possible scenario may be the creation of a medical chart for the rights and the duties of citizens concerning food, alcohol, tobacco and drugs, supported by laws and penalties.

An example of such key enablers lies in the control of meals and diet. For the control of the rate of sodium chloride in soups and meals, patients and people on diets, can rely on the *salt pencil*, a small and autonomous pen. It is the first member of a family of domestic food quality detectors. It is based on the odour detectors used in Japan to control the freshness of fish. The probable evolution of this device will be a *multi-sensor pen* capable of detecting the consumption rate of sugar, fat, glucose and other ingredients.

It is possible also to add a code detector to this pen so that it reads the content of the menu or a plate from a wireless tag on a sticker on each plate in the restaurant or on the menu. By plugging the pen into a computer, a *bad conscience* of the patient is obtained in the form of remarks such as, "don't eat this, or don't drink that".

The prevention principle applied to food is not new: in *Don Quixote*, Sancho Pança was promoted governor of the island of *Baratiara*. The official physician of this island (Pedro Rezio de Aguero) controlled the quality of each meal. Sancho Pança found that each of these meals was particularly dangerous and was forbidden. Finally, Sancho Pança had nothing to eat and he dismissed the physician. A future scenario may be that each patient is obliged to use a food pencil to be dietetically correct. A subsidiary question arises however: is the stress and the anxiety that arises from this correct dietary strategy more dangerous than the food itself? Will future biomedical sensors for health monitoring be friends or spies?

Conclusions

The progress of sciences and technologies, for example, genetics, information, materials, and telecommunications will give citizens and physicians new tools and methodologies for early diagnosis, treatment and personal health management and wellbeing. The new devices will be increasingly sophisticated, and be able to do numerous and complicated functions.

The design of these new tools will have to focus on simplicity of use, ergonomics, and automatic control of the quality of functioning. Without the aspect of good design and ergonomics, only engineers would be able to use these new biomedical devices.

The areas of home care, ambulatory monitoring, drug delivery, surgery, and rehabilitation engineering, will all probably make use of the capabilities offered by micro-technologies. For example, wrist devices or smart clothes could significantly help in the areas of chronobiology (the study of rhythms related to biological, physical, chemical, hormonal, thermal, activities of the body) and chronotherapy (detection of best individual response through daily life monitoring and optimisation of therapy with *right time, right dose* drug delivery). These developments will have the possibility of interacting with developments in many medical fields.

A major challenge of the new forms of medical delivery described will also lie in the management of the numerous actors involved (suppliers, physicians, patients…). To date, the supply of medicines has had a unique interlocutor: the pharmacy. In the future, a large range of actors will be providing these new forms of medicine, and each one will have the conviction that their roles are essential. It will be necessary to co-ordinate all these actors, and also to change the patterns of behaviour of the administrations and also of physicians. In addition, a new evaluation of health costs and ethics will also be necessary.

One also has to be aware that despite the very fast progress of informatics and new materials for designing new wearable biomedical devices, the number of *usable* sensors is actually small. The time-to-market of developing new sensors is also long; usually up to seven years. The limited number of sensors and the long time to design and validate them is an indication that these developments will not happen overnight but will involve long term and committed research and development effort.

As a final point, training on new health devices will have to be provided to physicians and to patients. This has to be given in schools, colleges, universities, and also on television, and should become an obligation for physicians throughout their careers.

If some of the above points are taken into account, citizens could benefit significantly from new generations of health monitoring tools. By the year 2020, citizens are likely to experience completely different healthcare and wellbeing environments.

Acknowledgments

The author wishes to thank Joseph Lauter, Phillips, for discussions and suggestions on this text.

Chapter 10

Before the Cyborgs Come

Marc Bogdanowicz

Introduction

Body-friendly information and communication technologies is a provocative expression and deliberately so. It echoes the often wished for user-friendliness of technologies, but also raises concerns about intrusiveness. *Intrusive* information and communication technologies, an alternative and more negative term, can be used instead of electronic implants. However the ambiguity of the term body-friendly information and communication technologies seems to offer much more scope for discussion than the alternative term.

This chapter aims to examine the relationship of Western societies with the individual body, and how this evolving relationships may affect and be affected by the development of miniaturised and *body-friendly* information and communication technologies. While the scope of the chapter is wide ranging however, there are many issues that are not addressed. These include such related issues as death and burials, beauty and pain, spirituality and faith, etc. The main area addressed is that of information and communication technologies related body repair and body enhancement.

A Brief Scenario

The location is Paris, and the date is 7 November 2025. Vedonan likes the long walk through the city up to his working urban area. Even though caught in a shower of light rain, Vedonan is quite oblivious to the external world, lost in his own thoughts. The tune mildly delivered by his ambifon™, a micro-device embedded in his ear, is rather relaxing, and Vedonan cannot but feel happy. Today is going to be a good day.

The day had started with the successful reload of his Tactoo™, an intelligent skin, that Vedonan had had implanted with his first revenues from his MC4 franchise. The design of the Tactoo™, a full-sized dragon covering most of his back, had become a cost with time, because it had to be reloaded quarterly, but this cost is well balanced, in Vedonan's opinion, by the sun tanned look and the healthy skin appearance obtained without having to bother with time consuming and costly skincare sessions.

Vedonan has had his usual healthy breakfast, but he is also using the time spent walking to improve his physical resistance and general aspect. Body embedded micro-containers, activated by a signal emitted manually from his wristwatch, inject, on-demand, adequate levels of ProKf™ and Botan™, as recommended by his doctor. Additionally, monitoring information is instantaneously captured and processed and any malfunctioning is immediately fed back to Vedonan and the closest Health Support Unit. Healthier than coffee or other drugs, the products improve enormously Vedonan's heart and respiratory rhythm, optimising the effects of the walk, and helping him to look younger.

While entering his working urban area, Vedonan makes a rapid call to Ala, his girlfriend. A year ago, he had been embarrassed wearing those horrible Glassphones™ to connect with her. Now, using his enhanced memory and his jewellery-inserted mobile the connection is perfect and Vedonan feels truly touched when Ala looks at him, straight in his weblens.

He had been thinking for a while about investing in a SeMe™, an organic based camera implanted on the skin, but he still feels a little uneasy about such a device. He did not dare share the idea with his girlfriend yet, even if such a photograph album may demonstrate his own emotional commitment to her. Best to hire a SeMe™ in the short-term to check first the benefits.

Two Assumptions

To examine the potential of body-friendly information and communication technologies, it is necessary to make some assumptions about the increasing role of individualism as a legitimate value in society, and how this may affect peoples' representation and experience of their own bodies.

Assumption 1: Towards the Wellbeing of the Body – About Repairing Bodies

Western populations live in increasingly individualistic societies; the individual is central in assessments of what is good or bad. Self-perception, and the perception by others, as being a successful and happy individual is regarded as a legitimate and essential life goal. This trend may be seen as a consequence of growing wealth. Western societies offer such a range of opportunities that the majority of the population is confronted with an overwhelming number of individual opportunities rather than the hard collective choices resulting from the scarcity of shared resources. The success of the individual has become a reality that supersedes, or becomes an apparent precondition to, the survival of the group. Of course, a more global and ethical view may suggest that this is a result of social blindness considering the life conditions of the vast majority of humankind.

In such an individualistic environment, the story of a person's own construction, the *self-made man* fantasy, is strongly on the agenda. Furthermore, the role that the body plays, as representative of the *self*, in these circumstances is that of an interface. It is the locus of social relations; people showing themselves to others. It is also an expression for individual differentiation from others; people being unique among others. The body is both the *self*, and the performance tool for individuals to tell their own story and achievements. In the Western world, the human body in such a perspective is increasingly perceived as *fundamentally unachieved*; something to be adapted, improved, supported, and, ultimately, constructed and reconstructed.

Constructing and reconstructing the body, in Western societies, already has a history. It has for generations been part of a range of banality with such activities as healthcare, surgery and more recently cosmetic surgery, dental intervention, prostheses, chemicals, external aids such as eyeglasses and contact lenses, and embedded supporting devices such as heart pacemakers, etc. Interestingly, all these examples refer to body repair or compensating activities, and as such show a high level of acceptance and development of body engineering in society. Most cases have found early support from the scientific medical community, thus gaining legitimacy.

Such body reconstruction, aimed at repairing, echoes peoples' claim for a *good life*. This can mean feeling happy through cosmetic surgery and the resulting improved self-esteem, or feeling efficient through eyeglasses and the resulting increased labour productivity. But it can also mean achieving the good life through the maintenance of ageing bodies. Caring for the body is a dominant value. It has become a norm, inculcated since early childhood; regular brushing of the teeth can be seen as a simple example of such early teaching about the importance of body care.

Some developments in body care demonstrate that there is never an agreed status quo about the application area of such values. The progressive exploration of innovative reconstruction and repair activities questions the limits that society, in a heterogeneous rather than consensual way. In cosmetic surgery, what is a *good reason* for removing fat from the body using liposuction? In the area of organ donation and transplants, who owns the body parts? With the targeted use of medicines such as Viagra, what is a legitimate aim? When electronic devices are implanted into elderly people to compensate for the loss of memory and to make geographical positioning easier, what are the ethics of control? Is cloning for healthcare reasons a legitimate use of genomics?

Where do claims for a *good life* stop, if anywhere? How much do people reflect upon the paradox between claims for a long life expectancy and the concept of to-be-repaired bodies? Life expectancy has rightfully become a building block of the United Nations Development Programme Human Development Index exercise, as it was itself inspired and guided by the principles developed by Amartya Sen about the definition of quality of life. Life expectancy is not yet regarded as something that people are entitled to, but it has become a claim, or at least a benchmarking measure among countries and regions. Is entitlement to the maintenance of an ageing body one of the next frontiers? The development of body-friendly information and communication technologies is widening the scope of technology-based wellbeing of the body, by offering new opportunities and therefore new challenges.

Assumption 2: Towards Better-than Wellbeing of the Body – About Enhancing Bodies

A second assumption is that *body-enhancing* technologies, rather than simply repairing ones, will progress further over the period up to 2025. These technologies will be aimed at improving peoples' bodies beyond their natural capacities, and at pursuing the transformation of the cosmetic image. The project of enhancing is about taking people and making improvements upon what nature has provided. This is what the psychiatrist Peter Kramer famously referred to as *better than well*.

A spectacular example of capacity enhancement technologies, is night vision implantation through surgical intervention. In a similar vein, sportsmen may be operated on to improve their eyesight for a specialised use. Such technologies do exist. Less spectacular, but much more

118

publicised and controversial, are the various chemical diets based on drugs, hormones, etc., developed for amateur and professional sports people. Even more generally, the use of legal and illegal drugs influencing brain functioning has spread across a series of contexts from higher education students, such as Ritalin to enhance intellectual capacities, to night clubs addicts who use power-drinks and pills to enhance resistance and emotionality.

The vogue for tattooing is another good illustration of the growing success of body aesthetics in Western societies; better being through beauty. Tattooing was once considered a practice associated with primitivism of non-western populations or with prostitutes, delinquents, and prisoners. It developed through informal networks that were mainly limited to marginal strands of the population with little public visibility. At the end of the 1970s the punk and skinhead movements, to make a statement, appropriated this practice. But tattooing has progressively become a more mainstream activity and is considered to be part of body aesthetics.

Tattooing as legitimate behaviour may well have started gaining its first signs of legitimacy in Western societies in the late 1980s. In modern societies, tattooing is almost taken for granted and is interpreted by anthropologists observing Western societies as one phenomenon among many, such as bodybuilding, body-piercing, cosmetic surgery, etc. Categorised sometimes as body art, those more or less permanent and strong interventions on the individual's body illustrate the growing trend of transforming interventions.

These are metamorphosis processes interpreted as a way of defining individuality and, when made publicly visible, projecting an image, often provisional and contextual, towards others. The body becomes a possible locus of *oeuvre* about the self and relations to others.

There is a direct relationship between the expanding so-called mosaic society, a multi-layered pluralist society, and the growing necessity for people to reconstruct for themselves an individual world of values, certainties, and belongings. And while tattooing and piercing are practices that can still be challenged as being extreme examples, there has been an impressive growth of cosmetic interventions. There are many examples of this, such as the success of chemical-based body enhancement using Botox, growth hormones, and anabolic steroids. The role of diets and the multiplication of fitness and bodybuilding centres is another indication of the growing legitimacy and importance of such cosmetic activities, and the focus on the body as the intimate *and* interaction incarnation of people identities. Furthermore, interpreting these activities as *modern primitivism*, a tribal ritual behaviour, is a misunderstanding of their contemporary aims and social context.

119

These activities, recuperated and adapted, are benefiting from the interest of upstream trend-makers. But in the future it will be the marketers of mobile phones, soft drinks, fast food, etc. targeting the well-off youth in Western and other fast developing countries, rather than trend setters that will be interested in these activities.

Cosmetic interventions are an aesthetic of luxury, but made reproducible, join the circuits of mode and mass consumption, focused on self-esteem and seduction. Beyond the obvious examples of surgery, diets and fitness centres, some early signs of more innovative trends of creative body art can already be seen. They further question the use of the skin and the body as an expression and communication device.

All such activities, often, but not necessarily targeting the youth, open progressively the door to body interventions which are not aimed at repairing, but rather at expressing and enhancing. The body has taken a strong role for defining an individual *better-than-wellbeing*, not only in terms of health of an ageing population, but also in terms of individual and collective identity, performance, communication, entertainment and even immediate fun. Seen as rather unethical and often rejected by adults, in particular as parents, such focus on the body, and its accompanying body interventions for *non-repair purposes* will be on the next generation's agenda.

While technological progress, including information and communication technologies, will allow for delivering a growing range of body intervention, of *body-friendly technologies*, these will develop *de facto* in society, By 2025 they will be assessed as legitimate for both repair and enhancement.

Technological Trends – Before the Cyborgs Come

There is technological evidence to claim that the supply of body-friendly technologies will develop in the next few years, benefiting from progress in a number of areas. The manipulation of individual atoms and molecules, known as nanotechnology; the embedding in artefacts, of software that provides intelligent-like behaviour; and genomics, the study of the human genome, the complete collection of genetic material, to establish its sequence and function, are all relevant examples.

Miniaturisation, and work at the ultimate frontier, nanotechnologies, is part of the basic research agenda, and increasingly that of applied research. But this feature is not an essentially relevant one for body-friendly technologies. Larger devices can be worn, or be integrated into the body. These are not micro components, but *macro* ones: and there are long-standing existing experiences of these, so much so that the devices and practices are sometimes taken-for-granted. Examples are heart pacemakers and other metabolism-supporting devices, prostheses, measurement instruments, etc. These have shown that individuals can adapt very deeply to the embedding of non-human, non-organic components and tools in their everyday life.

Extreme experiences, such as those enabled by electronic implants, or wearable personal computers, have helped provide an important stock of knowledge about the obstacles to comfort, use, and finally complete integration of macro and microelectronic components. Body compatibility of such components, in particular miniaturised components, and longer-term embedding of large-scale devices, such as artificial skin for example, may well offer new challenges for research at the boundaries of the organic and the non-organic, the so-called wet frontier.

While it is not known if fully organic *intelligent components* will become, some day, a reality, both compatible non-organic components and genome-based organic ones are emerging. Imagine a three-dimensional genomic printer, at hand in every household, as a possible example of ultimate visionary statements in the area of body parts repair and enhancement.

Microelectronics has been driven by what is called Moore's Law, which predicts a doubling of computing power every 18 months. Implied in this is increased miniaturisation: putting more transistors on to integrated electronic circuits. As a result, computing capabilities, for example, processors with integrated sensors, have become cheaper, smaller and faster and they can be embedded, potentially, in every object or device. There is already invisible computing available in products such as cars, household appliances, entertainment equipment, mobile telephones and many others. This embedding will increase exponentially, and visible computing, for example activities done on personal computers, will move to the background.

Following this reasoning, embedding information and communication technology devices in bodies is, technologically, a further step on the same trajectory and encompasses the same assets and obstacles.

Whatever the size of devices, be it nano or macro, or the compatibility, be it organic and non-organic, or the functionality of the devices, body repair or enhancement, two categories of devices define two different visions of body-friendly information and communication technologies. There are external devices, such as eyeglasses incorporating an equivalent to a personal computer screen, and there are internal devices, such as pacemakers. Embedding implies internal devices.

The application of external and internal devices leads to the use of the term Cyborg. This encompasses both types of devices, but implies much more. Rather than referring to simple embedding, the term embodiment is used where the boundary between body and machine is further reducing. And it can reduce up to a point where there is a confusing overlap of the natural and the artificial, the *Cyborg Dilemma*: the more natural the interface, the more people become unnatural. In Haraway's founding paper [1] on Cyborgism, it is stated, "A Cyborg is a cybernetic organism, a hybrid of machine and organism, a creature of social reality as well as a creature of fiction." In her remarkable Cyborg Manifesto, the author, an important Californian scholar in feminist studies, makes a claim in favour of the Cyborg's built-in androgyny. *Cyborgism* as defined above, as well as the feminist claims developed by Haraway, is however beyond the scope of this chapter.

Conclusions – From Body Repair to Capability Enhancement

A significant dichotomy that articulates peoples' reactions to body-friendly information and communication technologies is centred on the images created by repair versus enhancement. Repairing technologies, for example, to use eyeglasses, pertain apparently to the general field of healthcare, while enhancing technologies, for example, to obtain night vision capability, is seen as an exaggerated move, driven by rather ambiguous motivations about self and others.

This provocative dichotomy is the first to be evidenced, but surprisingly, people may discover that they are used to and tolerant of a second type of enhancing technologies: those that are part of a beauty care package aimed at improving how people sense others. It can be argued that surrounded by such *beauty care* technologies, people have become unable to notice them. In earlier centuries, beauty care was mainly household craftsmanship leading, during the Victorian period, to [2] "proposals of law allowing husbands to annul marriage with wives who trapped them with scents, paints, artificial teeth, false hair." The 20th century has witnessed the rise of a beauty industry worth an annual 160 billion United States dollars turnover and glamorously growing at 7% annual growth, with some companies showing 14% annual profits growth over several decades. This industry includes such large multinational companies as L'Oréal, Nivea, Elizabeth Arden, and Helena Rubinstein, launched at the beginning of the 20th century, and some latecomers such as Revlon or Estée Lauder. The beauty care industry has the enhancement of the body at the core of its mission. In Western societies, the repair (equated with good) versus enhancement (equated with bad) dichotomy does not stand as firmly as may be thought.

A second explanation to people's resistance is that it is the enhancing of an individual's capacities, and *not* of its *appearance*, which makes people a little nervous about those technologies. Imagine an individual, a competing one, able to see 20 kilometres into the distance, to hear conversations through doors, to have expanded memory capacity or sexual pleasure, to taste the flavour of air, or to feel the touch of microscopic layers. To be stronger, or to be smarter, or ...

Does the difference start to be unacceptable when it comes to changing the individual's innate capabilities rather than external appearance? Where are the limits on each of these territories to be placed? Is it so that this needs to be seen only as a reward to an individual's effort, in education, sport, etc. in a reversed view about nature and nurture relationship? Or are people triggered by the issue of the definition of humankind: the *Cyborg's dilemma*, its *androgyny*, often alluded to in science fiction, a Frankenstein syndrome, that does not take in account all the earlier steps that have already taken *de facto* in enhancement technologies? How far into making a body out of parts can people go, and still be human? How far can capabilities be extended, or organs added, for people still to feel a belonging to humankind? Is it, ironically, the human-made machines that make people feel closer to the animal than to humankind? How different can others become, and still be accepted in the community?

A third hypothetical explanation is that capability enhancement will generate such differences that enhanced people may not be socially acceptable? How will judgement about differences be made, while maintaining claims about equal opportunities? Once stated in such terms, the issue of body enhancement touches upon the understanding of equity. On what basis will that difference be perceived as socially legitimate? As soon as speaking of equity, there arises the issue of entitlement and access. It is hardly surprising if considering, for example, the results of a series of studies about the effects of beauty, which showed that, beauty matters and confers important social advantages. It contributes towards being perceived as more intelligent, having better earnings, being more likely to get married, etc. Being beautiful is being well. Becoming more beautiful is being *better than well*.

Beauty is not only a societal trend, possibly powered by heavy celebrity endorsements, but has also become a significant market, on which Americans spend more than on education [2]. In such costly circumstances, entitlement to body care may become a valued, and thus valid argument.

The entitlement to *better being* may well become even less disputable, if additionally it includes *capability enhancement*. As argued by some [3], about brain enhancement technologies, "many people believe the enhancements would be unethical because some of us would be able to get an improved brain and some would not, which would be unfair. It is certainly possible – in fact, probable – that if nothing were done to ensure access to brain-enhancing technologies, inequities would arise. The solution though is to provide fair access, be it to teachers, or implantable chips, not to do away with the idea of improvement."

Finally, it may well be that body enhancement, by the improvement of capabilities, or by mere aesthetics, also transforms peoples' perception of themselves, their sense of self, their relation to others, and their socially built identity. Ultimately, the senses can be seen as interfaces to the world, and the body, in particular its sensitive envelope of skin, as the interface people offer to the world. In that relation to the world, enhanced senses and capabilities create a *quasi-secondary skin*, a digital envelope with modified senses for the individual and sensations for the others. The senses may become more intrusive for others, even though apparently more distant because they are partly mediated by technologies. Technologies blur the limits of socialising tools and territories, and affect strongly the apprehension of social distances in face-to-face contexts, and possibly beyond [4]. The potential of enhancing peoples' *sensors*, as well as enhancing their *envelope* confronts everyone with the issue of understanding of themselves, of self-consciousness, but also of understanding of individual's relation to the others, and the world.

Before the Cyborgs come, people had better master the humanity of their bodies.

Acknowledgements

The author wishes to thank for their creative support, S. Lo Sardo, L. Beslay, C. Centeno and Y.Punie.

References

[1] Haraway, D., 1985. *A Cyborg manifesto: Science, Technology and Socialist-Feminism in the late Twentieth Century*. In: Simians, Cyborgs and Women: the Reinvention of Nature. Routledge. New-York.
[2] The Economist, 2003. *The Beauty Business*, May 24th-30th, 2003, pp.69-71
[3] Scientific American, 2003. *Better brains. How Neuroscience will enhance you*, Special Issue. Scientific American, n°289. September 2003
[4] Altman Irwin, 1975. *Environment and Social behaviour*, Brooks/Cole Publishing Company. Monterey, California.

Chapter 11

Tapping the Mind or Resonating Minds?

José del R. Millán

Introduction

Brains interfaced to machines, where thought is used to control and manipulate these machines. This is the vision examined in this chapter. First-generation brain-machine interfaces have already been developed, and technological developments must surely lead to increased capabilities in this field.

The most obvious applications for these technologies are those that will assist disabled people. The technology can help restore mobility and communication capabilities, thus helping disabled people to increase their independence and facilitate their participation in society. But how should this technology be employed: just to manipulate the world or also to leverage self-knowledge? And what will the technology mean for the rest of the population? These are some of the questions that are addressed in this chapter.

Interfacing Brain and Machines

The idea of controlling machines not by manual control, but by mere *thinking* has fascinated humankind, and researchers working at the crossroads of neurosciences, computer science, and biomedical engineering have started to develop the first prototypes of *brain-machine interfaces* from about the mid-1990s (see Figure 11.1).

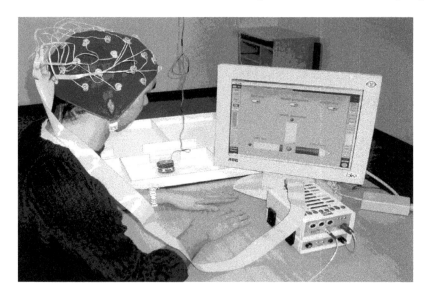

Figure 11.1: Brain-machine interface based on the analysis of electroencephalogram (EEG) signals, i.e, the brain electrical activity recorded from electrodes placed on the scalp (the spots on the cap worn by the person). The user is mentally driving a mobile robot between rooms in a house-like environment, making it turn right, turn left, or move forward. *Source*: José del R. Millán, Copyright 2004. Reproduced with permission.

The promise of this technology is to augment human capabilities by enabling people to interact with a computer through a conscious and spontaneous modulation of their brainwaves after a short training period. Indeed, analysing brain electrical activity online, several groups have designed brain-actuated systems that provide alternative channels for communication and control. Thus, a person can select letters from a virtual keyboard on a computer screen and write messages. Researchers have also been able to train monkeys to move a computer cursor to desired targets and also to control a robot arm. Work with humans has shown that it is possible for them to move a cursor to the corners of a screen and even to drive a mobile robot between rooms in a house model. To do so, all that it necessary is for the person to simply imagine body movements, or other mental tasks such as relaxation, rotation of geometric figures, and generation of words beginning with the same letter, without needing to perform any physical action.

The motivation for this *direct* interaction modality is that it has been widely shown that motor and cognitive tasks are encoded in a distributed way by networks of local brain areas and that different mental tasks activate local brain areas to a different extent. This extraordinary body of increasing knowledge provided by the neurosciences, together with recent progress in biomedical engineering and information technologies, makes it possible to monitor and extract relevant features of brain activity. It also enables the recognition of patterns associated to different mental tasks that are then transformed into actions of the brain-actuated systems. All this can be done in real-time.

There is a problem however. The *signatures* of the mental tasks to be recognised are unknown and individual. But this is not an insurmountable barrier. Machine-learning techniques can be applied to train the brain interface and follow a *mutual learning* process where the user and the interface are coupled and adapt to each other. The brain interface learns user-specific brainwave patterns describing the desired mental tasks, while the person, who receives feedback indicating the output of the brain interface, learns to think in ways enabling the interface to better understand the user.

Although brain-machine interfaces are still in their infancy, they are no more in the realm of science fiction. It will not be long before it is possible to operate mentally complex systems that will restore mobility and communication capabilities to disabled people, thus helping them increase their independence and facilitate their participation in the information society. This is the main driving force behind the development of this brain technology. But how can brain technology truly support independence and integration? How can it augment peoples' residual capabilities? Brain technology should *not* substitute human residual capabilities, and should *not* take over automatically from humans. On the contrary, such a technology should push people to use fully their mental capabilities, and should require people to deliver voluntary mental commands to the machine, which will then perform external actions for them. If children do not make their muscles reach their limit, they will never increase their physical strength. Similarly, if brain technology simply relies on basic evoked potentials, that is to say, the automatic responses of the brain to external stimuli while the person is passively driven by the external input, for example flashed visual stimuli, then it will hardly help to develop new skills that, when engaged voluntarily, will compensate for functional impairments.

Of course, these issues are also relevant for healthy people. However, they are more pressing for disabled people since the former will start using brain-machine interfaces only when their performance becomes sufficiently high, as with speech recognition systems, at least in certain domains such as games and entertainment.

Why should brain-machine interfaces be limited to recognising cognitive states? Why not also analyse affective states to determine whether a person feels frustration, dislike or satisfaction while interacting with machines so that the machine changes its behaviour to serve better the users? In short, intentions and emotions may be conveyed to machines, for example, to control them when manual operation is problematic, to detect material fatigue to prompt a safety-critical system to increase its level of automatic control, and to recognise affective states to augment the richness of virtual interaction. But beyond such real-world applications, these interfaces may enable the human brain to develop new skills so that computer systems complement their users, instead of requiring peoples' passive conformance to technology.

The brain-machine interface, of the type described, is not just a matter of *tapping the mind* to read someone's most secret thoughts. The brain-machine interface proposed can only determine whether a user is performing a mental subtraction, but not the numbers involved in this arithmetic operation. A brain-machine interface will eventually be able to recognise a user's state of mind, but not the content of the mind: it will know that users wish to move their hand forward and then grasp something, but it will fail in guessing why. And, in any case, the elements of the dialogue between users and their brain interfaces, that is to say, the mental states chosen by the users, the patterns learned by the interface, and the mapping from mental states to actions, will remain private. Moreover, because of the mutual learning process, the patterns characterising the mental states are individual and so only detectable by the interface of the users.

Should Brain Technology Explain or Portray?

The bandwidth associated with most experiences, such as admiring the first steps of a baby, manipulating a delicate object, the frustration of failing to communicate a point, etc., vastly exceeds any digital counterpart generated by the codification of these experiences and their recognition by computers. Nevertheless, scientific and technological progress will certainly reduce this gap and machines may eventually recognise, in real-time, many, if not the myriad, of the cognitive and affective states that people experience. But, admittedly, attaining this goal will take a long time. Moreover, even when it will be technologically feasible, people will acquire the capability of conveying intentions and emotions to machines incrementally, much like new-born babies take years to learn to co-ordinate their bodies.

If there is no clear limit to how powerful brain technology may become, then is it not beneficial to humans to employ it, preferably as tiny neural implants, to augment capabilities and experience richer interactions with people and machines? But, what about the *mutual learning* principle of a brain-machine interface?

People must learn to think in ways that facilitate the codification and recognition of their intentions by the machine. Feedback training drives this process whereby peoples' mental strategies are positively or negatively reinforced depending on the response of the brain-machine interface, that is to say the mental state it has recognised. In other words, if the user is concentrated on a given mental task and sees that the interface has correctly recognised it, then he will likely continue employing the same strategy in the future; whereas the user will change it if the response of the interface is incorrect. As a result, they learn to *regulate* their brain electrical activity so that the machine can codify a distinct pattern for each mental state that is easily differentiable from others. This is why the full realisation of the brain technology dream, that is to say conveying voluntarily to machines *any* intention and emotion, may remain just a dream. Surely, technology will one day allow representing and recognising most mental states of a given user, but to do this it will first be necessary that the user generates electrical activity reliably, which in turn depends on satisfactory recognition rates of the brain-machine interface.

To see the possible limitations of brain technology, it is worth asking, how should this technology be employed, just to manipulate the world or also to leverage self-knowledge?

In the first case, real-world applications will certainly be successfully realised, that, for disabled people, will be extremely useful for them as well as for their relatives. But, a brain-machine interface will do it best if it makes people mobilise voluntarily their mental capabilities. This purpose must be at the forefront of development efforts. Otherwise, in the quest for efficient mental control, thinking will be restricted to those states the brain-machine interface can codify and recognise *here* and *now*, which is better achieved if the technology relies on (more or less) automatic brain processes. And if there is no awareness of this difference, then there is a danger of shrinking the mind and adapting to machines, which is quite the opposite of the original goal! After all, thoughts shape minds. At this point, people will wrongly perceive that the dream of brain technology will have completely succeeded, simply because the interface seems to handle perfectly the usual cognitive and emotional states. This is the scenario where, somehow, people reduce their thoughts to what technology can only deal with: objective, measurable, quantitative aspects.

For such a brain-machine interface to work it is necessary to have abstract classification rules that extract the important components of brain activity and discard the highly variable components. It is well known that brain signals change naturally over time. Modern brain-machine interfaces work in this way. The underlying assumption in this approach is that variability amounts to noise and that this background activity is neutral or, at least, sufficiently controlled. However, this variability corresponds to fluctuations in cognitive and emotional context. Thus such kinds of classification rules, or *explanations*, enable manipulation and control of the world, but this predictability only exists in closed systems because, background activity, the cognitive and emotional context, is never neutral or under control. Whenever people engage in an interactive experience, it takes place in an open system. There is always a context that a brain-measuring device will fail to capture in its entirety unless people consciously or unconsciously remove it, thus effectively shrinking the mind to what can be quantitatively measured, represented, explained, and predicted.

To grasp the context of an interaction in its wholeness, the alternative is to attend to both measurable patterns and to the dynamic interconnections between them. An *explanation* puts strong emphasis on quantification; a *portrayal* deals with qualities. Portraying is an active process where the person continuously interprets every quantitative item in relation with the whole context, which requires systematic observation and experimentation with variations of conditions (both inside and outside for brain technology). Thus people can play an even more active role than before, because they have not only to voluntarily perform mental tasks, but also have to be aware of and to investigate context.

This distinction between explanation and portrayal parallels the debate on how to use *objective* (or third person) measurements of the *brain* to investigate the *subjective* (or first person) aspects of the *mind*. A reductionist view explains mind as the result of brain processes and disregards any first-person account that cannot be correlated with third-person data. Prominent neuroscientists and philosophers like Edelman and Dennett (among many others) lead this view. There is however also a dualistic interpretation, held by phenomenologists like the philosopher Chambers and the late neuroscientist Varela (to name a couple). In this view, brain structures and processes certainly provide the necessary conditions for mental states, but they are not sufficient to account for the whole experience. Also advocated is a *mutual constraint* approach, where first-person accounts and third-person data jointly catch the essence of an experience or interaction.

In this alternative portrayal scenario the quantitative and the qualitative aspects of interaction can be brought into balance through an inner work that no brain technology can do, but which it can leverage. *First-generation* brain-machine interfaces classify brain electrical activity into different mental states to compensate functional impairments and augment human capabilities. Humankind will tremendously benefit from this type of brain technology. But, in addition to a purely brain technology that only pays attention to objective brain activity, it is possible to go further along and develop a *second-generation* brain technology that encourages mutual constraints between objective physiological activity and subjective experience. This new brain-machine interface will *not* make decisions, but only suggestions to the user. The interface will simply monitor brain activity, and perhaps other kinds of physiological signals such skin conductance, heart rate and blood pressure. Whenever a salient pattern is detected, it will be brought to user's awareness for interpretation with respect to the context. Implicit here is a phenomenological distinction between awareness of brain activity and consciousness of the whole experience, because the user can only assess the inner significance of this physiological pattern through an act of consciousness of his thoughts and feelings. And this process of bringing salient patterns to user's awareness for interpretation is again a mutual adaptive process where both the brain interface and the user learn from each other over time. In particular, this adaptive process constantly tunes the pace and type of relevant physiological patterns according to individual preferences. As a result, a personal *language* of conscious states, and their related physiological patterns, will emerge. This will be a language that is progressively acquired through the disciplining of conscious activity, which is triggered by the awareness of particular physiological patterns.

A key aspect of this second-generation brain-machine interface will be its potential to deal with unconscious events, which may open a new road to self-knowledge. Subliminal perception demonstrates that, although people are not aware of certain stimuli, these stimuli exert an important influence on cognitive processes, behaviour and even social interaction. Furthermore, it is clear that emotional processes precede and modulate cortical cognitive processes, which in turn modulate emotions. Bringing salient patterns of physiological activity to awareness will make people more conscious of their inner drives. This will lead to direct brain interfaces for balanced emotional-cognitive interactions with the surrounding technology, as well as with people. Is this perhaps paving the way for a *resonating mind* technology?

To illustrate this point, consider a simple example related to epilepsy that affects many people. In the coming years it will be possible to develop neural implants to detect the onset of epilepsy seizures and prevent them by delivering an electrical stimulus to the brain. The principle is quite similar to a heart pacemaker. This wonderful device will operate independently of the user's degree of awareness. This is, no doubt, useful. It can be advocated, however, that brain technology should go further. It should help users to understand and prevent critical circumstances by making people aware of why and how these develop so that they can be avoided.

131

Finally, what type of framework could enable the development of such a brain technology encompassing quantitative-objective and qualitative-subjective aspects? The scientific method developed by Goethe, the well-known German poet, is worth exploring. This Goethean science [1] bears similarities to phenomenology. It deals with the qualitative aspects of phenomena and, quite interestingly, in Goethean science the experimenter plays a central role, being engaged in a participatory relationship with the observed phenomena. Goethe's way of science begins with the whole phenomenon as it is experienced and asserts that its qualities belong both to the inner and outer worlds, which are an indivisible unity. Then, the experimenter investigates systematically the phenomena to move from naïve observations to grasping their complete meaning, a process that requires discipline and cognitive maturity. Goethean science stands as a good candidate framework for second-generation brain technology, because it sticks to the actual human experience from the first ordinary observations to the deepest theoretical insights.

Conclusions

"Its intention is to portray rather than explain," Goethe said about his scientific method. It is an approach that makes it possible to go beyond fragmented and de-contextualised measurable brainwave patterns because it focuses on the unity of the conscious experience. In this case, a second-generation brain-machine interface will build on the power of technology to analyse complex data (such as physiological measurements related to unconscious states) to leverage the user's ability to catch the inner meaning of an experience. Moreover, as a by-product of integrating objective brain signals and subjective mental states, such a brain technology would give rise to a language of neural correlates of inner awareness and intents, which could be ultimately conveyed to machines in the same way as with first-generation brain-machine interfaces. But, now, people will have gained self-knowledge along the way, and they will have truly augmented their minds. Otherwise, as Talbott [2] has convincingly argued, if people employ technology just to manipulate the world, then their unaware use may lead them to abdicate consciousness.

References

[1] D. Seamon and A. Zajonc (eds.), 1998, *Goethe's Way of Science: A Phenomenology of Nature.* SUNY Press
[2] S. Talbott, 1995, *The Future Does Not Compute.* O'Reilly & Associates

Part IV: New Directions for Power and Participation

Chapter 12

Towards Democracy without Politics?

Ignace Snellen

Introduction

There is a fundamental divide: it lies between the function of politics and that of democracy. When speaking about democratic politics this fundamental chasm is often forgotten; in a democracy, politics and democracy are usually seen as two sides of the same coin. But they are not.

Until recently, the fundamental divide was disguised in the cloak of *the general interest*, for which particular interests would have to retreat. However, information and communications technology applications in the public domain, which inform citizens about *the real circumstances*, make this disguise, increasingly futile. There are an ever-increasing number of technologies that facilitate this. Databases deliver statistical information on which *evidence based* policies are founded and allow analyses of the circumstances from every possible angle. Group decision technologies, such as, for example, information systems containing geographic related information, and computer generated representations of reality, enable citizens and their representative interest organisations to participate in planning discussions, and to structure those discussions. Tracing and tracking technologies make it possible to maintain an overview of the activities and performances of public services and authorities. Desktop technologies facilitate the instant organisation and mobilisation of large segments of the population. Network technologies provide access to information, services, people and technologies.

The *freedom of information* is ever expanding, not only with respect to governmental information, but also to information about private actors such as enterprises. Large numbers of people, and their capabilities, can be reached at the same time in a cost-effective way. The use of email, chat rooms, electronic dialogue systems, instant polling and referenda, all accelerate the dissemination of opinions and insights. Together these information and communications technology applications support a shift from representative democracy to consultative democracy and a drift away from traditional policymaking.

In this chapter an attempt will be made to explain why, in a society where information and communications technology applications are deployed to the full, the practices of politics, even parliamentary politics, in the perception of citizens, are increasingly irreconcilable with the fundamental principles on which a democracy is based. The contention is that in an information society, the conflict between the principles of democracy and the practices of politics will become increasingly visible, because the division of pleasures and pains among citizens is becoming increasingly transparent. Transparency makes legitimising an unequal division of pleasures and pains in circumstances of equal claims, the essence of politics, and guarding the integrity of the polity, increasingly problematic. The irreconcilability between democracy and politics will lead, at least in the sectors of society where pleasures and pains are distributed, to democracy without politics. Politicians will become marginal. Their role will be partly taken over by non-elected officials and the judiciary, and partly relegated by civil society (participatory civil society).

To substantiate these contentions, the principles of democracy will be confronted with the basic character of politics, and a distinction will be made between politicians' perception of the nature of politics and the perception held by many citizens. Against this background, examples from the United States and The Netherlands are highlighted, which point in the direction of a democracy without politics.

Core Functions of Democracy and of Politics

In a democratic state, in which the population is supposed to rule itself, albeit through representation, the following principles are adhered to: the majority decides; the minority accepts the decisions of the majority; and the majority takes the convictions and feelings of the minority as much as possible into consideration. This can be put differently and perhaps more ethically: the basis of any democratic arrangement is, when it is necessary there is unity; when it is not necessary there is freedom, and in all circumstances there is solidarity. This can be called a positive of democratic polity.

Politics, on the contrary, is ruled by a recognition, which may be moral, but more often is simply prudential. It is a recognition of the power of social groups and interests, a product of being unable, without more violence and risk than can be stomached, to rule alone. In politics, the freedom of a group will be established at the moment when its power or its existence cannot be denied and must be reckoned with in governing a country as it is. It is not a notion of solidarity, but of calculation that is involved in politics. Politics is not as such motivated by principle, except in a dislike of coercion, which can in turn be thought to be a matter of prudence. This can be called a negative of democratic polity.

The Systems World versus the Life World

At the background of this distinction between politics and democracy there is also a difference in orientation. Politics, as described here, is oriented on the maintenance of the polity as a more or less integrated system. Democracy, however, is oriented on a say (it means an equal say) of citizens in the creation and maintenance of their own circumstances as a collective. What in essence is the role of politics, that noble art? There are two answers; one from the perspective of the system world of policymakers, and the other from the perspective of the life world of citizens. Politicians define the essence of politics from the perspective of their system world, a world of policy categories. Citizens define the essence of politics from the perspective of their life world, the world of daily experiences.

With respect to the system-world of policymakers, David Easton, the American political scientist and famous systems analyst, has formulated a definition of politics that is generally accepted in political science. According to this definition, politics is "the authoritative allocation of values for a society".

The more the allocations decided upon and realised by political actors are accepted as authoritative and legitimate, the less tensions will arise within society, and the better the political system will be able to maintain itself. As a systems analyst, Easton focused especially on conditions for the continuity of the political system. How can it be ensured that political systems do not succumb, despite the many conflicting demands placed upon them?

The definition that policymakers give to politics can be characterised as a top-down control approach. In this definition, the maintenance of the integrity of a society is the fundamental goal of politics. All political activities are, in the end, oriented towards this fundamental goal. A peaceful settlement in circumstances where not everybody gets what they want; this is the essence of politics. In the life-world of ordinary people, however, a more *bottom-up* phenomenological approach to politics dominates; at least, if people are prepared to make positive expression about what politics does to people. Seen from the life-world of the citizens, politics can best be defined as unequal division of pleasures and pains in circumstances of equal claims.

When politicians are involved, the average citizen expects an unequal sharing of the burdens connected to collective amenities, such as highways, industry parks and airports. If the equality of claims is recognised, for example, the people who are adversely affected by a neighbourhood development project, are fully compensated, no politics is needed. In such circumstances compensation can be defined on the basis of empirical research and market principles with respect to the positive and negative effects of the amenities.

However, in circumstances of scarcity of resources in which not all wants can be satisfied, politics is needed to make the unequal sharing of pleasures and pains acceptable, and to ensure that peaceful compromises are reached. As a consequence, politics are seen as only necessary in circumstances of inequality of outcomes. Is, therefore, a lack of trust in politics with the average citizen a surprise?

In so far as it is possible to speak of politics in circumstances of full compensation, it is not so much a matter of division of pleasures and pains, but of guarding that all stakeholders, and all elements of importance, are taken into account. Those parties who profit from a project have to compensate; those who are put at a disadvantage have to be compensated.

A Growing Tension Between System World and Life World

There is a growing tension, not to say estrangement, between the way politicians perceive politics and the way citizens perceive it. According to politicians, the role of politics is to keep the peace and to ensure that people stay on speaking terms, despite the fact, that in circumstances of equal claims on pleasures and pains, unequal allocations of value take place. According to citizens, the role of politics has to be, to take care that a fair deal is made among the interests of the different stakeholders. According to politicians, politics has succeeded if the unequal sharing has been made acceptable to the party that is short-changed. One of the tricks of politics is that the winner does not boast of victory in the deal, thus making it possible for the opponent to claim not to have got the worst of it. If the political agreement between the contesting parties has to be vague, and open to different interpretations about the deal that has been struck, so be it. Political agreements do not have to be clear, as was believed by many politicians in the late 1960s and the early 1970s; on the contrary they have to be unclear, vague, and multi-interpretable to fulfil their political function well.

However, in as far as citizens have confidence in politics, they expect the contrary; transparency in the political realm, and equality in the democratic realm. Therefore, the disparity between the system-world approach of politics and the life-world approach of citizens is a contradiction between the order perspective of governments and the democratic perspective of citizens.

In the United States this tension has resulted in, for example, the development of an *environmental justice* movement. This challenges the unequal distribution of environmental pleasures and pains for all kinds of physical projects: airports, traffic, etc. Ethnic minorities, and groups which are politically less agile, have to bear the environmental burdens of collective amenities. In the same vein the European Union Expert Group on the Urban Environment remarked in its 1996 report *European Sustainable Cities*: "high (population) density […] accentuates negative social and welfare effects of economic activities, such as pollution and transport. The poorest and most disadvantaged residents of cities often also live in the worst local environmental conditions, while those who can afford to, will buy a better local environment elsewhere".

Examples from The Netherlands

In view of this growing tension, the history of some huge cost overruns of some infrastructure projects in The Netherlands is interesting. The projects are the *Betuwelijn* and the *Hogesnelheidslijn*. The *Betuwelijn*, a railway line, is intended to connect Rotterdam harbour, the biggest in the world, with the Ruhr area in Germany, one of the most industrialised parts of Europe. The *Hogesnelheidslijn*, another railway line, is destined to become a fast connection from Amsterdam Airport to the existing high-speed train networks in Belgium, France and the United Kingdom. Amsterdam Airport is supposed to position itself, or to maintain its position, as a *main-port*, whatever this may be, for a large part of Europe.

Neither of these two mega-projects is being developed in favourable physical conditions. The *Betuwelijn*, as a west-east connection, cuts across beautiful landscapes and disturbs what is left of pristine nature in The Netherlands, a densely populated country. The *Hogesnelheidslijn* runs north-south and cuts across the whole conurbation of the Randstad.

Despite widespread discussion by the public at large, and a failing preparedness of private partners to participate in the financing of the projects, the Dutch Parliament agreed to both projects. At the time the decisions were taken, the costs of the first project were estimated at about €2.3 billion (1992 figures), and those of the second project at about €3.4 billion (1997 figures). The costs of the first project were eventually estimated at €4.7 billion and those of the second project at €4.6 billion. For both projects taken together, an additional overrun of at least €1 billion is expected. This in total, is an overrun of about 100%.

Failing Politics

Explanations why such cost overruns happen are easy to find in the theoretical political science and public administration literature. Three explanations stand out: faulty estimates; lack of knowledge on the part of officials; and retardation of the projects by citizens' opposition. A closer look at the Dutch examples mentioned above shows however that there is a different explanation of the budget overruns. The overruns appear to be a consequence of compensating for all the damage caused by the projects. Noise barriers were installed, tunnels constructed, and all kinds of compensations for material and immaterial damage were promised. The minister, who was accountable for the budget overruns, excused these by saying that the compensations were given in full agreement of Parliament.

The consideration and settlement of *all advantages and damages* is essentially a new characteristic of these projects. According to the politicians' view of the role of politics, the unequal distribution of pleasures and pains discussed previously, it can be concluded that, *politics did not play its traditional role.*

An indication, also seen on other occasions, that politics does not fulfil its proper function any more is the growing part of non-elected officials in interactive policymaking. For larger projects, as mentioned above, officials from the *executive branch of government* bring the interested parties together, lead the projects through their different stages, come, as the case may be, to conclusions and agreements, and sign-off the results of the interactive policy process.

Politicians Becoming Marginal

In the processes mentioned above, politics did not function, and politicians became marginal. Politicians have problems in defining their role in

140

interactive policy processes. They prefer to keep out of the processes, reserving themselves for the political negotiations at the end of those processes. But creating an opening for re-negotiations at the end of the process may jeopardise the results of the whole interactive policy process, have a negative effect on the legitimacy of the outcome, and affect the willingness of citizens to participate in future interactive policy projects.

Putting the results at risk may backfire on the relationship with the participants in the policy process, who will experience such an intervention as undemocratic and unreliable interference in the outcome of the negotiations with the officials. Thus, such an approach may have a devastating effect on future relations.

The message, contained in the cost overruns of the projects, presented in this chapter, and in the developments around interactive policymaking is clear: politics and democracy are increasingly growing apart and running at cross purposes. Politics as the authoritative allocation of value, in practice meaning unequal sharing in circumstances of equal claims, is incompatible with democracy as recognition of having an equal say. Experiences with interactive policymaking leave no doubt that democratic procedure alone does not legitimise the outcomes of political processes, as Nikolaus Luhmann, the German sociologist contended. The life-world approach of politics is not procedure oriented, but output oriented. In the life-world, the development of a project through interactive policymaking is only legitimised when all positive and negative consequences are taken into account and taken as a basis for compensation.

The *Hollowing-Out* of Politics

In practical as well as theoretical discussions, much is made of the so-called *hollowing-out* of the state; central government losing power and authority to public and private supra-national bodies on one hand, and to lower layers of government and to civil society on the other. More than 60% of laws and regulations in European Union Member States originate in Brussels.

Governments themselves have furthered this *hollowing-out* by the formation of agencies at a distance from the ministries, by outsourcing even their core functions, and by privatising many of their traditional activities in the public sphere. In this way these activities are placed outside their political span of control and into the realm of contractual relations. In circumstances regulated by contractual relationships there is no room for politics in the sense of unequal allocations for equal claims.

This active hollowing-out by state authorities themselves may be interpreted as an early recognition by politicians that their role is being constantly diminished. This process is often called *displacement of politics* (to other authorities than the traditional ones), but can be better described as *replacement of politics* (by de-politicised arrangements in the public sphere).

Some Explanatory Elements

What are the elements in the background of the replacement of politics? Without suggesting an order of priority, the following can be mentioned.

First, there is an increasing *level of education* among the populations in modern countries. An enormous knowledge reservoir is available outside the circles of official professionals, who participate in public policymaking around a specific project. A single uninvolved specialist may be able to give counter-expertise and keep the official consultants and policymakers busy for a long time. This counter-expertise can be deployed by a contesting party in the media, in political forums, as well as in administrative court procedures. As a consequence of this, the opinions of experts are much more contested than in the past. They do not have the legitimising effect they had before. The internet as a medium facilitates the communication of the mass media, and the public at large, with the experts.

Second, politicians have become marginal: public officials take on their role. Supported by web sites, discussion groups, videoconferencing, and other information and communication technology facilities, public officials know, often better than the politicians, about the life-world problems of citizens. The wide range of information and communication technologies, which are available to the public officials, further reduced the relevance of politicians.

Public officials are primarily motivated by a *professional ethos*, not by a political ethos. Their objective is not political in the sense of unequal division of pleasures and pains in circumstances of equal claims. As long as they are working closely together with politicians they will leave it to them to take care of the allocation aspects of a policy. But, when they negotiate a project on their own, they will tend to strike a fair balance among the different opposing interests. Only when politicians participate in the policymaking, and set the boundaries, do the officials have to remain within the limits of the unequal allocations set by their political masters, which is often a very uneasy circumstance.

Third, during the past few decades a wave of *juridical involvement* has occurred in most modern countries. An increasing number of judges (non-elected in most countries) are supposed to solve highly contested political issues, which politicians themselves do not succeed in solving. In these circumstances, judges function as rule-makers. In the spheres of social security, labour regulations, and the protection of the socially weaker parties, for example, with respect to large infrastructure projects, judges have become especially active. The judges, just like the professional officials in governmental bureaucracies, are unwilling to fill in the role of politicians. Equality before the law, not the honouring of unequal allocations in circumstances of equal claims, is the direction in which judges will look for solutions. Principles of decent administrative behaviour, such as the principle of proportionality, or the principle of adequate motivation, are dominant. They are oriented on democratic equality and environmental justice, more than on the reaching of peaceful compromises, which is the leading principle of politics according to politicians and political scientists.

Fourth, the use of *computer applications* and *internet* has increased the transparency of the activities of governmental services and policymakers, and the background against which they may be judged, to such an extent that often policies of unequal allocations are not feasible any more. The increased transparency is a consequence of the use of computers. When computers are used in the implementation of governmental services two parallel processes take place: the *process of automated service delivery*, such as the provision of a subsistence grant, and a *process of registration* of the distribution of the services. The process of registration that runs parallel to the service delivery is a reflexive process, called *informating* [1]. The informating characteristic of information technology arises because computers not only undertake the tasks that they are programmed to do, but also generate information about these tasks. Thus events, objects and processes become visible, knowable and shareable in a new way. This is of utmost importance for politics and policies, which allocate unequally in circumstances of equal claims.

The transparency created by the *informating* computers is enhanced by the use of all kinds of purposed *tracking, tracing and monitoring systems*. Performance indicators about public services, such as hospitals, schools, fire brigades and so on stand out as examples of this growing transparency. Through benchmarking, their relative performance, as compared with other services, is ascertained. If performance indicators are used, less doubt will exist about who are the winners and who are the losers, as well as about the inequality of allocations of value in circumstances of equal claims.

Fifth, another side effect of the use of computer applications, such as the internet, is a *low threshold for involvement of people* in policymaking processes. Interactive policymaking is already mentioned in this respect. Networks of organisations and interested people participate in the different stages of a strategic public policy formulation. The internet may be used in the implementation of the formulated policy to facilitate the participation of the neighbourhoods which are affected by the policy. Computer applications, such as *email, discussion groups and simulations* are often applied for this purpose. A lower threshold for participation also means that people expect their opinions will have impact on the final result of a common policymaking process, according to the democratic principles sketched above. Right or wrong, information and communication technologies appear to promise the realisation of participatory democracy.

Conclusions

Will politics endure in Western democracies as the central mechanism through which an unequal division of pleasures and pains takes place? On the basis of the developments sketched in this chapter, the answer to this question is that the scope for politics in modern democratic societies will be greatly reduced. The transparency of the information society will increasingly limit the room for politics to distribute pleasures and pains unequally, at least in democratic polities. Supported by information and communication technologies, public officials, judges and other intermediaries will replace politics on the basis of non-political principles.

Politics will, however, not completely disappear. Two roles may remain to be reserved for politics. A first role may be the creation and maintenance of the institutional arrangements of the information society. A second role may be a procedural one: to assure a level playing field for stakeholders in policies and projects. According to this scenario, the *quid pro quo* of market mechanisms, handled by professional, non-elected, public officials, or other intermediaries, will take over the function of politics and politicians. In such a way democracy will be defended against politics. Taking into account the rate of change between 1980 and 2000, the developments sketched in this chapter may be fully realised by 2020.

References

[1] Zuboff, S., 1988, *In the Age of the Smart Machine: The Future of Work and Power* (Basic Books New York)

Chapter 13

A Win–win Strategy for Europe in The Knowledge Society

Marc Luyckx Ghisi

Introduction

"When vision vanishes, people perish"
Bible, Proverbs: 29:18

Almost all values of the modern rational capitalist system are in rapid transformation, but in silence. It is more usual in discussions to underline one or two aspect that are slowly being transformed, but this chapter highlights that *all key values are disappearing or have already gone.* All the foundations of industrial capitalism are rapidly disintegrating, but meanwhile *business as usual* prevails. Is this interpretation wrong? Have events been completely misunderstood? Is this exaggeration? Why such silence and such an absence of reflection and of action? Only time will reveal the full answers to these questions, but in the meantime presented here are some possible answers.

The New Values of the Knowledge Market

The values on which the knowledge society is based and built are very different from the values and procedures of industrial capitalism, although there is a strong temptation to use the new tools with the old values. Table 13.1 shows a general vision of the shift in values, which is underway. The table presents the chief characteristics of a positive view of the knowledge society compared with industrial capitalism. But, as the third column indicates, all the new values emerging in the knowledge society can be subverted into their opposites. Each item in this table will be addressed in the second part of this chapter.

INDUSTRIAL CAPITALISM	KNOWLEDGE SOCIETY: POSITIVE SCENARIO	KNOWLEDGE SOCIETY: NEGATIVE SCENARIO
Competitiveness is linked to availability of capital and top technology.	Human creativity, institutional change, and new vision are more important.	Efforts to exploit human creativity in the old structures and the old industrial vision.
Aim: producing and selling many cheap material goods.	Aim: produce quality of knowledge, thus push human creativity and networks. Immaterial assets.	Danger of manipulation.
Trade: either the item or the money for the item; what is sold is lost.	Knowledge that is shared is not lost. Exchange and sharing of knowledge in networks are the only way to increase knowledge. *Win-win* logic.	Danger of taking without exchanging.
All industrial policies are based on scarcity and exclusion.	All policies are based on abundance of information and inclusion, because sharing is the only way to produce more knowledge.	People try to steal knowledge without sharing. Dangers of viruses and pirates of new kinds.
All industrial policies, defence and business, are based on secrecy. Patenting is the norm.	Disappearance of secrecy and patenting! Information always *leaks*.	Refusal of this evolution. Soft Fascism. Wars and violence.
Capitalist debate: who owns the means of production? The right-left debate.	The capitalist debate is over because the means of production has become the human brain.	Subtle or violent manipulation of human brains.
Human capital is not an asset: it is a social cost.	Human capital becomes a central asset in production, management and new measurements and accounting.	Management as manipulations of human capital, to make it submissive to machines and old style profits.
The concepts of *industrial progress, growth* and *competition* are quantitative.	Progress, growth and competition become qualitative.	Refusal of this qualitative definition of progress, growth and competition.
Objects on the market have no ethical value.	Knowledge has an ethical value.	Manipulation of ethics and meanings, even religions.
The strategy is mastering and domination of nature and markets.	General strategy is reconnection and sustainability and qualitative growth.	Towards a new and worse mastery and domination!

Table 13.1: Important value shifts with two scenarios.

Towards an Immaterial Society

Industrial society aims to produce and sell a maximum number of material goods, and the industrial economic approach is limited to a materialistic view. Economic discipline is built on reducing everything to numbers, or even equations. The challenge for economists is to find new ways or new approaches of placing human behaviour in equations. And the only possible measurement in capitalist society is a quantitative and material one.

Now, there is a problem, because knowledge is immaterial. Some economists are making great efforts to express and measure knowledge into quantitative terms. Their work however does not seem to convince the majority of the economics community.

Economists do recognise openly that an increasing part of the economy is *intangible*. Baruch Lev states in a book [1] on intangibles: "An intangible asset is a claim to future benefit that does not have a physical or financial embodiment. A patent, a brand, and a unique organisational structure [...] I use the terms intangibles, knowledge assets, and intellectual capital interchangeably." Lev also observes: "Intangibles are frequently embedded in physical assets (for example, the technology and knowledge contained in an aeroplane) and in labour (the tacit knowledge of employees), leading to interactions between tangible and intangible assets in the creation of value. These interactions pose serious challenges to the measurement and valuation of intangibles. When such interactions are intense, the valuation of intangibles on a stand-alone basis becomes impossible."

The classical capitalist quantitative (material) measurement methods are not working. The economy is already in another value system. And the difficulty is that shifting to an immaterial qualitative approach will suppose a change in economic methods and axioms. Economics may have to become a multidisciplinary topic, involving philosophers, sociologists, anthropologists, psychologists, politicians, and even theologians: men and women.

The main obstacle to this rethinking of economics is the *clerical* behaviour of the corps of world-class economist. They do not seem very inclined to accept new ideas and fundamental changes in methods. In the modern world there is a new dominating class functioning like the medieval clergy. Economists are a good example of this modern functioning. They behave like the theologians at the end of the Middle Ages. When one of them begins to think out of the box, he is ostracised and reduced to silence. Herman Daly, former research chief at the World Bank, gives an excellent example of this ostracism in his book [2]. He reports that since he published his first critical article he has never again been invited to any world congress of economists.

These kinds of practices are not very tolerant, but they are structural since they are embedded in the modern approach to economics. There must however be tolerance for human behaviour. It is unfair to accuse people. However there is another obstacle, which is in everyone;

147

the materialistic approach to life has become embedded in everyone. Materialism has become second nature, it is in peoples' minds, and it is in the modern approach to life, so that immaterial information is not perceived. It is just not seen. Everyone will have to open up again to another set of values.

Beyond Trade Towards Sharing

Trade is a recent idea. It is a transaction where goods are exchanged for money, and nothing more. Once this exchange has taken place, the transaction is considered as completed. No follow-up is foreseen. This concept of trade seems eternal, because people have never known anything else.

However in the Middle Ages, in Europe, the concept of commerce was very different. It was much richer and holistic and was mainly based on exchange and gift. For example, if a farmer needed seeds and his neighbour had plenty, then the neighbour would give the needed seeds in exchange for something, or for money, or for free. And the farmer would accept to remain in a debt of honour. Which means that, in case of necessity, it is agreed as evident that the farmer would come and help his debtor, or that he would give his neighbour a present on the next good occasion.

If the farmer went to the market, in town, and bought seeds, he would have to pay, but he would have also used the trip to the town to gather information on agricultural methods, political affairs, etc. He would also perhaps have looked for a good husband for his daughter. The exchanges in city and town markets were much larger than monetary transactions; they included exchange of knowledge, of human relations, marriages, etc.

It is only during the industrial period, in the 19th century, that the concept of trade became so narrow. Society shifted from commerce to trade. What has been eliminated completely is the community-building idea of reciprocal debt. This notion of debt has been considered very negatively by industrial capitalism, perhaps under the influence of Puritanism. Popular wisdom today places pride in having no debts. There has been a complete reversal of values.

In the knowledge society, when people exchange knowledge, they do not lose it, and the receiver is linked by a debt. The advantage to the donor is not necessarily money. More important is the knowledge that comes back, enriched by the receiver's creativity. This is why new entrepreneurs are insisting so much on the compelling necessity of sharing any information received by their employees. In some firms in Silicon Valley, if an employee holds on to knowledge for more than 24 hours

148

without sharing this with others, that person is automatically dismissed. This new rule means that in most of national and regional administrations, the majority of the personnel may potentially be dismissed immediately. This is also why there is such an insistence on the crucial importance of networks of excellence. As Veran Alle shows eloquently, networks are the place where value is *created* in this new society [3].

There is thus a radical change in the very basic concept of modern industrial trade, in which it is impossible to *have both the item and the money for the item*. In a certain sense, in the knowledge society it is possible to have the *knowledge and the money for the knowledge*. There is a shift to a new logic of exchange and sharing. This means also that money is losing its central position in the knowledge transaction, because a knowledge transaction is possible without money. Money is also quickly dematerialising and disconnecting from post-industrial production. It is becoming increasingly speculative and abstract. Thus it loses its social usefulness. Is Society witnessing the end of the industrial concept of money? What is the future?

With a company such as Microsoft, there is a lot of money involved. But the way Bill Gates has made his money seems new. He had knowledge, understanding the importance of the user-friendly approach of Apple Computers, and selling it to the IBM system, but he had little capital and no infrastructure. It has been enough to make a fortune. However, taking the case of software that operates computers (computer operating systems) there is the established Microsoft Windows and the newcomer Linux. The latter is open-source and capable of being improved by users. Comparing the two, Microsoft still appears to be industrial. Will Linux win in the long run? Is Linux much more knowledge-based than Windows? These are still open questions.

Beyond Scarcity and Exclusion

Capitalism and its money system are based and built on the values of scarcity and exclusion. The whole of the market functioning is also based on these same values. One company has a new product and the other does not. The whole of the concurrence and pricing system is also based on this scarcity. If goods are not scarce, it is not possible to get a high price for them. And the consequence of this scarcity is the exclusion of those actors on the market who have not got a similar patent or product available.

A very different set of values is emerging. In the knowledge society, information is overabundant. The challenge is to transform this information into knowledge, which is less abundant. Only a person can do this, or better, several people. And so it is a question of survival to circulate information to a maximum number of people. The fabric of knowledge is built on inclusion. The more people who are included the better and quicker information will be transformed into knowledge. The behaviour found in industrial capitalism, trying to cultivate the scarcity of information, will rapidly result in knowledge becoming obsolete! A shift in values is therefore obligatory.

Thus a new proverb can be created: "Knowledge is like love; the more people give, the more they receive!" This may be shocking to capitalists, but in truth it is difficult for the majority as well, because people have so well internalised scarcity and exclusion as guiding values. These values are deeply embedded in peoples' minds.

This new logic, which is quickly invading society, can have a very positive impact in geopolitics. Why not apply this inclusive approach to Africa? Why not share with the poorer continents, information and knowledge? A tremendous return may result and because of this there may be hope for a new start for them. This will naturally presuppose also that there will be a new redistribution of income: humans cannot be creative if they are hungry and anxious for the survival of their children. The eventual return on knowledge may be unexpectedly high.

Is this a utopia? These countries may be able to switch more quickly to the knowledge age, precisely because industrial values are not so deeply embedded in their minds and in their structures. Their so-called *traditional* or *under-developed* societies are still based on a strong sense of sharing, giving, and including. These values are exactly the right ones that will allow a jump into the knowledge society.

Beyond Secrecy and Patenting

Secrecy and patenting are core values of the capitalist system: secrecy before applying for patents is the logic. This point is very much debated. Many thinkers are still defending the patenting system and there have been extended negotiations on intellectual propriety rights within the forum of the World Trade Organisation, where the West is fighting to defend intellectual propriety rights. And it seems a very legitimate fight.

However, Harlan Cleveland [4] addressed the issue in 1985, when he stated that "information always leaks". This means that secrecy will become increasingly more difficult: "Information is porous, transparent. It leaks: it has an inherent tendency to leak. The more it leaks, the more we have, and the more of us have it. The straitjackets of government *classification*, trade secrecy, intellectual propriety rights, and confidentiality of all kinds fit very loosely on this restless resource."

Information does indeed leak. And there will be more and more leaks, for example, on the web. It is even possible to learn through the web, how to build a nuclear bomb! It is becoming increasingly difficult to keep information secret. And this difficulty will probably increase, precisely because of the ultra rapid development of information technologies.

Knowledge is the central asset of the new society. If secrecy is not anymore possible, what type of structures will there be? Once again, people are so embedded in the old system, considering it so evidently eternal, that there are difficulties in trying to conceive something else. Perhaps there is a need to rediscover the notion of collective propriety and co-operative management, which tribal societies have been using for millennia.

An excellent example of this is the international agreement on the oceanic bottoms which after years of fighting, has been determined in the United Nations' Convention on the Law of the Sea, in 1982, and the subsequent agreements and programs following the Rio Earth Summit in 1992. Perhaps the time has come for humanity to rediscover old truth and create new concepts leading to a more sustainable world.

The worst scenario will be the West pushing to enforce rules for the protection of intellectual propriety, worldwide.

Individual Ownership of the Means of Production

This is the most destabilising new characteristic of the knowledge society, because it means the end of capitalism and of Marxism, and of the right-left debate. Here lies the theoretical basis and explanation why the left is so much in crisis in Europe and in the whole world. Indeed, the whole strategy of Marxism and of the left was the fight for the ownership of the means of production by the workers. Meanwhile the right was fighting for the ownership by the entrepreneur or by the owner of the capital.

This is all over, because the means of production in the knowledge society are the individual brains of employees. This means that every evening employees are going home with the means of production. Every evening, entrepreneurs remain alone with their capital, their factories, but without the main means of production. There is still capital, but it is far from being the central asset. Society is not anymore capitalist.

The new challenge for the knowledge entrepreneur is to make sure that the means of production are coming back to work in the morning. This also explains why management is shifting towards human-centred management. It is a question of survival for the enterprises, if they do not want to lose their best tools of production. There is thus a re-humanisation of management.

However the human brain alone is not productive. Humans must interact to create new value. This is the fundamental reason for so much discussion about networks. Networks of creative humans are indeed the value creation tools of this new society.

When Human Capital Becomes Central

Human capital is becoming central. Many entrepreneurs have learned this, by the facts, when they have lost the best brains of their enterprise, and thus, one important part of knowledge creation. They have been forced to completely change their management style. This is the optimistic scenario. And happily it happens often.

However, some businesses have been forced by market pressures to abandon the *new* management practices, and to go back to the old vertical, short-term profit-centred management. But these old practices are not the future.

However there is another scenario, which must be taken seriously. It consists of modifying humans, through life engineering, to make them conform to the technological system. Andrew Kimbrell, founder of the *International Centre for Technology Assessment*, in Washington DC has said, "Corporations, academics, and researchers came to realise, albeit slowly, that current technology is not compatible with life […] To deal with this historic dilemma, the techno-utopians and their corporate sponsors outline a breathtaking initiative. This initiative was not to change technology so that it better fits the needs of living things, as we were so eagerly advocating. No, they had and have a very different and stunningly self-serving approach. They decided to engineer life, indeed reality itself, so that it better fits the technological system. It is in this chilling context that the enormous significance of the current revolutions in technology can be fully appreciated. Here we have the key to the otherwise bewildering high-tech headlines and to much of our social malaise."

Thus a shift of values does not necessarily imply a rosy future. Every value can be used for the good or evil. This depends on the free choice of humans. And the evil forces in people and in society cannot be underestimated.

Towards Qualitative Progress and Sustainability

Another basic value of industrial capitalist society is an unshakeable faith in progress. In the pre-modern agrarian society, the dominant time value was stability, and change was seen as undesirable. The astronomers Copernicus and Galileo had negative experiences as a result. In modern and industrial society progress has superseded stability, almost to the point where stability is subject to ridicule. And capitalism has added a turbo drive to this concept of progress, by introducing the new undisputed value of unlimited quantitative growth.

The problem is that in a finite world, infinite growth is mathematically impossible. Many people feel this, but people prefer not to mention it, as the benefits of growth continue to be reaffirmed.

The good news is that in the knowledge society, knowledge can be of excellent, good or poor quality. This means that knowledge, like human creativity, are measured in qualitative terms, and very poorly in quantitative terms, precisely because the productivity of knowledge is linked more to its quality than to its quantity.

Peter Drucker observed in 1993 [5]: "Above all, the amount of knowledge, that is, its quantitative aspect, is not nearly as important as the productivity of knowledge, that is, its qualitative impact. And this applies to old knowledge and its application, as well as to new knowledge." This little quotation is very important. It is the signal that there is a new logic, based on quality. This is a new landscape, in which the economic rules are not yet known. But this also means that the basic concept of progress will have to be refined. People will have to accustom themselves to a qualitative definition of progress.

This will be another turning-point for the global society. This new definition of progress is changing the way society will be seen in the coming years. This means that there is a shift underway from a society that aims at producing the maximum quantity of goods, and finding a market for them, towards another society that aims at increasing the quality of knowledge. Does this mean that more globally, the aims of world societies will be to increase the quality of life for everybody? This is one possible option, which is probably the only way to prepare a sustainable future.

One of the main problems in society is that people feel compelled by market logic, to produce everyday, more objects, and in so doing to continue the exhaustion of nature and environment. In a framework of purely quantitative progress, sustainability is impossible, because it implies stopping the system, and this is not acceptable. How to conceive this limit? There must be a halt somewhere, somehow.

Qualitative progress may be this stop signal, this new red light, but in a way that is acceptable, and accepted by the key actors in the system: enlightened business people. If society is not anymore focused on quantity, but on quality, a sustainable society in the future is possible. This shift towards qualitative progress is thus giving humanity the new indispensable concept for imagining a sustainable future.

In philosophical terms, this means also that people may be leaving the materialistic framework, in which everyone was raised, and that people may be heading towards a post materialistic society. What then will be the new aims of society, if they were not anymore linked to material progress? Society may make the choice of focusing on human qualitative development. This may seem strange to many, but it may become more self-evident by 2015. Nobody knows the future, but it is important to prepare for it.

Ethics, Meaning and Transparency

In the industrial logic, objects have no ethical connotation. For instance, a block of steel can be produced in a German factory, where all workers are protected by strict social laws, are very well treated, and earn a very good living. Or it can be produced in an Indian sweatshop. No difference can be seen however: it is the same block of steel.

In the knowledge society, objects are increasingly linked to information, to knowledge and to meaning. People are interested to get information from the World Wide Web on how *Nike* shoes are produced, by whom and in what circumstances. The same applies to food such as chicken; people want to know how the chickens are raised.

Probing deeper it is clear that a *Microsoft* program is not the same as a Linux program. The first, despite its qualities, is sending a subliminal message of closeness and exclusivity. This program cannot be rearranged creatively, and eventually enriched, by customers. It is expensive and compels people to buy the new versions, which are not always fully compatible with older hardware material, which is then rendered obsolete, etc. Linux programs however, are open-source, and they are thus open to adaptation and improvement by customers. They are much more human-friendly, and thus more in tune with a positive future. This example shows how much meaning is invading business life and public debate, in general.

Another excellent example is that of Coca-Cola who were confronted in 1999 with a number of minor crises. One of them happened in Belgium. Some children became slightly ill after drinking Coca-Cola at school. The Coca-Cola management at the Belgian, and at the European and world levels, managed this crisis as a problem with a product, an object. They treated Coca-Cola cans like pure objects with a defect. They withdrew millions of cans from the European market, and sold them to Africa, where they do not seem to have produced any harm. This *object led* management was a good and cheap way out of the problem.

However, when the media informed the public of this behaviour, there was a negative reaction and the share price of Coca-Cola lost, in a very short time, 50% of its value! What had happened was that, in the eyes of the consumers, a can of Coca-Cola, which is 10% brown liquid and 90% brand, lost some of its immaterial value. Indeed this carefully constructed brand is about equality and integration among the races, a world of harmony and justice, hope for a better world, for the young generation, etc. These are ethical values. Such a brand cannot be managed like a material object. Management must reflect the values of the brand itself. This is what the upper management had not understood. They simply had not taken the immaterial dimension into consideration. And this damaged the General Manager's career and he was forced to resign.

This example shows how deeply society is already in this new way of doing business and in the new logic. It is around, but everyone is like the Coca-Cola General Manager, still desperately trying to solve problems with old tools.

From Command and Control to Reconnection and Caring

In industrial and capitalist society, command and control were important. They were so evident that these methods were not even discussed. And the tools of production, capital, and industrial technology had to be commanded and controlled to be efficient. In this machine-centred society, humans were invited or forced to adapt to the machine: machines were commanding their rhythm.

In the knowledge society this modern, rational and patriarchal type of management is rapidly becoming obsolete. Why is this so? The answer is because suddenly people have realised that it is not possible to control knowledge, and it is certainly not possible to control human creativity, at least if it is accepted not to transform human nature.

This is another huge transformation. It is not only a shift in values, but it is the deepest transformation in the way power is used for over 5,000 years, when patriarchal societies first emerged. Since this time power has been exerted in a vertical, command and control way. And suddenly, this means of exerting power has become obsolete, because it is not able to foster human creativity: a strange circumstance. Events seem to move faster than peoples' conscious understanding. They are thus obliged to reinvent power. And it is normal that in such a period of transition, women are found to be far better then men at human resources management. Women have not completely forgotten the way power was exerted in the pre-patriarchal society, the matriarchal one. Men instead are more identified with the patriarchal power structures. Their challenge is more important and difficult.

In a certain sense, the knowledge society is like a turbo drive, an accelerator of this shift from a patriarchal society towards a new women-men partnership society. And what is the new landscape of power? One key element is that power will become more enabling, enhancing both life and creativity. This is for men a new world, or at least for their yang dimension.

And there is another very important element. Patriarchal power, because of its command orientation, considered itself above nature. It was thus cut off from nature, from feelings, from life itself. It was like exerting power in a void [6], over nature, not inside nature. This power position has permeated the whole of the modern world, which is a model of domination. And to exert power in a life enhancing way, people must reconnect with nature, with feelings. This is a completely different way to relate to reality. Once again it is understandable that women are before men in this transformation.

The good news is that, if this shift is going on further, it is paving the way to a new vision of the world, which leads to sustainability. This new structure of power is leading people towards a positive and sustainable future in a much easier way.

However the more this shift is occurring in the shadow, the more that existing power structures will feel threatened. They will have the feeling that their foundations are crumbling. And people must thus be ready for desperate, violent, even extremely violent counter reactions, aimed at keeping this mastery and this control. People must be ready to live in the coming years in a contrasted landscape, with significant change and with very reactionary responses to these transformations.

The transformation has started, and it is unlikely to be stopped. However nobody knows the future!

The Negative Scenario

A transformation of values is clearly happening. This is something that is occurring deep within society. However any value is like an axis and the main axes of society are moving into the knowledge society. But on each axis, it is possible to move towards positive or towards minus. Every value can be lived and applied in a positive or in a negative sense.

It is thus evident that a negative scenario is possible. It is even probable that humanity will first try the negative scenario, because it is the direction where the *business as usual* policy is leading. And it is also more similar to peoples' everyday world, which is not rosy. It is indeed very probable that people in power will do everything they can to maintain command and control over the political and economic circumstances of the world. Never in history, has there been an example of a dominating class giving power spontaneously to a dominated class. This soft scenario is highly improbable.

This chapter has not tried to present an idyllic paradise, as a probable scenario. In practice, a refusal of the changes may lead to more harm than the understanding and progressive acceptance of the transformation. What is important in such a period is to prepare people for tomorrow's debate. What are the new questions? What are the new dangers? How to envisage a post-capitalist society? How will it function? How to rethink economy, power, inclusiveness, trade, secrecy, scarcity, human capital, qualitative progress, ethics in business and public management, reconnection, etc.? How to avoid the danger of subtle manipulation of the highest values and of human nature? How to prepare for these new dangers?

These are important questions that civil society needs to be explicitly aware of. Public opinion has probably already a passive knowledge of these changes, sometimes more than politicians. People intuitively feel the changes. It is urgent to foster an interesting debate on the collective and individual futures. The aim of this chapter is to help the public to think openly what they already implicitly know. And speaking openly what it feels inside, civil society will be able to participate in a constructive debate on the society of tomorrow, its dangers and tremendous opportunities.

Sustainability and Inclusion in The Knowledge Society

The shift in values is important and one of the most important consequences of this shift is that *sustainability and social inclusion* are moving within reach, in the immaterial world of the *intangible assets.*

Information and communication technologies have resulted in deep transformations of society. But even deeper changes can be expected. Power increasingly lies in the availability of human creativity in interactive networks (human capital) and less in the ownership of capital and technology. Why is this so?

To transform information into knowledge, capital and technology are necessary but not sufficient: human creativity is necessary. Verna Allee [3] has said "the electronic economy in California collapsed because they looked only at technological progress. They had not understood the importance of the *institutional transformation* of the companies and of society. They had not changed their *vision.* Most of those *top* companies were dinosaurs in terms of human management. This is the reason they collapsed. Others like Cisco or e-Bay had enormous intangible assets and human capital. They are prosperous."

Another feature of the knowledge society is the importance of inclusion. People are deeply rooted in the industrial mentality. It is difficult for everyone to understand that the exclusive logic of the industrial society is silently being transformed into an inclusive one. This is a 180° turnaround. If knowledge is not shared, it is impossible to increase it, because machines cannot do this: it is a distinctly human activity. Worse, if knowledge is not shared, it loses value. It is affected by a negative interest rate. This is the new logic permeating *networks of excellence, intelligent territories, learning regions, lifelong learning*, etc. The more people are included, the more a region will become intelligent. This is *win-win* logic. But there is something even more shocking: the entrepreneur of the 21st century may become a champion of inclusion in the knowledge society. Indeed the more people that are included the more qualitative knowledge an entrepreneur will produce. In affirming that the knowledge society must be competitive in an inclusive way, Europe has chosen the right way forward, even though many of the important actors in business, in administrations, in Universities, and the public, have not yet fully understood this new challenge.

Classical economists are increasingly speaking of *intangibles* when they refer to the knowledge society. It seems that one important part, possibly the major part, of the economic system in United States and in Europe, has become intangible. This means that the classical economic tools are not efficient anymore for measuring and managing this growing part of economies. Classical tools are becoming rapidly obsolete [4,7].

Importantly for the knowledge society, sustainability is a key intangible asset. But most economists have a problem with sustainability. Indeed in industrial policy circles it is often stated that there is a trade-off between sustainability and profit. Industrial economists consider that sustainability is a cost and they are right. If an enterprise wants to become entirely sustainable then this does have a cost. However, in the knowledge society sustainability is such an important intangible asset that although money is spent for sustainability, a win-win logic is everyday more possible and probable.

The story of *Interface*, the Carpet Company, which became 95% sustainable, is a good example [8]. Enormous sums of money were spent on reorienting the whole production system, but this does not appear to be the main reason that *Interface* became the world leader in carpets. Why was this so? What happened?

It seems that the personnel, the clients and broadly the stakeholders, became so deeply proud of their enterprise that its energy was transformed completely. The enterprise suddenly acquired a new and deeper meaning, a new image, because it was contributing to the survival of nature and humanity. The brand, the reputation, the meaning, that is to say, the non-financial assets of the company increased by 1000%. This is a huge increase of intangible value! Here the win-win scenario is coming to the fore: the more companies are sustainable, the more they acquire intangible added value. Yet this intangible value is not visible in the old measurement system. But in the knowledge society intangible value becomes everyday more important, surpassing sometimes financial value.

Indeed, in the knowledge society, the non-financial assets, or intangible assets, that is to say, those that are a source of future benefits that do not have a physical or financial embodiment, are growing in importance. This is happening because knowledge is more important, and the way to measure knowledge is mainly qualitative and non-financial, thus intangible. But intangible assets are something that cannot be recognised very well with the old tools. Thus, while sustainability is a cost in financial terms, it is an intangible asset in a knowledge-based enterprise. Now, if the importance of the non-financial assets increases, this means that sustainability is a key element of a win-win strategy for Europe.

Figure 13.1 illustrates that intangibles grow in importance in the knowledge economy as information and communication technologies enable greater communication of indicators and increase transparencies. The potential is for greater citizen participation and wider accountability between sectors of society, as new intangibles, sustainability, and social inclusion grow in relative importance.

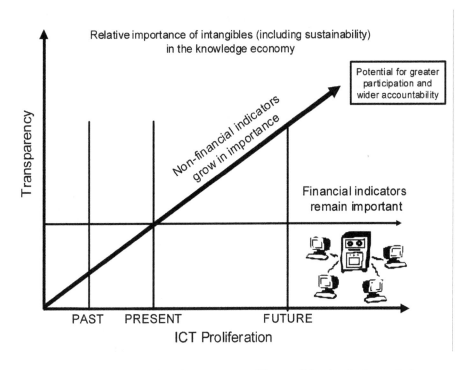

Figure 13.1: The growing importance of intangibles in the knowledge society. *Source*: Marc Luyckx and Verna Allee, Copyright 2003. Reproduced with permission.

Figure 13.1 also shows that society has reached the point where the line depicting non-financial assets and measurements crosses the line depicting financial assets. While financial assets will remain important measurements, non-financial assets and measurements will become predominant in the future.

In the classical industrial approach, sustainability is caught in a *win-lose* game, which is correct if only the line depicting financial assets is considered. No *win-win* is possible. However, in the knowledge society, the line depicting non-financial assets and measurements indicates a huge growth in the importance of intangible assets. And sustainability is an intangible asset. So at the moment when intangible assets become increasingly more important, sustainability, which is a very important intangible, becomes a key success factor in the knowledge society. This is a *win-win* game. More sustainability implies more intangible assets, which implies increasing *new* competitiveness.

For similar reasons social inclusion, which is embedded in the new logic of the knowledge society, also becomes a very important and crucial intangible. If an enterprise is considered as socially inclusive, it will produce increasingly valuable knowledge, and the intangible brand will increase enormously since the enterprise will be considered as a very positive social influence for society at large. While social inclusion is a cost in the industrial logic of *win-lose*, here more social inclusion leads to more knowledge creation, and hence more intangible assets. This again is a *win-win* outcome.

Conclusions

The knowledge society, which has begun to emerge, is a different world. It is not anymore relaying on secrecy, and material and quantitative growth. It is based on qualitative growth and qualitative measurements and qualitative assets. It requires a sharing of knowledge because this is the only way to create value. It is redefining the very concept of trade and its relation to knowledge. Unhappily people are still trying to manage this new society in an industrial way. This is probably the case because there is not enough discussion about the new values at stake.

A second very important conclusion is that the knowledge society is potentially more sustainable and socially inclusive. Indeed, sustainability becomes a realist aim for companies because a new *win-win* scenario becomes possible and is working effectively in some first experiments at companies such as *Interface* and others. Sustainability is possible because companies are not anymore imprisoned in the old *trade-off* between profit and sustainability.

References

[1] Lev, B., 2001, *Intangibles: Management, Measurement, and Reporting* (Brooking Institution Press, Washington D.C.)

[2] Daly, H., 1989, *For the Common Good: Redirecting the Economy Towards Community, the Environment and a Sustainable Future* (Beacon Press, Boston)

[3] Allee, V., 2002, *The Future of Knowledge: Increasing Prosperity through Value Networks* (Butterworth Heinemann Elsevier Science, USA)

[4] Cleveland, H., 1985, *The Knowledge Executive: Leadership in an Information Society* (Truman Talley Books, E. P. Dutton, New York)

[5] Drucker, P., 1993, *Post Capitalistic Society* (Harper Business, New York, p. 186.)

[6] Garcia Marquez, G., 1998, *One Hundred Years of Solitude* (Harper Perennial Library)

[7] Cleveland, H., 1997, *Leadership and the Information Revolution* (World Academy of Art and Science)

[8] Anderson, R.C., 1998, *Mid Course Correction: Toward a Sustainable Enterprise: The Interface Model* (Chelsea Green Publishing, USA, ISBN 0-9645953-6-2)

Chapter 14

Ecological Humanism and Technology as an Enabler for a Better World

Alfonso Molina

Introduction

Technological visions are usually imaginative and exciting and open up realms of unheard of possibilities and frontiers where reality and fiction tend to blur and merge. Technological visions however are often devoid of soul and cast humans as secondary players in a historical plot inexorably unfolding towards the envisioned technological future. This chapter portrays a different vision, one that that highlights the potential for a much better world. The vision gives humanity the lead role in shaping an information and communication technology based knowledge society.

The Starting Point – Globalisation

Globalisation is the result of the content, directions and dynamics of many circumstances and processes that have shaped the development of society. These include the attitudes and preferences of individuals. At a higher level, they include elements such as the computerised working of the international financial system, and the increasing importance of knowledge, technology and networks in all spheres of life. Together they form a powerful force of societal development that makes globalisation the future, one that belongs to a historical continuum that has seen humanity drawing closer together, particularly over the past 300 years.

The knowledge society is stimulating the networking of people. It involves tangible and intangible elements and aspects, impacts, relationships and interactions on a global scale. This process of globalisation however, is not fulfilling its potential to generate a quantum leap forwards towards the development of a civilisation capable of growing and living in harmony with itself and with the planet. And the reason lies in the governance of globalisation, which is based on maximising power. This gives preference to certain global activities and developments over others. The result is that the potential of a *global village*, in which freedom, democracy, justice and peace reach global plenitude in harmony with the planet, is not fulfilled.

Globalisation is not a negative thing in itself. Rather it is the tribal aspects of globalisation that favour the powerful regions, nations, organisations and communities that is problematic. For many developing countries this has meant crises, unfair subsidies and protectionism against their main, largely agricultural, products.

Ecological and Humanistic Globalisation

The vision is of a better world in which social and planetary responsibility plays a significant role along with the globalisation of solidarity. In this vision, the 21st century will be a crossroad century. It will be a century in which humanity will have to change and pursue an effective and balanced globalisation. Multiple issues, often interacting, will have to be addressed. These include finance, production, trade, profits, power, responsibility, solidarity, goodwill, health, education, jobs, knowledge, culture, experience, etc.

Harmonious globalisation will help shift the evolution of societies towards sustainable development and the knowledge society for all. It entails the globalisation of the best of humanity for all people and the planet. It involves the globalisation of efforts to combat all evils. For this reason, it is preferable to call it ecological and humanistic globalisation. This provides the holistic perspective required for an effective move to sustainable development.

Ecological and humanistic globalisation is a shift in world-view and implies evolving towards governance and institutions that favour human and ecologically centred processes of development. In practice, it means less emphasis on maximising power, and more emphasis on social and planetary responsibility in the governance of individual and social behaviour.

The Challenges of Achieving Ecological and Humanistic Governance

The implementation of ecological and humanistic governance is a complex and difficult process and requires a holistic approach.

Holistic governance is more than just legislative rules. It is the whole collection of rules that condition and influences the behaviour of individuals, communities, organisations and societies. So governance is much closer to culture. It is something deeply ingrained and resilient to change without a strong and compelling reason, negative or positive.

Here lies the depth and extent of the difficulty for humanity to change. Ultimately, it is people that must change. Just like the transformation of a caterpillar into a butterfly brings about a new and more beautiful expression of the same creature, humans need to become different. And this difference is a focus on ecology and humanity.

Everyone who embraces the dream of a better society for all, has a pivotal role to play because, in the words of Gandhi, "we must become the change we want to see."

Making Dreams a Reality

The development of information and communication technologies and the knowledge society in the 21st century is giving rise to new concepts based on the use of the internet, such as electronic government, electronic democracy, and electronic citizenship. New forms of information and communication technology based organisations, decision-making, campaigning, communicating, interacting, etc. are also emerging. This is a great opportunity to advance towards ecological humanism and, particularly, towards a knowledge society for all. It is in times of challenges, opportunities, threats and changes, that humanity is often best positioned to undertake the deep soul-searching needed to find ways to work and progress towards a better world.

The key is to *place people and the planet at the centre of reflection and action.* There needs to be a sharing and joining of forces to build, in an innovative way, on the opportunities opened by the new technology and the many initiatives aimed at including people in internet based activities (such as electronic government, etc.).

The path forward may consist of people doing two contradictory actions, simultaneously!

One of these is to dream and aspire for a better world, for instance, in the form of a knowledge society for all. A world without poverty, that is free, just, democratic, transparent and peaceful and a society in which environment and people are at the centre of developments. The other thing that people need to do is to seek to advance the realisation of the dream in a practicable way, but in accordance with the magnitude of the challenges, difficulties and opportunities.

Many people across the world are implicitly pursuing dreams and practicable steps in their thought and actions. This force must be multiplied a thousand fold through many movements working for a better world. And in this vision, technology has a fundamental part to play.

The Fundamental Role of Technology

Often, technological visions are devoid of soul. In contrast, the vision described in this chapter gives humanity and the environment a central role and technology is placed at the service of people and the planet. Since this future is not guaranteed, the vision is simultaneously a goal and a challenge, which can be stated as:

> *To bring about a knowledge society for all, in which democracy, social and environmental responsibility, cultural diversity and achievement, transparency, justice and peace constitute the dominant governance of sustainable human and planetary development.*

No Escape from Making Hard Choices

The future of society and the world is not pre-determined. People can shape it, taking advantage of the opportunities and benefits brought about by new technologies. For this to happen, however, technological visions and developments must be infused with a soul. Ecology and humanism must be the *reason for existence.*

This means everyone has to make choices and journey towards ecological humanism governance and practice. It means embracing new values. Reductionism needs to be rejected, and the borders that separate people from one another and from the environment need to be removed. Life with all its contradictions has to be embraced, and enjoyment and enrichment achieved through cultural diversity and the simple fact of living together.

Scientists, technologists, researchers, and others engaged in envisioning and building technical infrastructures, processes, products, knowledge and environments, need to reflect on what they are doing. They should consider their constructions, and the social drives that are shaping them, and the legacy they are creating for future generations and the environment.

Difficult as this is within the established order, scientists, technologist, senior managers, leaders, and others have a degree of power and choice by virtue of their expertise and positions. This can be used to direct talents and efforts to generate knowledge, products, and processes that improve the lot of people and the environment and, ultimately, foster a society where intellect, actions and spirit are integrated in harmony.

Among the many processes already pointing in the direction of ecology and humanism are the United Nations Millennium Goals, Agenda 21, and the Universal Declaration of Human Rights. In technology development, there are already examples to draw on for inspiration. For instance, the environmental movement and the *appropriate technology* movement are very much epitomised in Schumacher's book *Small is Beautiful*. These movements have represented humanity's efforts to put people and the planet at the centre of technological development. Their impact has been significant, yet not enough to alter substantially the negative consequences of the established order. Technological advances offer new possibilities and opportunities to move forward to establish a new order in the 21st century.

Technology – Enabler of a Better World

Technology is creating completely new and intelligent utilities, media, communication, instruments and networking. As a result, new dimensions of activities, learning, working, transacting, innovating, designing, inventing, imagining, feeling, and so forth, are emerging on a global scale. This new environment based on a mixture of the computerised and the physical offers completely new places to undertake human and planetary activities and interactions.

This new environment will embrace everything, and everything will be its content: life and death, memories and dreams, space and time. This environment will encompass messages of the planet and space in a universe of new awareness, knowledge and, above all, new relationships, governance, behaviours and actions. The beginnings of this new universe are emerging and the 21st century is likely to witness its growth and global expansion. The seeds are in the rudiments of imaginative concepts, inventions and trials, as well as in that which people can be, but cannot yet become.

To place in perspective the socio-technical environments of the 21st century, three historical developments can be distinguished. These are deeply interrelated in their potential to enable increasingly significant societal transformations.

The first is the emergence and continued development of digital components, subsystems and systems. This started in earnest in the 20th century and will continue for a long time, feeding into the future.

The second is rise to predominance of networking of these components, subsystems and systems, primarily through the internet, leading to the emergence of new forms of economic, social, political, cultural expressions. This development is characterised by the migration of activities into a world of computerised data, referred to as cyberspace, and the discovery and learning of the most effective ways to exploit the new environments for a great variety of purposes. It is the beginning of a network environment, based on the internet, for such things as electronic commerce, electronic business, collaborative networking environments, electronic learning, etc. This is accompanied by new forms and expressions of community interactions, polling, advocacy and protest, and to a lesser extent, participatory politics. People can use the internet for communicating, discussing, debating, mobilising across the globe, and rapidly joining forces around crucial issues. People can participate in areas from which they have previously been excluded.

The experiences of protest and direct action web sites demonstrate the potential of networking and relationship environments in the world of computerised data. These not only bring people together with common interests, but beyond this, they provide a basis for monitoring, communicating, protesting, and stimulating actions that may stop or make it difficult for the established world order to continue unchallenged with its developments.

Most importantly, this networking has witnessed towards the end of the 1990s the birth of new forms of technological developments fundamentally based in changes of governance. These changes affect the ownership of intellectual property and, consequently, the established way in which business and profit are pursued.

This innovative and radical development is the *free and open-source software movement*, abbreviated to the term *open-source software movement* for ease of further reference. This has given rise to new electronic governance of creation, development, distribution, and diffusion of software. These developments point firmly towards ecological humanism.

The radical idea of the *open-source software movement* originated in the 1980s, and started with the development of computer operating system software. This type of computer program is what operates a computer, and enables other software such as word-processing to function. The most well known computer operating system is Microsoft Windows, but there are others.

The word *free* does not mean that the software is free in the sense that no fee is payable. *Free* means that there is freedom to do whatever people want to do with the software. This is not normally feasible. When people buy something like Microsoft Word, they do not buy the computer programming code on which it is based, nor are they allowed access to this code. They just acquire a license to use the programme. In contrast, the *open-source software movement* provides access to the original computer program code, and making modifications becomes possible.

This approach fundamentally challenges the *proprietary* way of doing business. The 1990s saw the full blossoming of the *open-source software movement*, particularly with the development of a new open-source computer operating system called Linux. This technical development enabled a great pulling together of many ingredients already available and truly released the energies of the *open-source software movement* to the point of threatening to alter profoundly the socio-economics of the software industry and with it all dimensions of the knowledge society.

The *open-source software movement* opens the possibility for the development of software capacities by many more individuals, organisations and regions, and consequently promises a much more widespread reach of benefits of the knowledge society than will ever be possible based on the predominant power-maximising governance. Most importantly, the *open-source software movement* has opened an avenue for a huge number of technologists, developers, and others to come together to release their creative social energies. These people are not driven by unbridled profit-maximisation, but by a much fuller set of human motives much more akin to the spirit of ecological humanism. These developments will be multiplied by many millions of people, as the third wave of technology-enabled purposive action-oriented environments begins to spread to all of society creating the tangible and intangible conditions for people to increasingly shape the 21st century.

Finally, the third historical development will take everything the component and networking developments have achieved and will shift this into an unprecedented scale of societal creation and trials, spreading the structured action-oriented environments and mixing computerised and physical ingredients and processes. This experimentation and societal learning will go well beyond the confines of business and other purposive organisations, for example, educational institutions. It will embrace the thus-far largely fragmented domains of the public and customers, creating, as never before, structured places for learning, innovating and changing the world with mixes of positive programmes of action, protest, cultural manifestations, etc. In these places people will create and find the instruments, processes, action and aggregate force to influence and change behaviour away from the established order towards ecological humanism.

This will be the essence of many *global movements* conceived as loosely co-ordinated social forces helping with innovations and transformations in targeted areas directly fostering the realisation of a knowledge society for all. There can be many such global movements and they can interact to form larger forces for innovation and change for a better world. These targeted movements can all be seen as expressions of a general ecological humanism movement focused on people and the planet. They all work towards the eradication of poverty and associated evils, the flourishing of justice and peace, and the sustainable development of human capacities for the benefit of all people and the environment.

One such movement can be focused on the human and ecologically centred development and implementation of information and communication technologies for all. It would make an important contribution to halving poverty by year 2015, and to eradicating it by year 2030. Ultimately it would advance the *knowledge society for all*, a society in which democracy, cultural diversity and achievement, transparency, inclusiveness, and justice and peace constitute the driving force of sustainable development.

Many new elements, concepts, tools, products and systems are emerging that will facilitate the rise, spread and synergies of different movements' action-oriented environments, particularly in the form of writing, publishing and communication tools, which are available to all through the *open-source software movement*. Witness for instance the rise of web logs, wireless internet access locations, community media, electronic advocacy web sites, and public community information and discussion web sites offering facilities for personal and community interaction with public authorities. These are all part of new technology-enabled processes and tendencies. They point towards the spread the accountability and transparency of decision-making and hence into new forms of democracy, even within environments dominated by the maximisation of power.

The 21st century will see the flourishing of these tendencies and developments, along with and enabled by, constantly increasing *intelligent interactivity* within and among the realms of devices, systems, people, life, the planet and space. It will see intelligent interactivity evolve to become increasingly powerful, with greater integration. This will happen as a direct result of the interaction among imaginative concepts, inventions and trials and the agonies of the crippled opportunities and developments of what people could be but are yet not able to be. And the worse circumstances become, as a result of the pursuit of maximising power, the stronger and more extensive will be the transforming force of the qualitative leap.

Clearly the direction and content of technological development will not remain untouched by this process. Just as governance that seeks the maximisation of power drives technological development in directions that support this goal, so it will be with new governance for purposive action-oriented physical and computerised environments for human and planetary development.

The new electronic governance of the *open-source software movement* provides a clear indication of this. The same dynamics will apply to technology, or technologists, developers, scientists, and others, driven by the need to generate solutions consistent with human and planetary development. These may include, new mass-customisable components such as highly accessible and affordable multilingual, terminals and screens that understand meaning; new ultra-low energy consumption devices accompanied by ultra-long-term energy batteries and systems; combined digital and genetic (*diginetics*) products for preventive vaccination or elimination of diseases; nanotechnology, involving the manipulation of individual atoms and molecules, for eliminating or reducing disability-based exclusion; new technologies for enhanced understanding of animal language and *knowledge* with a view to respecting their rights to the planet; new preventive *diginetic* anti-disaster packages to anticipate and deal with natural and human-made disasters such as droughts, earthquakes, pollution, etc.; new learning technologies and contents for multicultural communication, understanding and ultimately peace; new technologies and structured environments to facilitate enhanced democratic knowledge and opinion formation and participation in decision-making at all levels of the global society.

These types of technologies are all consistent with the drive by ecological and humanist governance. This governance itself however is likely to be both cause and effect of the structured action-oriented purposive physical and computerised environments with their enabling flows of activities, learning, working, transacting, innovating, designing, inventing, imagining, feeling, and so forth, on a global scale. For this reason, technologically enabled action-oriented environments will have a role as fundamental to the rise of ecological humanism as they do for the evils of maximisation of power.

Conclusions

The changes from seeking dominion over the earth and its inhabitants to ecology and humanism, supported by technology, may be the most dramatic socio-technical innovation of the 21st century. Everything else can be easily seen as part of this great play unfolding in the theatre of history. Thus far the music of this play, the leading lyrics of its singing, has been maximisation of power. The foundations of this world are changing, and it is largely in the hands of people to compose the new music and lyrics of a better world: the music and singing of ecological humanism in the 21st century!

Part V: The Distant Horizon

Chapter 15

Transport in 2030: 20,000 Leagues between Two Cities

David Jeffery

Introduction

Laura takes a journey between two cities in two different futures: one is optimistic and the other a potential nightmare. The first vision describes the optimistic future. This is based on a sustainable transport system consisting of shared non-polluting vehicles, improved vehicle safety, and satellite based guidance and information systems. The second vision describes a frustrating nightmare world: chronic congestion is the norm; information systems are autonomous and uncoordinated; the environment has been seriously damaged; and rapidly increasing travel costs have reduced accessibility and increased social exclusion.

The descriptions of these two visions for transport and travel in 2030 are each followed by explanations of how the different positions were reached. In each case some analysis of the issues raised is presented. The nightmare vision shows in particular, the possible consequences of not facing up to the issues and planning for them in a timely manner.

The Optimistic Vision

Laura got up early. Ahead of her is a drive from her home in the new town of Breslac on the outskirts of London, to Brussels for a meeting. Breslac-Enviropark, to give it its full name, was specially developed by planners in response to a competition for an environmental and sustainable community. The name Breslac was formed from the first letters of seven words: business; residential; education; shopping; leisure; and commercial. And these six different types of areas are co-located within the town so that all facilities were within easy reach and the need for travel is minimised.

When Laura needs to communicate outside Breslac, she normally uses videoconferencing, or travels by train. Cheap flights are a thing of the past: they now include the full environmental cost and are used only for intercontinental journeys, or where speed is essential, or by the very rich. But Laura's normal modes of communication are not appropriate in this case. She needs to demonstrate a new prototype three-dimensional body scanner. Although portable, and not large considering what it does, it is too bulky to carry easily on public transport. Also, she will be travelling with her colleague André. So she has decided it is best if they go to Brussels by car.

A cyber-car belonging to the *car-share club* has been reserved. Laura and her neighbours are all members of this club. It is a condition of living in Breslac-Enviropark that residents do not own their own cars, but share environmental and pedestrian friendly cars powered by hydrogen fuel cells. A fuel cell is an electrochemical device in which the energy of a chemical reaction is converted directly into electricity. Unlike a battery, a fuel cell does not run down or require recharging; it operates as long as the fuel, in this case hydrogen, is supplied continuously from outside the cell.

Her route, which will take her via her office in Breslac, and her expected journey time, were planned for her when she made the booking for the car over the internet. A parking place at her destination in Brussels was also reserved at the same time. She paid for the transport services with her personal electronic transactor or PET for short. This also recorded details of the transaction.

While eating breakfast, Laura receives a message on her PET, advising that she should leave by six o'clock if she wants to keep to time. A lorry has shed its load causing delays on the route from the office to the hub, and a diversion has been planned for her, which will add five minutes to the journey. She forwards the message to André and is relieved to get an almost instant confirmation that it has been received and read.

Her cyber-car is waiting outside her home, running in standby mode, having itself been forewarned of the earlier start, and automatically making its own way, using its satellite navigation system, from its garage to Laura's house. Approaching the vehicle, Laura is pleased to see that the car has been freshly cleaned, and that it is the latest model fitted with the new mood adaptive media system that automatically senses mood and creates the appropriate in-car environment of music, lighting, texture and scents.

Laura activates the authenticate control on her PET to confirm her credentials. The PET and the cyber-car automatically recognised one another and *pair* using wireless communication. The car door opens, Laura gets in and speaks to the car, telling it to proceed to the planned address in Brussels, going via her office first.

The car acknowledges, having automatically read her preference profile from the PET and adjusted the seating position and instrument display layout and lighting accordingly, and sets off, again driving automatically, using the satellite navigation system. This takes her at a safe speed on the *cyber-ways* used by the cyber-cars. She travels through the housing, shopping and educational areas of Breslac-Enviropark, to the business zone and her office. André is ready and waiting for her when the cyber-car arrives. Laura tells the car to proceed. It does so, still under automatic control, until it reaches the ring road around Breslac-Enviropark. It then pulls into a lay-by, stops, and asks her to take over.

Cyber-cars are equipped with sensors to detect and follow vehicles in front at a safe distance, but outside the areas equipped for cyber-cars, the infrastructure is not guaranteed to be of sufficient quality to ensure errors will not occur and accidents will not happen. So on these roads, the law still stipulates that the driver is responsible and must take control and drive the car on the rural and inter-urban roads, or until it joins a road-train at one of the designated hubs on the motorway network.

At the hub, the car again enters automatic mode using satellite navigation, and tells Laura it will take over. It communicates electronically with the hub to confirm the driver, booking details and destination, and is guided into a marshalling area. Here, without stopping, it joins with other vehicles, heading in the same direction, to form a platoon of vehicles. This platoon then rapidly accelerates to match and merge into the road-train, a continuous stream of vehicles already on the motorway, and moving at 150 kilometres an hour in the fast lane with gaps among vehicles of only a few centimetres!

At each junction, vehicles leave the road-train and exit from the motorway. Most of the gaps left by these vehicles are quickly closed, but some are left to allow vehicles at the next entry point to join the platoon. Laura stays on the motorway until the Folkestone exit, where her car then automatically feeds-off into a stream leading to the Channel Tunnel train. She passes through a marshalling yard and eventually the car parks itself on the train in the place reserved for it, again all automatically.

As soon as the train is loaded, it sets off to cross beneath the Channel. On the other side of the Channel, the car automatically disembarks and, as before, joins a road-train on the motorway from Sangat, and heads for Brussels.

André says, "It's a good job you booked the slot for this trip. It is very foggy near the coast, and while our road-train was unaffected, the traffic on the normal roads was stopping and starting and travelling very slowly because of the reduced visibility."

Laura needs to take over the driving when the car leaves the motorway at Brussels. And she has no problem following the instructions given by the in-car navigation system to arrive at the out-of-town business park and the car parking space reserved and paid for, all as part of the booking. She uses her PET at the entry gate to validate her identity. The car then enters automatic mode again and drives to the reserved parking place in the section of the car park especially reserved for cyber-cars. She arrives after three hours and 27 minutes, reasonably within the tolerance specified for the journey time and taking account of the extra time needed to avoid the unexpected problem at the beginning of her journey. Her colleagues are waiting for her to help unload her baggage.

Her presentation is well received, so well that she is promised a first sale if she shows her scanner to the Company's board of directors in Paris the next day. So Laura and André, along with their new found colleagues, walk to the nearby stop to take the cab-track, first to the hotel where she and André will check-in, and then to the restaurant area in the city centre.

On the way she notices that there are no private cars in the city at all, only cyber-cars and cyber-buses. The transport provided by cyber-cars, and the cyber-buses, which are larger with more seats, but otherwise essentially the same, is augmented by cyber-trams, which are larger still, but running much faster and mostly on overhead tracks to keep them segregated from pedestrians

Just as in her hometown, these cyber-ways need much less road width than conventional roads for vehicles driven by people. As a result, much of the old road width is unnecessary and has been turned into gardens, pedestrian ways and meeting areas. This in turn means that Brussels, and especially the main through ways and arteries, has become much greener and quieter.

All three types of cyber-vehicles are part of the Brussels integrated cab-track system. The cyber-cars and buses act as transport for individuals or groups having the same origins and destinations. The vehicles are brought together at stops and stations where, like the road-trains she had used on the inter-urban journey over to Brussels, they join up with the cyber-trams. These travel through the city like a light rapid transit and subsequently break apart again to distribute the individuals and groups to their specific destinations. People or groups can therefore summon individual cars or buses to pick them up at almost any location and take them to any other destination in the city. Others can use the core tram units just like a conventional light rapid transit or Metro system and get on and off at the various main stops or stations along the route.

It is André who first notices there are no lorries to be seen anywhere. As a result, Brussels is not only greener, but is particularly clean, quiet and pedestrian friendly. But Laura is puzzled about freight distribution. How is this achieved? Her colleagues point-out a number of green coloured cyber-vans that they say are utility vehicles. These are specifically used for collecting and distributing goods and waste. The system uses the old underground Metro system as the main arteries for moving freight into and out of the city, and further extensions, escalators and elevators have been constructed to support local collection and distribution, often directly into the larger buildings and stores. However, a good number of the small cyber-utility vehicles are still needed to collect and deliver post and goods locally at street level. The system is highly reliable.

Laura lets the wonderful Brussels freight logistics system transport her scanner to Paris in the morning, while she follows on the high-speed train and André returns home on the Channel Tunnel train, this time without a car.

Looking Back from 2030 – How was the Optimistic Vision Realised?

Travel for personal contact was, is, and always will be, important. But there was only limited space for building new roads and this was simply unable to accommodate the increasing demand for private transport by cars and freight vehicles.

The prediction in the early 2000s was for traffic to double within 25 years. This was a direct consequence of increasing personal wealth and the falling cost of vehicle ownership, which also encouraged bigger lorries and four-wheel-drive vehicles instead of the smaller vans and cars suited to urban areas. Congestion, delays, and accidents on urban roads, in residential areas, and on motorways were growing and were increasingly recognised as unacceptable, as was the accompanying pollution from emissions and noise, and the visual intrusion. At the same time, journey times were becoming increasingly unreliable and unpredictable

But people still wished to travel and young people still wanted to have cars and to drive when they reached 18 years of age. There was also pressure from motor manufacturers for this to continue, although there was a growing trend promoted by environmentalists, to share rather than own vehicles.

Methods were therefore sought to shift the balance between private and personal transport; to reduce accident risk and pollution; to minimise the need for driver control; to increase throughput and journey time reliability on the roads; and to provide vehicles as part of a collective public transport system. Simultaneously, there were significant thrusts worldwide to improve the environment and quality of life for citizens through the use of non-polluting electric vehicles and engineering for safety, particularly pedestrian safety.

Progress was greatly facilitated by developments, particularly in information and communication technologies, which included fixed and mobile broadband communications systems, as well as the geographical positioning systems and satellite navigation systems. Together, they enabled improved mobile communications systems and services that, on the one hand, enabled public transport operators to locate and better manage their vehicle fleets, and on the other, enabled travellers to learn about travel opportunities, including disruptions and delays, in real-time. For drivers, these developments provided improved navigation, guidance and emergency call systems based on precise knowledge of the vehicle's position. The developments also provided driving aids that enables vehicles to automatically follow a vehicle ahead at a safe distance, keep in lane, respond to a speed limit transmitted electronically from the roadside, and stop if an obstacle such as a pedestrian was detected. These systems and services essentially supported the *supply* side of transport. The same technologies were also being applied to develop systems for managing the *demand* side. These systems provided automatic fee collection and road use charging as a means to restrict demand, especially in cities and other environmentally sensitive areas and in some cases also to raise revenues to support improvements to public transport.

The challenge for politicians and decision-makers was to learn how best to exploit these developments as tools to help implement sustainable development and transport policies.

In the 30-year timeframe considered here, cyber-cars were ultimately developed for city use and as part of an integrated public transport system, while road-trains were developed for the inter-urban parts of journeys, together with PETs and car-free cities. But in practice, progress was slow. Not so much owing to the technology challenges, but more because of social features such as public acceptance of new technologies; the risks perceived by politicians in implementing them; and the legal and institutional barriers. All these had to be overcome through a gradual process before the public and politicians alike accepted, for example, driverless cyber-cars in pedestrian areas.

Cyber-cars

Cyber-cars, buses and trams were being investigated in the early 2000s. These have been developed into non-polluting electric vehicles, capable of fully automatic driving, that ply city-wide following a guidance system to run on-street and through pedestrian areas; cyber-ways. They can be summoned to a particular location, or picked up at collection points, and will drive automatically to a desired location, avoiding obstacles such as pedestrians on the way. They can, in principle, also operate nation-wide, and even internationally as in the scenario, provided that a *roaming agreement* is set up among different operators. They are shared vehicles and a form of public transport, but for individuals, families or small groups who are willing to pay the price; rather like taxis. If Laura did not need to take cumbersome baggage with her, and was not accompanied, she could have taken a cyber-car to the nearest main line railway station, and transferred to public transport for the inter-urban part of her journey. Instead, she chose to take the car all the way.

Future urban public transport systems probably will not need railway tracks, but will run on-street mostly sharing the space with pedestrians, except where segregation is needed for speed and safety. In the scenario, the cyber-cars support cyber-buses and cyber-trams in the Brussels cab-track integrated urban public transport system. The cyber-buses are presented as demand responsive collective public transport that run on the streets, but which can merge at specially constructed interchanges and stops with cyber-trams running mostly on a raised track. The trams provide the main means for mass transit, that is to say, providing fast, segregated travel between stops in and around the city for large numbers of passengers.

The cyber-car can be used more widely, for example, on inter-urban journeys, and in road-trains. They are strong, lightweight, non-polluting vehicles using hydrogen fuel cells for propulsion. They were developed in response to the need to pave the way towards a smooth transition from fossil fuels to renewable sources of energy for transport, and to reduce pollution including noise, exhaust emissions and visual intrusion. They incorporate vehicle sensors for pedestrian and headway protection, speed management, and lane keeping. They also have advanced mobile communications, including mobile internet and advanced in-car information, and navigation and guidance systems. The latter respond to precise knowledge of the vehicle's position and at the same time enable the vehicles themselves to report their progress through the network and any problems they encounter. Finally, cyber-cars have precision guidance technologies, based upon a satellite navigation system, which enable the cars to follow cyber-ways, that is to say, vehicle paths precisely delineated around and through pedestrian areas.

All the above features, in combination, enabled improvements in performance, information and service levels so that journey times and reliability were eventually guaranteed.

Road-trains

Road-trains were considered before 2000. They were developed initially to help manage inter-urban journeys on motorways. Vehicles are controlled automatically, so eliminating driver error and reducing accident risks; enabling higher speeds and improved journey time reliability. Throughput is also increased. Typically for long journeys, the number of vehicles increased by a factor of four or five from a level of about 1600 vehicles each hour for each lane. In addition, because the vehicles can automatically keep to a prescribed path, much more precisely than a driver can, lane widths and the amount of land used for roads have been reduced. Two lanes each way on the trans-European motorways have been converted for exclusive use by road-trains so far, leaving two lanes each way for conventional driving. But within a decade or so these too will be converted so that manually driven vehicles, with all the attendant problems of journey time unreliability and accidents, will be a thing of the past.

Road-trains are very popular. They release drivers from driving so they can read or do other tasks. Time slot booking was introduced, as with airlines, to regulate and meter the demand for access to the road-trains. This also helped to further improve control and the certainty of journey times.

There were significant problems to overcome when these complex systems were first introduced, for example, determining a vehicle's fitness, that is to say, the integrity of its systems for joining a road-train. Vehicles must have enough fuel to complete the trip, and they must be able to follow the vehicle in front and brake as quickly as the other vehicles in the train. There were also problems with joining and leaving road trains, and it is still necessary to provide dedicated running lanes to segregate them from other non-controlled traffic, and to separate cars and lorries. But the problems are all solvable, and progress was greatly assisted by the introduction of the cyber-car that conforms to international standards for the operation of the necessary systems. Especially important was the capability provided by Europe's satellite navigation systems that allow cyber-cars to identify cyber-ways and to follow them with centimetre accuracy.

Personal electronic transactor (PET)

The essential components had been developed by the early 2000s, but were not yet integrated to provide a PET. The PET is a device that integrates the mobile telephone with a personal digital assistant and a satellite navigation location system to provide a portable and mobile personal information, entertainment and communications centre. At its heart is a multi-purpose smart card that serves as an electronic identity tag, purse and ticket. It is consequently very personal to the owner and contains the owner's details and financial information. It is extremely valuable and requires very high security against loss, theft or fraud, and also means for regular, reliable and secure backing up. The latest devices use retina and speech recognition, as well as an encrypted phrase or password to obtain access.

The PET stores personal preferences, for example, it can remember meals and seating preferences for booking train, air and theatre tickets. It can also remember the preferred seat position for the cyber-car, and the internal layout and colours of the dashboard, and head-up displays.

Car-free cities

The concept of car-free cities was invented in the mid 1990s and was supported by developments such as pedestrian zones, park-and-ride, and road user charging as implemented in Oslo, Rome and London. But, car-free cities did not become feasible until new freight logistics, distribution, and waste management systems were developed so that deliveries by lorries using urban roads could be avoided. Underground distribution systems were used in a basic form by the British Post Office in London in the 1900s, and schemes along the lines of the one in Brussels, were suggested in the 1990s for Tokyo.

The Nightmare Vision

Laura got up early, even earlier than usual, for her drive to Brussels from her home in the suburbs of London for a meeting. She normally tries her utmost to avoid travelling anywhere, except for the twice-weekly commute into her office by car. This is a journey of only 10 kilometres. Cycling or walking is occasionally possible, though dangerous, but the preferred trip by car normally takes anywhere between one and one-and-a-half hours, and occasionally two; most of the time is spent stationery, trapped on congested roads. So she, and her colleagues in the car-share club, who take it in turns to drive their cars to the work zone, have to leave early to be certain of making an appointment. They enjoy the company of the workplace, but for the most part are content to forego this and telework from home for three days each week.

The commuter journey is bad enough, but on this occasion she needs to take her colleague André to Brussels with her to demonstrate a new piece of equipment. Knowing the problems, he has come to stay at her place the night before, with the equipment, so they can make an early start together.

Over dinner, they discuss the alternatives. Videoconferencing would have been best, but this would not enable them to demonstrate the machine's full capabilities. André would have liked to travel by air. The flights are cheap enough, relatively, but parking the car at the airport is prohibitively expensive since the European Union decided to make air travellers pay, through airport car park charges, the full cost of the pollution caused by aeroplanes. Laura would have liked to travel by train, but the trains are very expensive, and increasingly unreliable. The output from power plants supplying electricity to the railways is no longer certain, nor are the outputs from those producing the hydrogen fuel used by the latest vehicles. Fortunately, she does not have a hydrogen-fuelled car herself. She does not believe in them since, although the cars themselves were clean, the plants used to produce the hydrogen from natural gas are not. They generate carbon dioxide and so contribute directly to global warming and climate change.

One week ago she used her PET to plan the route to Brussels and to book a space on Channel Tunnel train. She had no choice but to book in advance. An old system, one that had been used in the latter part of the 20th century to try to reduce pollution in Athens by restricting traffic, is widely used across Europe. Only cars with even-number plates are allowed out on even-dates and cars with odd-number plates on odd-dates. Even with this system, it is still necessary to give at least five days' notice and to pay in advance the high tolls and taxes imposed upon all inter-urban car journeys, particularly international ones.

The route plan produced by her PET told her that she must set off at five o'clock. She can expect to get to Folkestone to join the Channel Tunnel train at nine o'clock, and have a reasonable chance of reaching the vicinity of Brussels by around noon. She has fixed the meeting for three o'clock to give them some flexibility in case of unforeseen problems.

They set off, but have not been long on the road when Laura's PET informs her there is a problem on the southern section of the M25 London orbital motorway. A tanker has overturned and spilled vegetable oil on the road. The congestion is so severe that the emergency services cannot get vehicles there to clean up the mess and the road will be closed for at least four hours. It will be necessary to follow a diversion around the northern section. As this is a longer route it will add about one hour to her journey, but she should be able to take a later train and still arrive in Brussels at about one o'clock.

Everybody else receives the same information, and the vast majority of traffic heading for the southern section of the M25 has also been routed around the north. Consequently, when Laura eventually reaches the northern area, she finds that the congestion is far worse than normal. She consults the PET, but it can offer nothing. All the roads around the closed section of the M25 quickly become grid-locked and this soon extends into London itself. Nothing is moving.

Sadly they telephone Brussels and cancel the meeting. They begin to look for an opportunity to get out of the mess and head for home. Eventually they arrive at their office two hours later, tired, but also relieved, for in the meantime, they have learnt from Laura's PET that there is fog near the coast in France. The resulting traffic chaos would have slowed their journey and they would not have got to meeting in Brussels by three o'clock. The net result of all this traffic congestion is that there is still no sale in prospect. A good part of the day has been wasted and the future of the company is still uncertain. With the economy deteriorating daily, and the transport system in a total mess, Laura thinks, "How on earth did we ever let conditions and the quality of life get this bad?"

Looking Back from 2030 – How Did the Nightmare come About?

The inertia of institutional and technological arrangements in the early 2000s and the selfish requirements of individuals and commerce had been allowed to triumph over common sense. At the turn of the millennium millions of lorry kilometres were driven every year across Europe, by companies in various Member States, exporting bottled water to one another; a product with virtually zero intrinsic value, where the cost is almost wholly in the packaging and transport. A triumph of marketing over sustainability! Cheap flights were allowed to proliferate; not only did the cost of the air travel become cheaper than the cost of getting to and from the airport, but the pollution and damage to the environment became significant. A triumph of institutional inertia over sustainability! Politicians also allowed traffic to grow to unsustainable levels in response to public demand. A triumph of selfishness over sustainability!

As a consequence traffic congestion is the norm. Average journey speeds in vehicles on the inter-urban motorways, as well as in the cities themselves, are in single figures. Industry estimates the costs of delays to business at trillions of euro each year, and growing. Moreover, these add to increased production costs, which are also driven by rising energy prices. The development of renewable energy sources is not given sufficient priority. As a result, nearly all energy has to be imported by the European Union, which must eventually lead to its economic decline, relative to the oil producing regions, in a growing global economic crisis.

Costs generally have skyrocketed because fossil fuel production peaked in 2020 and natural gas in 2025, so prices, on a barrel or equivalent basis, have increased at a much greater rate than the growth in gross domestic product. Meantime, the world continued to fool itself that it was tackling environmental problems by producing non-polluting electric vehicles powered by hydrogen fuel cells. It was not recognised however, that even by 2030, it would be unlikely that hydrogen would be produced using renewable energy sources. In the early 2000s, the most energy efficient method of production was by reforming natural gas, which is non-renewable. But the efficiency of this was lower than using internal combustion engines running directly on natural gas. So low pollution levels could be achieved at the local level, but not at a global level.

Furthermore, the security of natural gas supplies is not certain, especially as about 40% of reserves are located in the Middle East and 33% in Russia. As a consequence, in 2030, it is no longer economic or environmentally sound to run private transport using fuel oil, or to provide public transport systems using diesel, or to run electrified railways fed by traditional coal or oil powered electricity-generating stations. So, across the European Union, accessibility to transport is already reducing and social exclusion growing.

But the transport system had been running at the edge for many years. All modes of transport are overcrowded in the peak hours. There is no spare capacity and even small disruptions have disastrous consequences. Clever in-car information systems have been produced. These were developed by commercial organisations, for example, the motor manufacturers and telecommunications companies, but governments took no central responsibility so the systems are autonomous. All drivers receive the same advice when there are traffic incidents, and problems are simply moved from one place to another.

Furthermore, successive governments failed to take necessary and sufficient action for fear that they would upset their electorates. Actions were therefore only taken in response to catastrophic events, such as the grid locking of a large city for many hours. Responses were then too late and not proportionate to the scale of the problems. So, for example, congestion charging in London was the result, rather than a solution based on a total re-think of the way taxes should be recovered from transport users, and spent for their benefit.

Conclusions

There is still time to act, but if something is not done soon, it will be too late to apply the proportionate measures needed to clean up the planet. Then even more nightmares may follow. For example, travel may be subject to a carbon tax, or perhaps each individual, family or company may be allocated an amount of travel, in an effort to ration their use of fossil fuels. Travel for leisure may be constrained and eventually, perhaps, forbidden in favour of essential travel. Additional taxes may be imposed on work that is not based on teleworking. Multiple official authorisations may be necessary to prove that a journey is worth the full fuel and environmental cost. Virtual entertainment may become the norm and be conducted at home. Family units may grow because children are frightened that if they leave home they will not be able to get back to visit their parents.

There is hope the world will see sense before the above happens. There is also hope that work to impose benign influences through proportionate and timely measures will lead to a better quality and sustainable lifestyle for all citizens.

Chapter 16

Restarting the Evolutionary Drive

Roman Galar

Introduction

History almost always follows trends. Sometimes old trends vanish and new ones emerge. And the shape of history is decided in these rare and relatively short periods. When envisioning the next 20 years, will there be a continuation of existing trends, or is one of these crucial periods of change looming ahead?

The latter option should be seriously considered. The sudden and unexpected demise of the Soviet Union brought about a uni-polar power structure, something that many find unbearably offensive, and dispelled the most obvious reason for international co-operation. The emergence of large-scale suicidal terrorism fundamentally challenges the logic of the consumer society, which assumes that there is nothing worth dying for. A number of trends that people have taken for granted, are dissipating in absurdity.

As anthropologists maintain, it was in Neolithic times when the important change in the direction of human progress occurred. The shift was from self-perfecting to face the challenges of the natural world, toward erecting barriers separating humankind from the external. As everybody realises, this way of development has proved to be extremely successful and amazing achievements accumulated in the process. Yet, the resulting bliss produced some nasty side effects. It is dangerous that modern society acts like a sanctuary, where punishment for stupidity is suspended. Amassed wealth is used to cushion people from consequences of irresponsible behaviour and reckless lifestyles. Alas, these consequences are not so much dealt with, as delayed and appear in the form of environmental issues, degradation of social capital, etc. It is also dangerous that many decisions on everyday issues get transferred to contexts so huge and complex that human intelligence cannot cope with them any longer, and has to be replaced by relatively crude procedures. As a result, the regulatory feedback between individual choices and their longer term effects, which was the dominant element of progress, barely works.

The hopeful expectation is that a relatively mild correction to the way society functions is still possible, and in effect the evolutionary drive of civilisation will be restored. It is argued that the development and spread of information and communication technologies may be the enabling circumstance.

Troubles with Trends and Expectations

The formidable progress experienced over of the last two centuries was accompanied by a number of trends that shaped a number of expectations. These trends were persistent enough to breed the conviction that their role was causative rather than circumstantial and, as such, they had to be encouraged in their own right. The expectations were approached with such flair that they have assumed the status of certainties. This model has worked for some time, but it seems to be challenged by a number of developments.

Important among these is the challenge to the hegemony of procedural democracy by the erosion of its base. While possibly the best system of all, democracy demands one precondition: the majority has to be reasonable; otherwise politics turn into a formal spectacle. To this end people have to distinguish needs from desires and immediate gratification from fundamental values. Unfortunately, this postulate is in collision with the consumer economy that is built on compulsory shopping.

Another point is that the synergy of free market and free trade seems less obvious than typically assumed. There is a rarely mentioned disparity between these two freedoms. The free market, rather than free trade, was historically more Western European; taxing the flow of goods has spread wealth around and built diversity. Free trade, rather then free markets, was more Byzantine: it attracted wealth to the metropolis and promoted standardisation. In the globally trading world, the competition of global firms with small local providers usually amounts to a clash of giants and pygmies. This certainly damages the buds of intrinsic development.

Technological progress may also be losing its dynamism. The public is made to believe that such progress is in the best shape ever. Yet, there has been an evident slowdown in recent decades. Acclaimed priority research programs such as thermonuclear energy, cancer treatment, artificial computer-based intelligence, etc. have all defaulted on their initial promises. Great projects tend to produce gadgets. The avalanche of incremental improvements and combinations is coupled with the growing deficit of breakthrough innovations.

The idea of assured economic growth may turn out to have been an unjustifiable generalisation of 19th century and 20th century experiences. Historically, periods of development were usually separated by much longer periods of stagnation. When innovative deceleration sets in, demand falters and those with money soon have it all and the others are not creditworthy. The crash of the new economy that occurred in 2001 deserves this reflection. Information and communication technologies, which were supposed to propel the world into new era of growth, suddenly attained the status of a utility.

The fixation on incessantly increasing competitiveness may lead to stagnation. Competition is obviously indispensable for development but its debilitating excess is bad as it destroys adaptability. The ultimate competitive victory in some areas means the end of competition in those domains. The ensuing lack of diversity leads to extinction of the wild population of related innovative ideas. Competitive fixation hampers visionary thinking too: is there no better mission for Europe than chasing the United States?

It may turn out that globalisation is not such an irreversible process as advertised. Attempts to *globalise* the known world by making it subject to a uniform set of rules reverberates across the centuries. Allures of the *final order* are strong, and incremental efforts in this direction are usually successful. Yet, in the longer-term, such attempts have never succeeded and typically ended in disaster. Why? The answer may be illuminating for modern endeavours. Globalisation is clearly an indispensable medicine for a number of the world's ills, therefore it should be administered carefully and in adequate doses.

The idea of the state-of-law is clearly showing its limits. The removal of basic uncertainties of the human condition by straightforward legal regulations may look like a good idea, but only at the beginning. Later on, it often turns out that the implemented rules have substituted for social capital. The procedural stance, *what is not prohibited is allowed*, replaces decency. The ensuing erosion of no longer needed values leads to relativism. Atomised societies become engulfed in the deterministic chaos produced by the ever-increasing body of law.

The significance of formal education has also begun to dissolve. Education has proved to be the key to personal success and general advancement. Hence, much has been done to provide more of this good thing to more people. Unfortunately, the form has been mistakenly taken for the essence. Obligatory curricula reduce the amount of knowledge in circulation. Objective grading leads to domination of codified, that is to say, easily computerised knowledge, over *know-how* and *know-who*. Higher education is confused with a longer education and biological mechanisms of learning are ignored.

The great social shift toward multiculturalism and consumerism also produces its own dangers. Cultural clashes have a very bad record and governance of complex social structures is certainly very difficult. Therefore, the quest for the lowest common denominator of social relations is understandable. What was overlooked is the substantial difference between the tolerant and the permissive and between the possible and the viable. There is also a Faustian twist in the consumer model of life, since it demands immortality to be consistent. The developing demographic crisis is going to expose how far the biological cycle of life and death may be ignored, and lead to a re-evaluation of the fundamental ideas of the welfare state.

The prospect of sustainable development is also receding. For years already the conscience of the rich and the despair of the poor of this world were mollified by the myth of the final convergence in the sustainable economy. There is little factual evidence to support this optimism. Some declare that the first Club of Rome's report about the limits to growth was a failure. Yes, the predictions have not materialised, but in the 1970s nobody expected that the disparities would be so persistent; they were generally expected to fade away. It may be only now that the developing world will begin to seriously assault the environment in its efforts to copy the European road to prosperity.

The acclaimed pursuit of happiness may not be an end in itself, but the happiness that suffering people long for is not the same bliss that consumers expect. The meaning of the feeling of bliss is obvious; it is the currency used by biology to pay for evolutionary sensible behaviours. For this reason, it is physiologically impossible to be happy all the time and it is dangerous to trust these feelings in circumstances out of evolutionary context. Attempts to overcome these limitations produce behaviours that would have surprised the philosophers of The Enlightenment. People are increasingly trying to reach happiness using simple techniques of direct stimulation of the brain's pleasure centres.

Finally there is overwhelming optimism. The main actors in the modern world declare and demand optimism as the principal virtue. Is this a residue of religion after all transcendence got washed away? The demand for optimism seems strange in the supposedly rational societies, where both optimism and pessimism should be regarded as forms of misguided perceptions of reality. From the other side it agrees with the New Age presumption that the Universe exists to keep people amused. It is also very convenient in professional politics where well wishing is rarely punished.

There is no doubt that each trend and idea contested here is sensible, even essential, but to a degree and in the right conditions. When implemented autonomously, as aims in themselves, and pushed to excess, they tend to act disruptively and bring havoc to the world. There is a tendency to accept these trends as right and ultimately victorious because they show, or have been showing, a strong growth effect. Yet, strong growth is also a characteristic of a cancer.

Looking for a New Renaissance

In the late 19th century and the early part of the 20th century, two great Frenchmen created two captivating and conflicting visions.

In 1896 Pierre de Coubertin's efforts to bring sports to the forefront of public interest made him the first president of the International Olympic Committee. Pierre de Coubertin is reported to have said, "Why did I restore the Olympic Games? [...] For the glorification of the individual athlete, whose muscular activity is necessary for the community, and whose prowess is necessary for the maintenance of a general spirit of competition." These must have been the most harmless and refreshing intentions, followed soon by terrific success. Some might have been annoyed by another confession that he made, "For me sport was a religion [...] with religious sentiment." But these were delightful old times, when even intelligent people might have believe that traditional religions were obstacles in social development.

Just before World War One, Romain Rolland published *Colas Breugnon*. The novel deals with the essence of life as perceived by an imaginary woodcarver from renaissance Burgundy. The book is one that resonates deeply with readers. For many it depicts a life worth living. Existence was quite grim in many aspects; no protection from diseases, the elements, marauding armies, and dreadful family members. Nevertheless, it was a very human and sovereign existence. The hero goes cheerfully through the cycle of life, engages in a profession providing both bread and fulfilment, tries to keep a distance from *wolves and shepherds*, misses no opportunity for fun, and has no doubts when his real duties call.

The condition of Europe is, to a large extent, an outcome of civilisation choices made at times when these two visions emerged. In particular, the shift in perception of life's attainments seems very important. The change may be expressed metaphorically as the triumph of Baron de Coubertin over Colas Breugnon. The shift in perception was from the subjective *I know who I am*, so inescapable in relations with God and fellow human beings, to the objective *I am what the impartial criteria show me to be*, so handy in streamlining organisations of mass-societies.

The effects of this shift are obviously evident in the wars and revolutions that tormented Europe in the 20th century. The bloodshed seems to be largely contained, but the other consequences of the shift are emerging. There are changes in general aspirations, from deeds decent and honourable, to ones spectacular and profitable. There are changes in perspectives, from encompassing the whole of life to concentrating on the next challenge. Formal success has become the principal driver of reality. The pursuit of inner satisfaction has been substituted by the race for external trophies that are supposed to make people feel satisfied.

These substitutions are not working as expected. In a way that is already well understood, they hamper formation of social capital and collide with the higher motivation systems. In effect, the innovative drive of civilisation is stalling, and everyday life is becoming increasingly dull. And so, it is possible to wonder, a bit perversely, if the levels of dissatisfaction in many rich countries cannot be achieved much more cheaply, with smaller Gross Domestic Product and less environmental abuse.

It may well be that such evolution was unavoidable. Perhaps the already much extended, but still poorly educated societies with inadequate information technologies needed this primitive social glue to function. The point is that people have lived through the times when not only disastrous effects of the de Cubertin's way become obvious, but also technologies may soon allow co-operative sophistication big enough, to make the Breugnon's way a workable possibility again. In such a perspective the future may be seen as ripe for the coming of a new renaissance.

The Basic Presumption of the Hopeful Vision

The pendulum has gone too far toward appearances. The future may be shaped by its return toward the substance. To achieve this society needs to give up projects of social engineering, and unbind the adaptive mechanisms that will detect the right path of development.

The usual attitude is that progress and innovations are making the world more comfortable. Therefore people have no other choice but to withstand their detrimental effects on other values, and to adapt. There is a progressive fatalism in action when people are told, for example, that the more scary projects of genetic engineering will materialise, because progress is unstoppable. Undeniably, a great flexibility in this direction was demonstrated. Yet, somehow, it failed to make people happier. Thus, it may be time to start thinking the other way round, and to use technology to adapt the world to essential human needs. Public opinion has already made a precedent, limiting the exploitation of nuclear power stations. It is also necessary to realise that these needs may be different from wants. This distinction is very clear with children; they often crave for what may be harmful to them and detest what is beneficial, for example, fast food rather than wholesome meals, or violent videos rather than inspiring lectures. As for adults, in societies where lots of people intend to stay young for ever, reaching the legal drinking age becomes de-coupled from reaching maturity.

Reasonable and satisfactory social and technological arrangement cannot ignore human nature, as it was formed by biological and cultural evolution. For thousands of generations people lived in small groups as hunter-gatherers and this shaped human neurological and physiological design. Therefore, it is only natural that people tend to be instinctively intelligent in circumstances resembling these formative conditions. Alas, instincts tend to mislead, because conditions that have emerged in the last few generations are very different. This opens large fields of abuse, as when mass media lead people to some sentimental frenzy or clever politicians place themselves in the father's role. Peoples' brains still carry the old designs and their incompatibility with the modern environment produces failures and frustrating mismatches. The surges of feeling good, which people crave so much in their pursuit of happiness, still happen when human brains interpret the real or virtual circumstances in the terms of the hunter-gatherer's advantage.

The core of a sensible future lies in placing human actions in human contexts, and in spite of the dominating clichés this realisation is expanding. A system is needed that, at the same time, is anthropologically sensible, maintains vital cultural values, and displays adaptive dynamism. The trick is to bring social structures and progress closer to the human scale of interaction, where humans tend to be intelligent, and to do this without jeopardising the more global equilibria. This type of vision has to imply a fair degree of human idealism, which seems to be a necessary social ingredient if there is to be hope for the future.

The adaptive dynamism in question is tantamount to social implementation of evolutionary mechanisms. The interest is in a system that strives to identify and use new possibilities of development, via experimentation, selection and reproduction of improved solutions. To explain this jargon it is necessary to describe some details of evolutionary adaptation; especially as the prevalent understanding of what evolution is, is still poisoned by some absurd concepts like *fight for survival*.

A Detour into Evolutionary Adaptations

The belief that a prosperous future depends on continuing outflow of clever technological and social innovations is common. It is quite evident that societies unable to produce such an outflow, risk becoming marginal and tend to be targets rather then players in the globalisation game.

In this context it is annoying that so little unifying theory of innovative processes exists. Not for the lack of trying. There was historical determinism, based on extrapolation of trends, where projections of the human will were supposed to overcome all obstacles. All this culminated in the much-touted futurology of 1970s, memory of which is clearly an embarrassment. What are left are some opinion averaging procedures like the Delphi process and foresight. In the background there are more serious theories of scientific discovery of Popper and Kuhn. Alas, these are more concerned with the logic of breakthrough inventions and the sociology of supposed discoverers than with the mechanism of fundamental shifts. They shed little light on the possible innovative policies, especially as they are contrasted rather than integrated.

Without integrating concepts, practical experience conveys a very mixed message. Modern organisations have been able to quicken the development time of some innovations, for example, the atom bomb and integrated electronic circuits, but they have failed dismally to deliver in many other cases, for example, a vaccine for Acquired Immune Deficiency Syndrome (AIDS), or an effective computer-based language translation. While innovative improvements are turned out each day in unprecedented numbers, the deficit of breakthrough innovations seems also without precedent in the last two centuries. To add irony to these circumstances, when some inventions do happen, they still surprise the establishment, for example, the personal computer and the drug Viagra.

The determination to escape from the *innovation predicament* is most visible in the resolve of Europe to develop the knowledge economy. What has happened creates a mixed impression. From one side there are usual attempts to do better by focusing still more intensely on selection of research targets and the organisation of co-operation chains. On the other side an interesting body of evidence emerges, which challenges the measures undertaken showing that the matters are more complex than previously imagined. It turns out that the correlation between traditional indicators of research effort, such as patents, publications etc. and innovative effects, is dissipating. Serendipity is still the winner as the instigator, or idea factor, of profitable innovations. Successful innovative firms are still based on culture of co-operation or social capital, rather than on procedure.

In the absence of a reliable theory of progress, it is worth considering why Darwin's theory of evolution is not used as a source of inspirations in decisions about progress. After all, its explanatory powers, about development of species, are practically unchallenged, and the complexity of evolved solutions is yet to be matched by technology.

There are a number of plausible reasons. Some people feel repulsed by the *cruelty* of Darwinian forces; however the cliché of the *survival of the fittest* is plain absurd in the light of the intrinsic diversity of wild populations. Some think evolution is about genetics only, yet Darwin himself knew nothing about genes. Conrad Lorenz's guess was that the main influence is pride; refusal to admit that blind random forces may shape the world, and resolve to control destiny and everyday experience of getting what people strive for. The Darwinian ideas of modification and selection are prevalent in thinking about innovative policy, but these are modifications channelled in the clearly defined directions and selection of the best results only. What else may be done?

It is enough to experiment with an extremely simple model of Darwinian evolution embodied in a computer program, to notice its appropriateness. Simulations reveal a number of emergent properties that correspond not only to the obvious, but also to the paradoxical aspects of real life development.

In particular, simulations reveal that even if evolutionary mechanisms work all the time, with the same pace, the emerging evolution is clearly a two-phase process. The first is an active phase where evolution progresses in a burst of successive improvements correlated with directional and practically irreversible shifts of traits. The second is a latent phase where evolution stagnates in some quasi-equilibrium; irrespectively that each generation produces diverse solutions, no trend emerges and no permanent improvement occurs. The term *evolutionary development* is often substituted for *gradual development*. The simulated evolution exhibits typical revolutionary dynamics.

It is important to realise that the mode of evolution is not dictated by its mechanisms, but by the specifics of the problem it *solves*. To understand this concept, consider a terrain with hilltops separated by saddles (adaptive landscape). The active phase of evolution corresponds to successive generations of individuals moving up a hillside towards some peak. This happens owing to random mutations producing still new types of individuals and random selection, which reproduces fitter (that is to say, higher positioned) individuals more eagerly. The latent phase settles when the peak is reached. Its top can be regarded as a locally perfect type. Evolutions still tests the area around the peak, *trying* to find still fitter types, but there are no higher points close to the peak. The chance of further progress opens only when a series of mutations moves population through the saddle, leading to the slopes of some higher hill.

In evolution the waiting time for such saddle crossing can be enormous; also there are practically no symptoms when and where such a breakthrough may take place. Naturally, the evolutionary search for improvements is a largely random trial and error process without any intelligence involved. Can intelligent humans do better than evolution?

What can be done, assuming that individuals correspond to alternative solutions of some problem, and fitness corresponds to quality? The interest is in finding the best solutions quickly and cheaply. To this end two things may be attempted.

In the active phase it is possible to analyse the course of improvements, detect trends and concentrate search on the forefront of these trends. This certainly speeds up the active, uphill phase, but it is of no use in the latent phase, as there are no trends to follow. In both phases it is possible to improve the quality of results by intensifying selection. This produces very good effects, but only to a moment.

Spontaneous evolution is characterised by soft selection. This means that though the odds favour the better adapted, even the poorly adapted may have some offspring. In other words, even not so good solutions may become the base for subsequent improvements. Conscious intervention may turn soft selection into hard selection in such a way that only the best are allowed to have offspring. Introduction of hard selection is a literal application of the supposedly Darwinian rule that *only the best survives*. Such selection significantly improves the quality of population, but also drastically limits its deviance. In consequence it makes the saddle crossings virtually impossible. This is the poorly realised and most important ability of spontaneous evolution. Only systems with soft selection can move toward saddles and enter the opposite hillsides, that is to say, produce breakthrough improvements that open a whole new area of innovative explorations.

The problem is that hard selection and soft selection both have their advantages. Assume that quality defines competitiveness, then it is obvious that when two systems are at the same stage of development, the one with hard selection is bound to win, as it provides better solutions. It is less obvious that, if such victory is somehow delayed, the system with soft selection can make a successful saddle crossing, enter a higher stage of development and turn the odds in its favour.

In the light of this dichotomy, hard selection, tantamount to striving for perfection, is a recipe for winning all the battles but the final one. Soft selection, synonymous to free choice (but not chaotic choice!) is very fragile when confronted with pressures to squeeze profits from standardisation. Does this explain the innovative achievements of highly segmented Ancient Greece, Medieval Italy and other *free countries of free people*? May this be a reason behind the evangelically puzzling observations of the new science of knowledge management that *the one who never failed is a failure*?

Some Aspects of the Vision of a *Happier Europe*

It is impossible to build a vision on extrapolation of existing trends, since some of them cannot continue much longer. Yet, possible comprehensive social equilibrium, which may emerge after these trends expire, can be pondered. The elements of such vision are proposed below. They may be more optimistic than probable and they are certainly based on the assumption that the security fabric of the world will be successfully maintained.

First, controversies between proponents of globalisation and regionalisation, enthusiast of nation-states and supranational structures are thing of the past. There is a commonly shared conviction that human lives run simultaneously in a hierarchy of social platforms, from the family circle up to the global arena. People recognise that they owe a proper allegiance to all of them, but concentrate mostly on the closest ones.

Second, naive convictions of baby-boomers that everything may be reduced to a competitive striving for success were ruined by bitter experiences associated with their old age and the downfall of welfare nets. Market and democracy, both evolutionary processes of trial, error and soft selection, work well within the framework of consistent systems of values and well-defined rules of social stability.

Third, the fundamental paradox of modern societies: growing efficiency that does not diminish the workload was resolved. Technology is consequently applied to reduce the amount of work necessary to acquire adequate goods and services. Some superficial services have disappeared. Diverse soft strategies of job sharing are widely introduced.

Fourth, the sphere of freedom between paid work and paid leisure has been systematically extended and people are getting back their own lives. They realise themselves mostly in this sphere, filling it with voluntary activities. Education systems recondition people to this type of existence.

Finally, systematic failures of social engineering made public opinion averse to such projects. The top-down attempts directed toward happiness for anonymous masses are practically prohibited. Local development is mainly due to local efforts. The free market is deemed more important than free trade, and what results are soft preferences for the local actors. The causative loop between efforts and effects functions again and straightens attitudes.

199

This is a renaissance rather than a futuristic vision. The main reason for choosing just such setting of social interactions, as described, is that it creates environment where progress propelled by evolutionary innovation may thrive, as it was thriving in the renaissance. This conviction follows from experience with evolutionary processes, which points to several conditions helpful for emergence of breakthrough innovations and fast adaptations.

First, progress may be identified with effects of spontaneous substitution, with better solutions superseding the worse ones. Soft selection is synonymous to autonomic, decentralised processes of choice, which are the core mechanism of the free market and democracy. As in evolution there is no supervisor in these processes. Elimination of the top-down *dirigisme* will enhance emergence of innovative solutions.

Second, progress is impossible without the background of diversity. The permanent co-existence of alternative solutions is necessary to gauge the relative effectiveness of various approaches and to divine the proper direction of change. The multi-layered social construction will provide politicians on different levels with pre-tested ideas and patterns of actions that might be propagated around.

Third, innovative firms from Silicon Valley are characterised as small closely interacting groups with minimum of planning and hierarchy. This is not surprising as the ability to cross saddles fades quickly with the population size. Small communities are much better breeding grounds for breakthrough innovations than the huge formalised institutions

Fourth, a fair degree of segmentation and compartmentalisation is fundamental for innovating as it allows ideas to mature before they are exposed to competition. The innovative powerhouses of Ancient Greece, 19th century England, and in the latter decades of the 20th century, the United States, all enjoyed a relative detachment. Archipelago models of evolution show that a much faster progress can be expected if evolution of a big population is decomposed into a number of small populations that interact sporadically.

Finally, as there may be no discernible signs of when and where breakthrough innovations may happen, a lot of patience and initiative is needed to prolong processes that are not bringing immediate profits and to widely disperse innovative attempts. The research and development efforts need to be inspired through gambling and breeding ideas, rather than cost estimates and careful planning. All this is much easier for people with lots of free time then the ones that are hard pressed by schedules.

The Promise of Information and Communication Technologies

There is a chance that information and communication technologies will become the enabling element of the new renaissance. How could this happen? Some people may react angrily to the opinion that such technologies will serve as a vehicle to the past glories rather than to some future utopia. They can produce evidence of the completely new vistas opening, many of them virtual. Fortunately the new economy in no longer included.

The abandonment of the Colas Breugnon's world was initiated by the advent of the age of technology. The new technologies turned out to be irresistibly attractive, as they rapidly increased the spectrum of generally available goods and greatly improved living conditions. Yet, these were also very crude technologies, which, to function, had to transform deeply the mode of life of whole societies. People had to be concentrated in one place to run large complexes of primitive machinery. They had to be made strictly predictable and controllable to enable functioning of big, inflexible organisations. To this end they were conditioned to be inhumanly punctual and disciplined, and to ignore seasonal as well as their own biological rhythms. It was a mission of education to pre-program all with some standardised knowledge first, to provide a ground for the seamless transfer of commands and reports, and to feed everybody with some specialised knowledge next, to make them act as procedural robots. To vent frustrations resulting from such an artificial life, new forms of intensive mass-relaxation were invented and introduced.

And so it remained. Most people in the prosperous countries oscillate between working hard to make some money and spending money to buy some fun. They have become more the watchers of other people lives, mostly staged, than the actors in their own life. It is little surprising that only one in five people in the advanced nations answer "Yes" when asked, "Are you satisfied with your own life?" This compares badly with the Mexican proportion of two in three. A popular saying in the former Soviet Union was "You can live but you won't be eager to reproduce". Perhaps this is an explanation of the recent demographic trends?

Can information and communication technologies improve such circumstances? At first glance they are making it worse. They allow big organisations to become truly global, enable increased control over employees, facilitate brainwashing of consumers, and invade the privacy of peoples' homes with prefabricated entertainment. If the industrial revolution eliminated muscle power, what might the information revolution eliminate? Yet there are signs that in doing all this, information

201

and communication technologies will push circumstances over the saddle and new vistas of development will be opened.

For quite a few years machinery has been becoming more universal, more flexible, more robust, more user and environment friendly, and cheaper: all owing to embedded microprocessors. This has begun to close the gap between the costs of mass production and of individualised craftsmanship. Allowing for some snobbery directed at customised and local products, and some scares about movement of jobs abroad, the techno-economic base for a highly sophisticated and low-scale local production may emerge. As a result, traditional communities where people live and work together providing most of the goods and services they need may become feasible again.

Modern societies live in the yoke of procedures. In a world too big to be ruled by common sense, procedures are used as brain bypasses. Computers and web sites are the long awaited tools that make procedures all encompassing, omnipresent and perfect. Fortunately for civilisation, once a procedure is perfect, it can be completely taken over by computers. It means a collapse on the appropriate job market. With time whole branches of procedural services and administrative functions will evaporate. A big army of the newly unemployed will ooze out of these structures. The dominating career model will change. A shift in politics may be expected. The discretionary domains will grow in esteem and importance and pressures will intensify to delegate decisions down, where common sense still works and jobs may be saved.

With lots of educated and articulated people joining the ranks of the unemployed, the atmosphere around job sharing may reverse rapidly. The realisation will spread that only a small fraction of total working hours is needed to produce all that people want to buy. A number of clever ideas resulting in the downsizing of the workload may be expected. The three-hour workday may not come at once, but the problem of unemployment should fade away. The civilisation of people with more free time than they can waste watching television may be spectacular. This time may be spent on voluntary activities to solve problems that are not solvable by markets and administrations.

The promise of an environment filled with instantly accessible information radically changes the mission of education systems. With unlimited volumes of codified knowledge available at the click of the mouse, the market value of such knowledge has to collapse. This knowledge will provide work for computers rather than people. Tacit knowledge, almost forgotten in the world of objective criteria, will come to the forefront again, together with the traditional, master-apprentice relations. Culturing and developing social capital will replace efficient pre-programming for the job market.

Internet piracy is undercutting the economic roots of big media conglomerates. Since stopping this piracy will probably turn out to be impossible, the media industry will have to adopt the methods used by complex organisms to fight parasites; namely protection by diversification. Conditions should emerge for cheaper, more varied and, owing to information technologies, still highly attractive productions.

Omnipresent computer webs may soften territorial limitations imposed on small, closely knit communities, which are the best breeding grounds for creativity and innovation. With the development of smooth multimedia communications, the emergence of high social capital groups situated on networks may be expected, as well as their growing impact on public affairs.

Conclusions

The elements of the vision presented are based on the conviction that evolution offers a proper reference for all kinds of development. It is obvious that some aspects of development may be managed better than random evolutionary forces may do. Yet, when it comes to the principal drivers of development, to breakthrough inventions, innovations and discoveries, no better way is known. This is why evolutionary algorithms are making a career in computer optimisation, and markets and democracies tend to win with systems based on *specialists who know what is best.*

The reason is that attempts to base development on the sequence of the best choices at every stage end in traps; that is to say, circumstances that cannot be improved by any small change. This produces development stagnation, which cannot be broken without compromising on the quality of that already attained. This effect is also well known in computer optimisation as a principal obstacle in the search for global optima. Escape from such traps demands soft selection and parallel trials. The algorithmic trick is not the absence of competition, but a softened competition.

The basic dilemma about progress is a freedom versus perfection issue, embodied here as soft versus hard selection. Aristotle's *VII Book of Politics* contains a strange comment about playing music; it is not commendable to try to reach perfection, as it is proper for slaves rather than free people. Conditions enabling soft selection are as natural in the culture of Colas Breugnon as they are alien to the culture of de Coubertin. The Olympic notion is that the outreach of competition has to be global and that precision of winner's selection must be extreme. The winner is the winner, if only by milliseconds and millimetres. There is something within peoples' brains that make this so irresistible, not only in sports but also in public tenders. Colas Breugnon could not have cared less about such things.

In the longer-term, innovative dynamics will decide, sooner or later, that the renaissance culture with its network of high quality concentrations of social capital will return. But will it return to Europe? Remodelling Europe into a network of strongly integrated and loosely co-operating communities and regions may restore its earlier innovative drive. Technology is suddenly making this possible. In particular, information and communication technologies may turn out to be a tool liberating people from procedures and allowing them to live comfortable lives in relatively small worlds which are best for their intelligence and creativity. If only the *successful people* could be limited in their ambitions. It is known from the Ancient Greeks that *hubris*, that is to say, *arrogant pride*, is the greatest sin of all.

Chapter 17

The World as Computer

Walter Van de Velde

Introduction

"Restart the world. Click here." So reads an advertisement for broadband access by a leading Italian internet access provider. This suggests nothing less than that the world is a computer. It illustrates the basic argument of this chapter: not only is the computational perspective increasingly influencing the jargon of science and technology, but also publicity aimed at the general public. In addition the *status* of the computational perspective is changing. Initially a *research instrument* (like a notebook or a calculator), it has become an *epistemological* tool (modelling nature *as if* it is computation) and is taking on *ontological* ambitions (implying that nature *is* computational). This ontological stance is a cornerstone for the *convergence* among the nanosciences, the biological sciences, the information sciences and the cognitive sciences, commonly referred to as NBIC. The hypothesis that binds these together is, essentially, a computational one. If the basic building blocks of world, atoms, cells, neurones, and so on, can be understood as computational elements, then they can be made interchangeable and interoperable.

This convergence is, however, only a first episode in which humankind is learning the *engineering* skills to turn this convergence into material practice. This focuses on the smallest things, which, though still dauntingly complex, are easier to deal with in the reductionist scientific tradition. But these techniques will eventually produce their effects at the scale of everyday life experiences. Everything becomes programmable through such things as smart materials, brain-machine coupling, community technologies and global sensor networks. In contemporary research the computational approach is preparing for the final move, namely to absorb everything: small or large, living or not, natural or artificial. It aims to become *metaphysics*: a theory of life, the universe, and everything else.

These developments raise many questions. One is particularly worrying: is computer science ready to assume this role that is, willingly or not, bestowed on it? The answer is a clear *no*, which can be interpreted both as a *warning* against going along without reflection, and as an *opportunity* for a radical and long overdue re-invention of computer science.

The Computational Sciences

Computational approaches are creeping their way into the sciences. Biology, sociology, linguistics, physics, economics, astronomy, chemistry, philosophy, neuroscience, anthropology and just about every other scientific discipline have their *computational* branches. These branches have their own communities, their own conferences, and often their own journals.

They are prototypical products of cross-disciplinary work, typically driven by researchers in computing that cross over into another field, like biology or chemistry. At first theses researchers may have been looking for inspiration to advance their own computer science. Genetic programming, a well-established technique for *evolving* rather than for writing programs took its inspiration from genetic evolution. Autonomic computing, a more recent proposal for achieving complex systems that *grow* as needed, maintain and even repair themselves, also taps into ideas from biology and ecology.

Computing has become a *research instrument* for the other sciences. Of course, computing is sometimes essential to cope with the enormous amounts of data generated by experimental laboratories, like in bioinformatics. But a computational approach takes a more fundamental methodological stance: it *models* the systems under study. Computational biology, for instance, uses computational techniques to model certain aspects of living systems like their metabolism or their evolutionary mechanisms. It is as if a cell-biologist gets a new microscope that enables living cells to be viewed from a new perspective: a computational one.

The least thing that can be said about the computational approach is that it has strong seductive power. Maybe it is the swiftness by which computational models can be tested and updated? Perhaps it is the lower investment threshold of computers compared with laboratory equipment? Or maybe it is the lack of any formalism in certain disciplines that make these disciplines more eager to adopt formalisms from the outside? It may also be that computing is trendy, and this attracts funding? Deep Thought, the super-computer in Douglas Adams' *The Hitch-Hikers Guide to the Galaxy* seduces Majikthise and Vroomfondel, two philosophers, into a computational approach purely for the enormous amount of popular publicity for the whole area of philosophy in general that the computational approach would create. Whatever the reason, the computational branches tend to attract quickly, critical mass, and to earn respect as visitors with a message of hope for rapid progress.

The Changing Status of the Computational Approach

The notion of computational modelling is key to understanding the computational approach. A computational model represents systems under study as data structures that, when processed by algorithms, mimic in astonishing precision certain aspects of the behaviour of the real systems, be they molecules, cells, neurones, markets, societies, or cities. The representations that are manipulated are abstractions from the systems under study. This is not too different from the way in which the notion of mass in classical physics abstracts from the concrete physical shape or material of an object. Exactly by virtue of being abstractions, they approach more precisely the essence of these systems. They capture the properties on which faithful computational prediction of behaviour can be based. These *essential* properties reflect all that needs to be known about a system to understand it.

The computational models are, in other words, *epistemological* tools. They help to fix the conceptual and terminological foundations of a discipline. For example, genomics and proteomics researchers produce part lists of cells, but they fail to capture the higher levels of organisation or the processes that make the cell function. Notations that allow descriptions of the interactions among the parts and their coherence, the engine of life, are lacking. To fill this void, algorithmic notation is becoming the new mathematics, a universal language that can be used by scientists across disciplines to formulate, exchange, test and change ideas.

The computational method is at first a particular methodology of doing science, where experiments are being done, so to speak, in the virtual. Computational models are, however, more than a black box simulation, which for some reason or another (and usually a statistical or a mathematical one) is effectively predictive. The beauty of a computational approach is in the transparency of the box: the computational notations *are* the theory, the computational theory. Refining the model of a cell for instance is like focusing a microscope until the image comes out crisp and clear, and *fits* the data.

Computational modelling is like a Trojan horse: the computational models have the notions of computer science in their belly, waiting to come out. And they do. Words like *code, memory, computation, state* and *program* are used in describing the best understandings in science. Computational science views systems through the eyes of the information scientist, that is to say, as information processes that interact by information exchange, based on the programs that they contain. This goes beyond earlier approaches in the sciences, notably the mechanistic worldview that dominated science since Isaac Newton until the end of the 19th century, and in applied science probably much later than that. Mechanisms have no *program* that determines their behaviour. They consist of parts whose physical interactions determine the behaviour of the entire mechanism. Programs, on the other hand, are coding particular pathways of interaction that can be switched *on* or *off*, a formulation that is used almost identically in computational biology. Here it is not the physical laws of interaction that determine causal propagation of dynamics, but it is information. This information is encoded in some of the physical parts of the system, like in the genes of an organism, or in the spin of an electron.

Once it is seen that a computational theory is sufficiently precise and predictive, it is easily asserted that the system that it describes *is* computational: its behaviour *is* computation, based on codes and programs that *are* in the system. It is as if some brilliant engineer created them with the writings of eminent computer scientists such as Shannon, Turing or Von Neumann in mind. Thus a phase has begun where the computational approach has become an *ontological* hypothesis. Not only does it make sense to look at a molecule, a cell or brain *as if* they were computation, but it can be asserted that they *are* computation.

The implications of this ontological stance are far-reaching, and not just philosophical. If indeed the systems are computational, the notion of their program is not just a metaphorical way of putting things. It implies, no less, that it is possible, at least in principle, to manipulate them to effectively reprogram them. By doing so, their characteristics and behaviour can be changed, at least in principle, without touching their essence. A living cell can be manipulated to change its program, and it will still be a living cell. It is *only* a matter of understanding the program and learning how to change it.

Rodney Brooks, of the Computer Science Laboratory at the Massachusetts Institute of Technology said that "Soon we will be able to program living cells in the way we program computers". This quote illustrates well, how the computational approach is rapidly becoming the driver of practical convergence among the classical strands of science that deal with the basic building blocks of matter (the nanosciences), life (the biosciences) and intelligence (neuro- and cognitive sciences). From a reductionist perspective, this convergence is based on scaling down the objects of study to the molecular, atomic and sub-atomic scale. Since it can be argued that this reaches down to the level of the basic building blocks that are common to the natural sciences, the convergence is at least conceptually no surprise. The dream behind this convergence is simple. If it is possible to achieve an understanding of processes at the smallest scale, and if it possible to be able to manipulate matter at this scale, then it becomes feasible to manipulate the processes by changing their material basis. Everything can then be *engineered*. Developments in genetic modification and in nanotechnology leave no doubt that this is not just fantasy.

Thus, scaling down is one way of understanding this convergence, but much like the parts list of a cell it fails to capture the systemic properties of larger wholes. More than being based on scaling down to common building blocks, this convergence is based on recognising a form of equivalence, of inter-change and of interoperation that is essentially computational. Science and engineering are rapidly moving into a phase of *computational engineering* in a generalised sense: gradually the tools and techniques are being mastered that allow manipulation of the basic computational building blocks of reality, in their different *accidental* forms. Neurones, smart materials, computer microelectronic circuits: the difference does not matter as long as they are computationally equivalent and materially interchangeable or interoperable. The language of computation provides the inter-lingua, both conceptually (a scientific convergence) and practically (for convergent engineering).

This convergence, which is commonly referred to as NBIC (nano, biological, information, and cognitive), is preparing the tools for programming the world. It is a key enabler for another and more ambitious goal, not driven by scaling down, but by scaling upward, looking at systems at the scale of living experiences within natural and human constructed environments and societies. The unifying metaphor of this second convergence is also computational: it revolves around the notion of programmability. Computational engineering provides the tools for programming systems *at large*. This is the *world as computer*: the ultimate realisation of computer science as a metaphysical hypothesis. Metaphysics is the branch of philosophy that is concerned with the most fundamental nature of reality and existence. The hypothesis and credo of world as computer asserts that *all* is computation and that *all* is programmable.

Computing the Future

It is plausible that the computational approach is strongly applicable to physics, genetics, biology and neurology. Smaller building blocks allow for simpler computational models, and some of them already exist. It is less clear perhaps, how the computational approach may be applied to the inhabited world of the natural, biological, cultural, technical, and social system that people live in. Reference to *the world* thus not only includes the environment, but also the full system of a socio-technical inhabited space.

If the world is a computer then what does it compute? Consider this simple hypothesis: *The world is a type of computer that constantly computes its future.*

In its slogan-like formulation, the hypothesis leaves some room for interpretation, so it may help to say what is *not* meant by it. There is no intention to argue that humans and the environment are the *result* of some computation that essentially goes on outside these. This view has been considered a lot in science fiction literature and was widely popularised in the movie *The Matrix*. It is of little practical interest, however, because it puts programmability outside human control. The dream is not of programming *a* reality, but of programming *the* reality.

The world as computer is not about fundamental physics either. The famous physicist Richard Feynman, and later David Deutsch, have argued that quantum mechanics is the basis for a universal computer, capable of computing any realisable physical process. Though different, the world as computer has some resemblance to this work since what Feynman and Deutsch did to the Church-Turing principle (a basic principle about what is computation) may also be possible to do to the Physical Symbol System hypothesis (a basic hypothesis about what is intelligence), namely to give it a radical physical interpretation. This will be further elaborated upon later in the chapter.

Information as a Means to an End

It is obvious that the world as computer hypothesis stretches the notion of *computer* beyond its limits. Surely the world is not a computer, in the form that this is known. There is foremost a need to think about computing in new and different ways.

Computation traditionally deals with information as a product, not as a resource. Programs are executed to produce output from inputs. For example, five is the output obtained from the sum of the inputs two and three. The program is correct when the input and the output stand in a well-defined relation with each other (5=2+3). But what is the meaning of this five? What happens after the five has appeared on the screen? If a program calculates control of the brakes of a car, and the car crashes anyway, what does it mean to say that *the program is correct*? Any computer scientist will point out that there is a difference between verification of a program (checking that it is correct) and validation of a program (checking that it is the right program). These are very different things that belong to different technological cultures. What happens around the program is not considered part of hard-core computer science.

Nevertheless, information is never a goal in itself but only a means to an end. The *end* is action in the world. Information is useless if it is not used, ultimately, to influence something people do, or do not do, in the future. Information informs the future. To make this more concrete, consider the following example. Imagine a wearable or handheld computer, designed to provide assistance in a setting like a large professional fair. The device would provide its user with spoken pieces of advice about interesting things to do in the near future. For instance, at a given moment it may produce something like "an interesting demonstration is starting in five minutes in the Rockefeller room". It might achieve this based on what it *knows* about the conference programme, on what is feasible for the user to do, and on what the user is interested in. Based on this, and on its perception of the whereabouts and activity of the user, it might target the right advice at the right moment to the user.

The important thing about this advice is that it creates an expectation for future behaviour of the user, namely that the user will be going to the Rockefeller room in five minutes. Information shapes a spectrum of likely future behaviours, a distribution in space and time of biases toward particular actions and behaviours. This can be called a *behaviour landscape*. It is shaped by the continuing experiences of the user as the person is confronted with the stream of informational and material *informants* of the future.

The meaning of the phrase, *the world computes its future*, is that it provides at all times the elements that are used by its inhabitants to *see*, that is to say, experience, their behaviour landscapes that reflect the expectations of the future.

Computing, Design, Architecture

The notion of behaviour landscape is obviously related to the everyday notion of landscape. Urban planners and the architects also use spatial organisation as a means to an end, the end being to a large extent the same for information, namely to bias future action and behaviour. Walls function as obstacles that constrain movement, or that constrain perception. Streets and sidewalks are ways of organising traffic at different speeds. But the architectural impact on behaviour can also be subtler. Think of the different behaviour patterns that are induced by churches, hospitals, museums, courtrooms, classrooms, and so on.

It is clear that a lot more is going on in architecture than managing a system of physical obstacles. The role of symbols and affordance in architecture is crucial. Affordance, a term from industrial design, indicates a perceivable property of something that influences and indicates how it can be used. In a classical study from the 1970s on the signs along the Las Vegas strip, the architect Roberto Venturi and his students showed how architecture might shift into an extreme of becoming all sign. Around the same time another architect (by training) Christopher Alexander, started to make explicit a program concerned with the *occupational* dimensions of space. In his view, a hall, for instance, is not just a room with a particular physical shape and dimension, but it is also characterised by the typical encounters and flows of occupants that occur in it. Alexander captures this in the notion of pattern and pattern language, a high level algebra for architecture.

A behaviour landscape may be viewed as a superposition of patterns. As people occupy space and unfold activity in it, the potential for behaviour *collapses* into a single or a small set of patterns. These may be stable for a longer or for a shorter time, moving as well through moments of indecision and choice, more generally of tension among elements of context, such as space, activity, identity, information, and values, and elements of expectation.

This deviation into architecture shows that computer science has to expand its realm of study beyond computing boxes. Incidentally, the work of Alexander has had a strong impact on computer science, but not in the way suggested here. Computer science adopted the notion of design patterns as a methodology for designing programs. It has not changed the object of study that computer scientists are concerned with: the algorithmic input-output boxes.

Turning to another notion that is alien to traditional computer science, yet which is key to its practical impact. Attention is the oxygen of information. Without attention information is dead; with attention it influences action. Figuring out how to program attention mechanisms will be key to programming the world as computer. But again this type of programming is not new. The theories of perspective are essentially theories about how spaces are seen, about how points become related by lines of sight. Ever since they started to be understood they have been used as techniques to manage attention. Modern architecture has created its own ways of managing attention. For instance, a Le Corbusier villa near Lake Lausanne is separated from the lake by a wall with a window in it. It seems as if the wall, which normally obstructs the beautiful view, is there for the sole purpose of being able to make a window in it, thus framing the view and focusing attention on its most interesting part. It is an attention mechanism. The use of shapes and colours for aesthetic purposes can also be added as a key element in *programming* attention mechanisms.

Convergence between the Informational and the Material

The argument presented has been for a parallel between the material and the informational worlds. Design and architecture provide examples of changing the behaviour landscape; that is to say, biasing the probability of behaviour toward a particular act or activity. Information fits in the same category.

Information however is typically not viewed as an architectural element, but it should be. Architecture however is typically not viewed as an informational element, but it should be.

The elements that can be used in shaping behaviour landscapes are numerous and all of them can be considered in a unified framework for a new architecture and computer science. Both realms provide the means to shape the behaviour landscapes, thus to program the world as computer.

The opposition between computing and architecture is one illustration of the direction in which computer science will need to expand. A methodological approach is needed that unifies material and informational programming of spaces and places. It enables the convergence between the informational and material means as ways to *bias* the future.

Communicating objects will form the atmosphere of peoples' environments. They will be a key element for programming these environments, if their meaning can be understood. Take the simple example of an arrow hanging against the wall. First it is a physical object. But it is also a sign. The meaning is the emergent property of the behaviour patterns that are formed when the sign is acted upon. For instance, the differently coloured direction signs that are found along roads indicate different types of trips that can be followed: fastest, most scenic, etc.

Communicating objects have to be understood as artefacts that emit the signs that influence behaviours in particular ways. What is needed is a framework for analysis and programming languages that work in such terms, not in terms of input-output relations and symbol manipulations that have been the fertile playground for computing in the previous century.

Allan Newell and Herbert Simon, two pioneers in artificial computer-based intelligence, came up with the Physical Symbol System hypothesis to characterise intelligent systems as a restricted class of Turing machines. The Physical Symbol System is an architectural (in the computer science sense) specialisation of the Turing model. The use of the word *physical* is to emphasise the *monistic* spirit of the model; that is to say, *mind* arises from *body*. It is however still a model of some abstract computational entity, albeit one that can be physically realised. It is not, however, a model of physical processes. What Deutsch did to Turing and Church was to replace *computing* (the abstract thing), with *finitely realisable physical process* (a concrete thing). The proposal is to do the same trick to the Physical Symbol Systems.

The world as computer can be viewed as a radical re-interpretation of the *Physical Symbol Systems* hypothesis. The statement that *the world is a computer* pushes this hypothesis to its limits: the world is the *Physical Symbol System* par excellence. The symbols are forms that, by association and arbitrary selection, and probably not by intrinsic meaning, have acquired a cultural meaning in the sense that they bias behaviour, in a particular way, of anyone who pays attention to it. Having the means to do this provides the necessary and sufficient condition for intelligence.

The mistake made by Newell and Simon was to see intelligent systems as a restricted class of Turing machines. Instead, they should have viewed it as a different class of *larger* system, one that includes the environments in which intelligence manifests itself. This is in itself not a new idea either; it is the basis of years of work on nouvelle artificial computer-based intelligence, launched by Brooks and others in the late 1980s. But the consequences of this have not been investigated, neither has it lead to a radical new conceptualisation of what computing is all about.

Conclusions – Is a New Science of Computing Needed?

So, is the world a computer or not? And does it matter?

This chapter has tried to highlight the changing status of the computational approach, in the sciences but also in common speak. The hypothesis that everything is computing surely is not proven, but the point is that many disciplines seem to implicitly embrace it. Pushing this perspective to its ultimate realisation is, it may be said, the *non-explicit agenda* of the Western technological tradition. In the future everything will be programmable: cars, kitchens, furniture, workplaces, plants, human bodies and minds.

Programming the world is, in a real but hardly stated sense, the objective of ambient intelligence research. Ambient intelligence is a vision that places human beings at the centre of future development of the knowledge-based society and information and communication technologies. Computing devices will be embedded in many everyday objects and these technologies will be almost invisible to those who use them, and interfaces will be easy and natural to use. But these environments are also pro-active: they are at the service of users because they anticipate their needs. Do they not also co-determine the needs of the users? The boundary is indeed fuzzy.

Information and communication technologies are shaping an environment that detaches people increasingly from the *natural* environment of *animals*. This technology-driven self-domestication is not necessarily a bad thing. But information and communication technologies are not the empowerment of humankind that they are often taken to be. By the dominating role that the computational approach is starting to take, the options for a technological future become ever more narrow. Programmability typically means more freedom for the designer, but less for the user. It implies environments imposing norms that are embedded for once and for all into the technologies.

This is the warning that was mentioned in the introduction to this chapter. Science and technology is well on its way to invisibly push a model, the implications of which on society are worrying, at least; even more so because computer scientists are not equipped to deal with this. If this is to have any chance of social benefit, and a long-term sustainable impact, a new computer science is desperately needed. The practical relevance of Shannon's and Turing's work has become weakened by the higher levels of abstractions of computing, and even more so by the radically new uses of computers beyond functional number-crunching type of input-output boxes. Computer science applies well to the building blocks for ambient intelligence, for example to intelligent communicating objects, but it is near to useless for understanding intelligent ambiences as computational processes, let alone for understanding tightly integrated biotechnological entities and societies. It has also become weakened by the advent of quantum computing where basic assumptions about information need to be revisited. Computer science thus needs to expand both upward to the *social plane* and downwards to the *quantum plane*.

This exploration is thus also a manifesto for a new computer science, for restating the problems it should focus on, and for repositioning it among other disciplines. It is not the objective of this chapter to develop this new computer science. Others are contributing elements to this. For instance, when Rodney Brooks referred to programming cells, he also mentioned that something fundamental is missing in computing to understand the living. He is thus talking about a different type of programming after all. Another computer scientist, Steven Wolfram, has proposed a *new science*, also taking a computational approach to non-computational sciences. He too aims at redefining what computation is all about.

The purpose of this chapter is to stimulate thinking about computing in ways that are different from the traditional one. The computational model *is* shaping the pseudo-natural environments that humans choose to live in, or more usually, that someone chooses for them as part of education and culture, but which are hardly understood from a fundamental perspective. If computer science wants to face this responsibility, which it should, then it needs to enlarge its object of study to the full socio-technical system of inhabited spaces, embracing much more of other disciplines than it has in the past.

Chapter 18

Creating Meaning: The Future of Human Happiness

Liselotte Lyngsø and Anne Skare Nielsen

Introduction

Working as a futurist and innovator involves talking to those who are in the business of changing peoples' lives. Managers who want employees to work in different ways, civil servants who want citizens to change behaviour, marketing people who want to change the buying patterns of customers, and so on. One thing most of these people have in common is that they approach change in a very rational way. They try to inform people and to persuade them with good arguments. They provide more possibilities, more information, and more technology and think that this in itself drives people to change. But come to think of it, technology and rational thinking does not change anything. It is only when meaning is created, that something happens. And this is a very irrational process. The world is not changed by technology, but by the pursuit of happiness, of laziness, of life quality, and wellbeing.

This chapter addresses the nature of the future of human happiness, and how information technology can help create happiness. Happiness is something that is attainable, but it is subjective since no-one can define the happiness of someone else. Happiness is rarely individual, but usually social. Thus, happiness is not just technology, for example, talking a pill, or doing what individuals want to do, alone in a computerised version of reality. Happiness is difficult to achieve, but is it not the case that happiness is what life is all about?

Who Knows What Happiness Is?

"To see a world in a grain of sand,
And a heaven in a wild flower;
Hold infinity in the palm of your hand,
And eternity in an hour."
William Blake, Auguries of Innocence

"[…] happiness is the highest good, being a realisation and
perfect practice of virtue, which some can attain, while
others have little or none of it […]"
Aristotle

The Earth from Space

During the space race, when the United States and the Soviet Union were
competing for *space firsts*, great efforts were made to put windows in
spacecraft. Why are windows fitted to spacecraft? They are expensive and
potentially dangerous, and they must have caused many engineering
problems. But even so, engineers with their rational minds can see that it
is quite meaningful to have a window for an astronaut to look out of when
in space. And the astronauts kept the illusion of being in control of the
craft.

Dolly and Dolly

Dolly the sheep caused a commotion when it was born, even though the
cloning of animals was not new in 1997. It is somehow reassuring though
that the scientists named the sheep after Dolly Parton. The cloned cell
was taken from the breast of the donor sheep: scientists are, after all,
humans too, and Dolly was not just a technological product.

The Girl with Golden Horns

In 1639 a young Danish girl found an ancient golden horn in her field, and
gave it to the king, who wanted to give her a gift in return. The girl could
have had whatever her heart desired, and she asked for a red dress. Did it
make her happy? Probably yes. If you ask a person in modern times the
same question, will they know what they want? And will one thing make
them happy? Or will they just wonder about all the things they missed out

on for the rest of their lives? It is not a question of people acquiring what they want; it is a matter of them getting what other people have!
Mother with Child

Nappies have become advanced products, filled with technological innovations. Past generations had to wash nappies and everything else many times a day, but modern mothers and fathers are free to enjoy the happiness of parenting. But do they?

Meaningful Technology

"So, what do you do?" This must be one of the most frequently asked questions when meeting someone for the first time. From an inward perspective living as a human being in modern times is a very complex and multifaceted task, but from an outward perspective the question boils down to this: what do you do? To do is to be, and to have something to do, even when it is nothing, has become a human right. Without doing there is no being.

It is a grand paradox that so much of what people are doing, and have been throughout the centuries, has been undertaken with the purpose of doing less and less. Machines are built to eradicate the brutal and harsh conditions of bodily work. Computers have made rational calculations, administration and management easier and more efficient. And in the future, complicated technologies such as artificial computer-based intelligence and cloning will move into areas of creativity, intuition, and integrity; areas that are perceived as exclusively and uniquely human.

In the future people will be transported further into space. It will be possible to download entire libraries into the DNA (deoxyribonucleic acid) of bacteria, and organs and tissue will be cloned for spare body parts. Science and fiction will join hands as never before. And perhaps one of the biggest wild cards of the future will be a change in the perception of life itself, as life becomes an unending and exploitable resource. For most people it feels like science fiction when they learn that it is possible to grow plastic in fields, create medicine in cows, and to make steel from spiders.

God created humankind in his image, and gave people the gifts of reason and technology as a means to find happiness. And people have used technology to create machines in the image of the human body, brain, and emotions. But have people found happiness? Are they closer to happiness? Or is the technological quest for happiness turning out to be fools gold at the end of the rainbow?

219

When trying to predict the future of technology and humanity, it is important to note that the development of the two go hand-in-hand. Technology is part of humanity, as people are part of technology. It is like a window and a mirror combined. Through the window a picture of a particular possible future is seen, but when the perspective is changed, a reflection of the viewer is seen.

Four Types of Societies

The industrial society relied on hard working bodies. Strong people were needed who could take nature and turn it into value. It was the time of blue-collar workers, who Karl Marx, amongst others, placed on the top of the pedestal. And people made heavy machinery and the conveyer belt, which destroyed the joy of constructing and building things together in a team. Workers rebelled, sabotaging the machines because they were seen as challenging what it meant to be human.

The information society depended on humans as rational brains. White-collar workers, bending their backs over bureaucracy and administration, turned value into something measurable and comparable. Hardware and software were created to help manage an exploding amount of information. Workstations, processors, and mainframes were constructed to provide assistance, and in 1997 a supercomputer called *Deep Blue* defeated the world chess champion Kasparov, and the world asked if this made computers human.

In the dream society, a person is not just body, and not just brain, but also emotional, imaginative, and intuitive. Value is added when emotions are attached to products, by not just communicating to rational and logical needs, but also by persuading the emotional and individual cravings and desires. And thus, artificial computer-based intelligence is recreated in the new picture. Humanoid robots are built to take care of the elderly and as *pets* that can watch homes and children. Strange behaviour and emotions are studied on deserted islands and in confined spaces stripped of all technological improvements.

And in the future, the next possible step may be to see human versus machine, not just as body, not just as brain, and not just as emotions, but also as a complex and living design. People will be constructors of meaningful solutions, capable of working in teams, creating, giving, and building value with the help of all their creations. Human happiness then, will not just be shaped through bodily work, through rational calculations, or emotional outreach, but through innovation. Happiness will be actively created for, with, and by other humans.

The question is now: what part does information technology have to play in this? The answer is a fundamental one.

From Technological Products to Meaningful Solutions

Assuming that Karl Marx was right, then people will be happier and have more meaning in their lives when they feel ownership of process and end product, when they feel part of something bigger, which they can understand and influence. Value and meaning does not just drop from the sky, but needs effort, organisation, and co-operation to come into existence.

The conveyer belt messed this up, and in many ways people are still standing by, observing its pacifying movements. Much technology is not perceived as holistic or as unified solutions, but as results, products, detached from their story, their meaningfulness, and their human side. Just because something can be made, does not mean that people want it. And so people stand by and become increasingly confused by the continuous stream of unending possibilities, products, services and gadgets.

It seems that more choices just make people more stressed. The stress is so great that some people long to sit on a deserted island in an undeveloped country, stripped of all the welfare goods of modern life. No job, no telephone, no bills, and no routines: in such a place, they believe, they can be themselves.

Scarce resources are not possibilities anymore. Nor is information, channels of communication, products, or even basic satisfaction. What is lacking are the immaterial aspects of life like time, trust, peace of mind, energy, control, and seeing oneself as integrated into a bigger picture. This does not mean that people do not need information, products, and basic satisfaction. It just means that this is not enough. They are required, yet not sufficient elements of human happiness.

The Value Chain of Technology

The value chain of technology has been broken. Technology brings about products, but not necessarily meaningful solutions. The chain of technological value creation needs to be reassembled.

Technology gives rise to products that should present some solution to people, and this solution is, or has the potential to become, meaningful to its users. The technology can be microelectronics, the product a mobile telephone, and the solution is that people can

221

communicate more easily. But the meaning is what fascinates and attracts people; all the social micro processes of *connecting people,* like chit-chatting, or sending text messages, or gossiping about big and small events. Meaningfulness again inspires further innovation to change, adapt and create new technology, products, and solutions. Meaning is something people intuitively create while using products, thereby revealing shortcomings, inadequacies, and potentials for improvement.

As an example, the tin-can was invented in 1848. However, the can opener did not arrive until 88 years later! The tin-can was a technological product and the can opener a meaningful solution.

Another example is *in vitro* fertilisation. In 1975 the first baby conceived through this technique caused a great deal of controversy. It was a technology that most people did not like. However, this has become a normal thing, with about 5% of babies born in Europe being conceived using *in vitro* fertilisation. This was a development driven by the fundamental meaningfulness of having a baby, and there used to be only one way of getting there; now there are 17.

It is possible that aeroplane pilots may become obsolete in the future, as technological advances make it safer and more cost effective to leave most tasks to computers. But aeroplanes still need pilots, because people do not want to travel in aeroplanes that do not have a human in the front seat. The technology is there, but passengers are not ready to trust this high-technology solution. It is not meaningful to them. This feeling may of course change in the future.

Modern biotechnology holds unending technological possibilities, but is perceived as scary and threatening by many Europeans. But tell them that scientists have successfully created a plant that changes colour if the soil is contaminated with explosives, and it becomes much easier to understand and discuss the benefits and risks of modern technological breakthroughs.

Information technology has largely been driven by technological feasibility and the inventiveness of engineers to come up with new products. Information technology has been subjugated to the 80/20 rule: 80% of users only exploit 20% of what an information technology product delivers, because most users do not want to invest more of their time in cultivating a relationship with an unfriendly and time-consuming piece of software. On the positive side this means that information technology, with its presence everywhere in everyday life, has a huge potential to become more meaningful and so help in creating more happiness in the lives of Europeans.

So What Makes People Happy?

In the following sections, two future images, *happiness created* and *happiness deserved*, are sketched. These represent different approaches to technological enhanced happiness. What direction is society heading in? What future do people want?

Happiness Created

About five million new products are launched into the marketplace every year and the number is increasing exponentially. So why worry about happiness? All problems will be solved eventually. Just lean-back and wait to get served!

If people feel worn out, they can stay awake for three days and nights using the drug Modafinil. Are people unhappy about losing their hair, looks and slim figure? Effective drugs are in the process of being developed. The ultimate quick-fix is the new tablet nicknamed the *Barbie Pill*. It was developed as a drug against sun induced skin cancer, but the side effects turned out to be quite interesting. The *Barbie Pill* makes people happy, sun-tanned, virile, and they lose weight. Can anyone ask for more? Maybe to forget or lessen the agony of some of the bad things that happened in the past? Enter memory management drugs; drugs that can be used to enhance memory, or to blur it, or to completely wipe out recollections that are causing post-traumatic stress disorders.

The experts report that, in the future they will able to genetically slow down ageing and that people will live much longer. Even when it comes to travelling in time, scientists have not been able to prove that it is *not* possible. So if people regret something that they have done, it may be possible to get a second chance of making things right.

The only person who enjoys change is a wet baby. People are experiencing: an accelerating rate of change; mobility; undefined risks; and lack of control. Something is needed that can lessen the pains of change, put people back in the driving seat, and provide power over the surroundings.

So what can soften the big transitions that society is undergoing at an ever-increasing rate? Possibly intelligent software that can allow people to screen away the things that are not wanted, and to give priority to those that are. There are many possible examples. For instance, televisions that can remove or tailor adverts according to viewers' preferences. Just as important, intelligent software that enables people to pay attention to the lifestyle that they want. Perhaps mobile devices can be designed that can beep when the owner stands near a potential friend or lover, thus avoiding the need to waste time in crowded noisy bars. Finally, an emotional sensing product may appear. These may warn people when their mood is about to change for the worse and also offer ideas how to feel better.

Likewise, surroundings need to be less threatening. One way to achieve this is to disguise anything new with old familiar settings. Seamless language and culture translations can be provided when people cross borders. When apart, images of absent family members can be projected into rooms as holograms, and people can be reunited in new combinations of fantasy and reality almost better than being together. Intelligent homes can take on the appearance of rooms from another age. In circumstances where radical changes are occurring, the final solution may be offering the ability to forget: helping people to forget may help them not to perceive circumstances as a change, but rather as a new beginning. People make mistakes, and so perhaps ex-criminals may be given new identities and memories, so that they can start all over again.

Predictions about the future have repeatedly shown that it is necessary to think the unthinkable to envisage the nature of change that will come about. Notions of happiness will be transformed to entail feelings that are difficult to grasp in the early years of the 21st century.

In the future, a life exceeding the wildest imagination may be possible. Who would not welcome a product offering artificial silence or mood enhancement through smell, sound and feeling? Not least, the sensation of being loved?

So imagine this. Wars and elections will be won based on contests to produce the most happiness. Emotions will be enhanced like everything else; making life's stages more defined, like the seasons. Happiness is often described as the end point of a journey that terminates where it began. To be content in the moment, sometimes it is necessary to lose the moment. Computerised versions of reality can provide simulations of hazardous actions, or dreams becoming nightmares, so that it is possible to learn the consequences of walking down a different road. Having an affair, yelling at the boss or robbing a bank, can be played out as a simulation and perhaps give people an appreciation of what they already have. Some will romanticise about the new scarce resources, and dreadful times past when people where miserable and fought for survival. Staged crying sessions and uncontrolled sorrow may be perceived as the ultimate dare or luxury as people discover that it is during an emotional crisis that they feel alive.

Happiness Deserved

Loss of intimacy is being experienced as a result of the weakening of the ties of lifelong family and friendship and the increasing rate at which people change jobs, partners, hobbies and location. Individuals have become more fragmented in a buy and dispose society. People turn to experts instead of friends to solve their problems. They use and dispose of other people as partners, and they search for meaning through buying things and shifting jobs.

Happiness is worthless if it implies an egocentric goal of feeling and looking better than the rest. The pursuit of individual gratification has not moved people very far forward. Despite getting richer and healthier, happiness in Europe peaked in 1984. This may be because happiness is the result of a meaningful process, hard work, and most importantly, the right attitude towards oneself and the surroundings. Consumption does not make people deeply happy, but giving something to others and belonging to a community does: not as charity, but as the heartfelt joy of donating and sharing something.

A priest speaking at a conference told a story of a man who drove his sons to soccer every week, always trying to communicate with them, but never succeeding. One day the man decided to talk about the suffering he had experienced when playing soccer as a young child. He talked about the scoring charts on the changing room walls, the nervousness of not knowing if one would be the last choice for the team, etc. That made the boys talk about their own experiences and from that day on, they were no longer silent in the car.

The priest had experienced the same thing with a top manager who had been on a management course. He learned that good managers always employ people who are better than them. The manager followed the advice and as a result felt inferior and miserable because the middle managers he had employed were far better than he could ever hope to be. In the end, the manager was on the verge of resigning and confided this to the three middle managers: he gave something. The middle managers were shocked as they had worked increasingly harder because the manager had not seemed to notice them. And they all worked happily ever after.

So how can technological developments facilitate and strengthen the notion of giving and belonging to a community as means to obtain happiness? Banks can provide an example of what may be possible.

The financial industries have replaced many personal services with technology and banks are, for most people, the antithesis to happiness. Nevertheless, if any organisation is in the centre of peoples' lives as consumers, it is the banks. They have information on every transaction that people make. What if people, by their own will, joined a new service allowing them to compare their private budgets with those of others? What if people compared their telephone bills, travel expenses, pocket money consumption, etc., with those of like-minded people. Suddenly there will be endless possibilities for saving money, endless hours of curious comparison and funny insights. Questions like "is this normal?" or "can money be spent more wisely?" may form the basis of the service. It is bound to be an online community, where people can talk and assist one another in saving money.

There are web sites that provide similar facilities in healthcare. People can share knowledge and advice on sickness and health: something that is normally taboo-laden. Private knowledge is of course extremely meaningful, and therefore valuable for others. When these services were started they were expected to become sites where people could get professional medical advice and acquire basic information on products and technology. In practice, however, 95% of all activities are inter-people related, being discussions of practical solutions and experiences. This is where the meaningfulness resides.

Happiness is not just something that can be bought or eaten. Happiness comes as a product of time and effort. And it is a social phenomenon that requires interaction with other people.

Conclusions

When the telephone was invented, it was thought that it would be used for listening to operas. However, what people use telephones for is social contact. The sense of community, trust and meaning has become increasingly blurred and there is an increasing need for active involvement, giving and belonging. Even so, many technological products are launched into the marketplace with little or no regard to the notions of wellbeing and happiness. Developing technology with a meaning such as the creation of happiness will only come about if people become more conscious about *meaning*.

Why are there so few toys that help children to learn to live and to be a part of community? Children in earlier generations did not learn anything *but* how to live and be a part of society. Why are an increasing number of young people experiencing lack of self-confidence and even depression? Young people have always been the ones who have been ready to challenge life and to conquer the world! Why do people look down on their elders, when in the past elders were held in high regard because of their wisdom and life experience?

Perhaps these things have happened because life has become more fragmented and specialised. Children have become something distinct, as have elders, as have everybody else. People can no longer be of much help to one another directly. Everything is mediated through the machinery of society and markets. Value creation has been displaced from families and personal relations to systems and institutions. This is why teenagers cannot see a future role for themselves. Their experiences in school and family life do not show them how to be of any value for the greater good of society, or for their loved ones. They cannot see how to deserve such status. Therefore many of then have stopped caring.

To create more happiness, people need to be reintegrated with society's systems for value creation. There is a need to find ways to involve children in work life when they learn and go to school, and also to find ways to do the opposite. People need to find ways to connect, to help one another, and to create value together in more direct ways than through anonymous markets and public institutions.

Information technology can help with this. If information technology systems are rethought in more open and value oriented ways, they can help children to approach their schoolwork in realistic settings. People and organisations can be allowed to give children some meaningful tasks to handle in school. And the children can organise their work with reality in mind. They can discuss things with one another, or with experts, using communication technologies. They can handle tasks and commitments with project management systems. They can share knowledge and build on one another's findings using state-of-the art knowledge management systems. Why create an artificial learning environment in schools, when reality has so much to offer?

Information technology can help society organise and use these many new interactions. Elders can offer advice, be involved and help. Specialists can lend a hand to non-specialists and vice versa. Education can be meaningful. And even banking can become fun. Information technology systems can help people reconnect, build trust, and participate in value creation, if information technology designers and system engineers begin to think beyond the *personal* computer; by thinking about: the *family* computer; the *community* computer; and the *friendship* computer.

In a complex world there is always the risk of losing control and producing unintended consequences. If information technology can be developed to allow people to stay ahead of society's creations, and themselves, and to see actions in a bigger picture, then society will certainly take a big step towards achieving a more meaningful and happier existence. The grand paradox though, is that nobody can define what should be meaningful to others. And a new ideology is not required to justify peoples' actions. The shortcoming of an ideology is exactly that it can excuse today's bad deeds, while it promises happiness tomorrow. There is no perfect knowledge of what makes people happy, and there probably will never be, so there is a need to always be in touch with the place where meaning is created: their reality. And modern information technology provides the perfect means to be just there. Not as an all seeing Big Brother, but as a friend fostering relationships and building bonds between users and producers, between society and citizens, between the real and the ideal. Rather than looking for a single headline ground-breaking new invention, or a quick-fix technology, it may be better to look at happiness as something that is actively being created all around, as an inspiration to everyone to create meaningful solutions with technological products.

A desired future cannot be created by just wishing for it strongly enough. It requires decisions: today. It entails risks: today. It demands actions: today. May everyone have much luck and happiness creating the future: together!

Acknowledgements

Liselotte Lyngsø is grateful to The Global Future Forum for sponsoring her to write this chapter.

Author Biographies and Contact Details

Laurent Beslay
Laurent Beslay works as technology adviser, at the European Data Protection Supervisor, Brussels. He holds a Post-master's degree (DESS) in Global Management of Technological Risks and Crisis (University of Paris, la Sorbonne) and a Master's degree in International Relations. He previously worked, for six years, in the Joint Research Centre of the European Commission (Institute for Prospective Technological Studies) as a project officer in the field of cybersecurity.

Contact Details:
European Data Protection Supervisor
60 rue Wiertz , 1047 Brussels , Belgium
Email: laurent.beslay@edps.europa.eu

Marc Bogdanowicz
Senior researcher at the European Commission's Joint Research Centre, Institute for Prospective Technological Studies. He leads a small research team specialising in the study of the relation between socio-economic and technological developments, under globalisation trends. Marc Bogdanowicz graduated in Educational Sciences and holds postgraduate diplomas in Social Psychology and in Organisational Sciences of the State University of Liège. He has published numerous papers and articles in the field of the information society and its socio-economic impacts.

Contact Details:
Institute for Prospective Technological Studies,
DG JRC, European Commission
c/ Inca Garcilaso, Isla de la Cartuja s/n
41092 Sevilla, Spain

Brahim Dahmani
Brahim Dahmani received a PhD in Electronics, Instrumentation and Metrology from Paris VI University in 1981. He worked as scientist in the French National Bureau of Time and Frequency Standards and joined Corning International Science and Technology Organisation in 1989 where he was in charge of identification and development of new growth businesses as external technology project manager. He launched numerous pioneering activities in microsystems and smart materials and actively participated in the strategic development of display activities within

Corning. In 2004 he set-up his own business, Lovalite, a micro optics company.

Contact Details:
Lovalite SAS
10 rue Auguste Rodin, 10440 la Riviére de Corps, France
Email: dahmanib@lovalite.com

André Dittmar

Director of Department of Biomedical Micro Sensors and Micro Systems of the CNRS of the INSA of Lyon (France). He is active in the research fields of micro, non invasive sensors for the Thermo-Neuro-MicroVascular parameters of the human body and microtechnologies in BME, and the study of vigilance, emotional response, mental workload and thermal comfort in man for local metabolism, microcirculation. He is a member of the World Academy of Biomedical Technologies UNESCO. He is also active in bio-inspired researches for the biomedical field.

Contact Details:
UMR 5511 LPM CNRS INSA Lyon
Bâtiment Léonard de Vinci, 21 avenue Jean Capelle
69 621 Villeurbanne Cedex FRANCE
Email: dittmar@univ-lyon1.fr

Roman Galar

Professor at the Institute of Computer Engineering, Control and Robotics, Wroclaw University of Technology. Starting from optimisation algorithms in 1970s, he moved to evolutionary simulations. His particular concern is with underlying dynamics of rapid adaptive shifts, which can be interpreted as breakthrough innovations or paradigm changes. He uses such computer-substantiated perspective in texts on the knowledge economy, innovative and education politics, cultural dynamics, etc. He is a co-author of the strategies of development for the city of Wroclaw and the region of Lower Silesia.

Contact Details:
Wroclaw University of Technology
Damrota 43/16, 50-306 Wroclaw, Poland
Email: rbg@kn.pl

Hannu Hakala

Director of Embedded Computing in Elektrobit Ltd. Previously he worked at VTT (Technical Research Centre of Finland) on mobile system development tools, embedded solutions, and automotive telematics. Prior to this he worked at Nokia on: in-car information systems, car audio systems and telematics solutions, wireless value-added service applications, and positioning technologies for mobile telephones.

Contact Details:
Elektrobit Ltd.
Kihlmanninraitti 1, 33100 Tampere, Finland

David Jeffery

David Jeffery BSc, CEng, MIEE, Minstp, FIHT, FRSA, is an electrical engineer with 40 years' experience in a wide range of transport-related matters, and a specialist in intelligent transport systems and services. Until he retired he was managing director of Atkins Transport Systems. He is now an independent consultant and visiting professor at the University of Southampton's Transportation Research Group.

Contact Details:
15 St Lukes Drive, Teignmouth,
Devon, TQ14 9GY, UK
Email: dj.jeffery@btopenworld.com

Paul T Kidd

Dr Paul T Kidd is a control systems engineer who has pursued a dual career, one in manufacturing research and the other in writing. As a researcher he works in the field of manufacturing foresight, futures, visions and research policy, and is involved in European and international research programmes. As part of his research he has been involved in human-centred manufacturing and associated skill-based technologies. In parallel with this he developed expertise in future generation manufacturing enterprises. He is also interested in new technologies that have the potential to enable sustainable business practices. His long-term goal is to contribute towards the development of a non-fossil fuel dependent manufacturing industry. As an author he writes about new technologies and the important related wider non-technical issues.

Contact Details:
Tamworth House
Macclesfield, SK11 8UP, No 4, United Kingdom
Email: paulkidd@cheshirehenbury.com

Kazimierz Krzysztofek

Kazimierz Krzysztofek's areas of research include: sociology of media, internet and international communication, human development, impact of information and communication technologies on arts and society, and cultural industries. During 1997-2000 he was member of the board of CIRCLE (European network of culture research and information centres). He is professor of sociology at the University of Bialystok and Warsaw School of Advanced Social Psychology, and a member of the Polish Academy of Science Committee for Forecasting *Poland 2000Plus*. In the late 1980s he was a Fulbright scholar at the Massachusetts Institute of Technology, and in 1996 a visiting professor at the Pennsylvania State University.

Contact Details:
Wandy 16/28, 03 949 Warszawa, Poland
Email: k.krzysztofek@chello.pl

Marc Luyckx Ghisi

Born in 1942, married to Isabelle, with six children. Studied Mathematics, Philosophy and Theology (PhD). From 1990-99 Marc worked directly for Presidents of the European Commission, firstly Jacques Delors and then Jacques Santer, as a member of the Forward Studies Unit, the internal *think tank* of the European Commission in Brussels. He is now dean of CBA Business School in Zagreb Croatia; a Member of the Auroville International Advisory Council, near Pondichery, South India; and a Member of the Eco-Cities Project, in China, Brazil and other countries.

Contact Details:
Sparrenweg, 10
B 3051 Sint Joris Weert, Belgium
Email: marcluy@scarlet.be

Liselotte Lyngsø

Liselotte Lyngsø is Managing Partner of the innovation and futurist company, Future Navigator. Prior to this she was Director at Fahrenheit 212, an ideas company owned by Saatchi. For eight years she worked as Director of Research at the Copenhagen Institute for Futures Studies. Since 2002 she has been a member of the Foresight editorial board, a board member at Bolius A/S, and part of the Vallekilde Globalisation Team. Liselotte works extensively with scenarios for the future consumer and co-worker, and with the consequences of new technologies on the way people think, feel and behave. Born in Denmark, she has a MPhil in Economics and Politics from St. Antony's College, Oxford University.

Contact Details:
Future Navigator
Prags boulevard 47, 2300 Copenhagen S, Denmark
Email: lll@futurenavigator.dk

José del R. Millán

Dr José del R. Millán is a senior researcher at the IDIAP Research Institute in Martigny, Switzerland, where he explores the use of brain signals for multimodal interaction and, in particular, the development of non-invasive brain-controlled robots and neuroprostheses. He is also an adjunct professor at the Swiss Federal Institute of Technology in Lausanne (EPFL). Prior to joining IDIAP, he was a research scientist at the European Commission's Joint Research Centre in Ispra, Italy, and a visiting scholar at Stanford University. His research on brain-computer interfaces was nominated finalist of the European Descartes Prize 2004. He was named Research Leader 2004 by the journal Scientific American, and the journal Science has reviewed his work as one of the world's key researchers in the field of brain-computer interfaces.

Contact Details:
IDIAP Research Institute
Rue du Simplon 4, 1920 Martigny. Switzerland
Email: jose.millan@idiap.ch

Alfonso Molina

Alfonso Molina is Professor of Technology Strategy at the University of Edinburgh in the United Kingdom and Scientific Director of the Fondazione Mondo Digitale in Italy. His research interests focus on theories of innovation and technology management and strategy, particularly on the *socio-technical constituencies* approach, currently applied to research on sustainable enterprises for electronic inclusion, information and communications technologies based educational innovation and free(libre) and open-source software (FLOSS). Alfonso has worked as an advisor and consultant for various Directorates of the European Commission and has published numerous books, papers and reports. He also designed a web site (www.e-inclusionsite.org) to contribute to the global e-inclusion movement and to raise funding for grassroots e-inclusion projects in poor areas of the world.

Contact Details:
Fondazione Mondo Digitale
Via Umbria 7, 00187 Rome, Italy

Roberto Saracco

Roberto Saracco, has 35 years research experience at the Telecom Italia Lab, where he has been involved in the various stages of the digitalisation of telecommunications. He is responsible for the understanding of the economic impact of technological evolution within Telecom Italia. He has led the World Bank FORWARD project in Latin America to foster the information society and stimulate business initiatives and has been involved in many activities of the European Union, included the Visionary Groups where he chaired the one on Super Intelligent Networks. He is a Senior Member of IEEE and Director of Comsoc for Sister Societies.

Contact Details:
Telecom Italia
Via Reiss Romoli 274, 10148 Turin, Italy
Email: roberto.saracco@telecomitalia.it

Anne Skare Nielsen

Anne Skare Nielsen is Managing Partner of the innovation and futurist company Future Navigator. By education she is a biologist with Master's degree in political science from Copenhagen University. Anne specialises in leadership, new value creation through customer insight, ethics and new technologies, as well as education and the future labour market. She regularly works with large international corporations. Anne is a member of the Danish Ethical Council, The Danish Ministry of Science Technology and Innovation's information and communications technologies forum, the Global Future Forum, and Strategy Lab. Anne has worked with futurology and innovation at the Copenhagen Institute for Futures Studies and as Director at Fahrenheit 212.

Contact Details:
Future Navigator
Prags boulevard 47, 2300 Copenhagen S, Denmark
Email: asn@futurenavigator.dk

Ignace Snellen

Emeritius professor of Public Administration at Erasmus University, Rotterdam. For the last 20 years he has specialised in the implications of information and communication technology applications in public administration. He has published several books on the subject and supervised many dissertations on the different aspects of informatisation. His main contention is that information and communication technologies are facilitating and furthering basic changes in all dimensions of the Executive, Legislature and Judiciary of (post) modern countries.

Contact Details:
Erasmus University Rotterdam
Jagerstraat 14, 2514BZ Den Haag The Netherlands
Email: snellen@fsw.eur.nl

Walter Van de Velde

Dr Walter Van de Velde approaches topics like wearable computing, context-aware systems and intelligent environments from a wide interdisciplinary perspective that includes interests in architecture, social science and anthropology. He was formerly co-director of the Artificial Intelligence Laboratory of Brussel's Free University (VUB) and Science Director of Starlab, a private research company that pioneered a new model of long-term research. Apart from being a guest professor at VUB he has working through his own firm CampoRosso as a consultant in science, technology, innovation and education. He now works for the European Commission.

Index

commerce, 81, 148, 185
communicating objects, 213
community, 39, 72, 76, 89, 91, 117,
  123, 147, 148, 160, 168, 170,
  175, 193, 205, 225, 226
community computer, 227
competition, 191
competitiveness, 191, 198
complex systems, 95, 96, 127, 182,
  206
complexity, 36, 37, 43, 74, 97, 112,
  196
compulsory shopping, 190
computational approach, 205, 206,
  207, 208, 209, 214, 215
computational engineering, 209
computational method, 207
computational model, 207, 215
computational modelling, 207
computational perspective, 205
computational science, 208
computational theory, 207, 208
computer applications, 100, 142,
  143
computer civilisation, 92
computer generated representations
  of reality, 135
computer operating system, 149,
  168, 169
computer programming, 100, 168
computer science, 125, 206, 207,
  209, 210, 212, 213, 215
computer-based language
  translation, 196
computerised data, 168
computerised knowledge, 191
computerised world, 95
confidentiality, 150
congestion, 184, 185, 186
Connectopolis, 80, 81, 82, 83, 84,
  87, 88
Conrad Lorenz, 196
consumer economy, 190
consumer society, 189
consumerism, 192
consumption, 225
convergence, 192, 205, 208, 209,
  213

Copernicus, *152*
cosmetic surgery, 117, 118, 119
creation of value, *147*
creativity, 43, 90, 93, 146, 148, 152,
  155, 157, 202, 203, 219
critical infrastructure management,
  74
cross-disciplinary work, 206
crossroad century, 164
cultural diversity, 166, 170
cultural framework, 70
culture, 90, 94, 99, 100, 101, 102,
  108, 113, 164, 165, 196, 203,
  215, 223, 234
customisation, 42, 47, 48, 49
customised, 40, 46, 47, 49, 50, 96,
  201
cyber-buses, 178, 181
cyber-car, 176, 177, 181, 182, 183
cybernetic organism, 122
cyberspace, 69, 74, 75, 95, 168
cyber-trams, 178, 181
cyber-utility vehicles, 179
cyber-vans, 179
cyber-vehicles, 178
cyber-ways, 177, 178, 180, 181, 182
Cyborg, 121, 123, 124
Cyborg Dilemma, 121
Cyborg Manifesto, 122
cycle of life, 192, 193
Darwin, 196
Darwin's theory of evolution, 196
Darwinian evolution, 197
Darwinian forces, 196
Darwinian ideas, 197
Darwinian rule, 198
Das Schloss, 79
David Deutsch, 210
David Easton, 137
debt of honour, 148
decentralised, 93, 199
de-coupling economic growth from
  energy consumption, 14
Deep Blue, 97, 220
Delphi process, 196
demand for oil, 17
demise of factories, 36

nuclear power, 194
off-shoring European production, 22
oil depletion studies, 16
oil reserves, 16, 17
Olympic Games, 193
omnipotent, 79, 99
On the Spot Manufacturing, 23
online catalogue, 47
open system, 130
open systems applied to human-
    computer interaction, 62
open systems concept, 62
open-source, 100, 149, 154, 168,
    169
open-source software, 100, 168, 169
optics, 106
optimism, 96, 192
organic intelligent components, 121
ownership of capital and
    technology, 157
ownership of the means of
    production, 151
parliamentary politics, 136
participatory democracy, 143
patenting, 146, 150
patenting system, 150
patients, 105, 106, 108, 109, 110,
    111, 113
patriarchal power structures, 155
patriarchal societies, 155
peace, 138, 164, 166, 170, 171, 221
pedestrian safety, 180
perceptions of reality, 192
personal computer, 121, 227
personal computers, 121, 196
personal digital assistant, 182
personal electronic transactor, 176
personal space, 70
personalisation, 72
personalised, 43, 71, 108, 110, 111
personalised drug treatment, 110
personalised environment, 43, 71
Peter Drucker, 153, 160
Peter Kramer, 118
pharmaceutical laboratories, 106
philosophy, 206, 207, 209
Physical Symbol System
    hypothesis, 210, 213

physician, 106, 107, 108, 112, 113
physics, 105, 106, 107, 206, 207,
    209, 210
Pierre de Coubertin, 193
piracy, 202
platoon of vehicles, 177
political, 84, 88, 93, 137, 138, 140,
    141, 142, 144, 148, 156, 168
political ethos, 142
politicians, 136, 137, 138, 140, 141,
    142, 144, 147, 156, 180, 185,
    195, 200
politics, viii, 135, 136, 137, 138,
    140, 141, 142, 143, 144, 168,
    190, 192, 202, 232
pollution, 139, 171, 179, 181, 183,
    184, 185
Popper, 196
population size, 200
portrayal, 130
positive feedback, 97
post materialistic society, 153
post-capitalist society, 89, 156
post-industrial production, 149
post-information society, 94, 100
post-mass production society, 89
post-modern, 79, 87, 92, 101
power-maximising, 169
pre-computer generation, 95
pre-modern, 101, 152
pre-patriarchal society, 155
printing of objects, 37, 40
printing on-demand, 39, 40
printing press, 34
privacy, 69, 70, 72, 73, 75, 79, 80,
    84, 86, 88, 201
Producer-Consumer Lifecycle
    Relationships, 26
production process in peoples'
    homes, 36
production processes, 36
productivity of knowledge, 153
Product-Service Systems, 22
professional ethos, 142
profit-centred, 152
profit-maximisation, 169
programmability, 209, 210
programming the world, 209, 212